CENTENARY
OF
MEDITERRANEAN
ARCHAEOLOGY
1897-1997

JAGIELLONIAN UNIVERSITY

CENTENARY
OF
MEDITERRANEAN
ARCHAEOLOGY
1897-1997

INTERNATIONAL
SYMPOSIUM
CRACOW
OCTOBER
1997

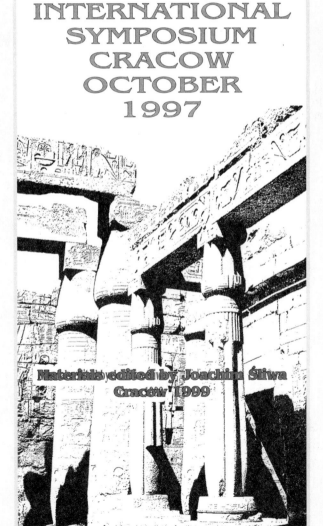

Materials edited by Joachim Śliwa
Cracow 1999

COVER DESIGN
Grażyna Szczurowska

TECHNICAL EDITOR
Wojciech Machowski

ISBN 83-86957-36-0

Printed in Poland
Oficyna Cracovia
31-571 Kraków, ul. Czyżyńska 21 a
☎ (48/12) 411-54-92; 412-03-21

Contents

Preface

On 9th June 1897 Piotr Bieńkowski then a young Privatdozent, was appointed to the Chair of Classical Archaeology that was being founded especially for him in the Jagiellonian University of Cracow. In the October of the same year he commenced his work as head of the research unit and academic tutor to the students interested in this new field of study. The graduates he educated in this, the first Chair of Classical (later Mediterranean) Archaeology in Poland (albeit at the time the country was not an independent state, but divided up into three partitional zones occupied by the neighbouring powers), would in future hold appointments to chairs of archaeology in other Polish universities, thereby continuing and developing the work Bieńkowski initiated in Cracow.

To celebrate the Centenary of our foundation, on 21st - 23rd October 1997 the Jagiellonian University Chair of Mediterranean Archaeology held an International Jubilee Symposium in the University's conference centre at Przegorzały, Cracow[1]. Among the papers delivered at this international assembly of scholars there were, of course, presentations of the history of archaeological studies at Cracow and of the academic biographies of the key personalities involved, but alongside the Cracovian subjects there were also contributions to the history of archaeology and collecting, early Egypt and the Levant, the results of the most recent excavations, and new studies on ancient art and culture. A second highlight of the event was the tribute paid to Professor Maria L. Bernhard, who was Head of the Chair in the years 1954-1978, on the sixtieth anniversary of the commencement of her academic work[2].

The programme which we reproduce below gives the full details of the proceedings and the papers delivered:

---

[1] We also had a special academic session, held on 5th-7th January 1977, to celebrate the 80th anniversary of the foundation of our Chair. The papers delivered on this occasion were published in various books and periodicals. See *Scholarly Meeting to Commemorate the 80th Anniversary of the Department of Mediterranean Archaeology of the Jagiellonian University*, Recherches Archéologiques de 1977, Cracow 1978, pp.74-75.
[2] A special publication dedicated to Professor Bernhard was issued for the occasion (*Studies in Ancient Art and Civilization*, vol. 8, Cracow 1997).

21st October 1997

Mediterranean Archaeology in Cracow (Chairman: Józef Wolski)

- Joachim Śliwa (Kraków), *Piotr Bieńkowski (1865-1925). Forscher - Universitätslehrer - Organisator der Wissenschaften*
- Janusz A. Ostrowski (Kraków), *Stanisław Jan Gąsiorowski (1897-1962). Student of Ancient Art and Museologist*
- Ewdoksia Papuci-Władyka (Kraków), *Le Professeur Marie-Louise Bernhard et ses recherches sur l'art grec*
- Krzysztof M. Ciałowicz (Kraków), *The Chair of Classical Archaeology, 1925-1993*

History of Archaeology and Art Collecting (Chairman: Aleksandra Wąsowicz)

- Juliusz Ziomecki (Wrocław), *Professor Edmund Bulanda (1882-1951)*
- Revd. Jerzy Chmiel (Kraków), *Biblical Archaeology at the Faculty of Theology in Cracow*
- Magdalena Blomberg (Łódź), *Les Polonais chargées de cours de la litterature et de l'art antique aux universités russes du XIXe siècle*
- Elżbieta Jastrzębowska (Warszawa), *Paul Styger (1887-1939) - explorateur des catacombes romaines et professeur à l'Université de Varsovie*
- Krystyna Moczulska (Kraków), *The Collections of Antiquities in Cracow*
- Stefan Skowronek (Kraków), *Research on Ancient Greek Coins and Coin Collections in Cracow*
- Jarosław Bodzek (Kraków), *Ancient Greek Coins donated by Stanisław Mineyko (1890-1924) in the Collection of the National Museum in Cracow*
- Agata Marczewska (Kraków), *Cypriot Antiquities in the Cracow 's Collections*
- Agata Kubala (Kraków), *Stefan Przeworski (1900-1940). Scholar of Ancient Anatolia*

22nd October 1997

History of Archaeology and Art Collecting (Chairman: Karol Myśliwiec)

- Tomasz Mikocki (Warszawa), *New Studies on Ancient Sculpture and Art Collecting in Poland*
- Witold Dobrowolski (Warszawa), *Lo specchio di Prometeo da Cracovia e veramente falso?*
- Werner Oenbrink (Köln), *Die ehemalige Skulpturensammlung des Grafen Karol Lanckoroński, Wien*
- Anne Destrooper-Georgiades (Athens), *The History of some Collections of Classical Coins in Cyprus*
- Monika Rekowska-Ruszkowska (Warszawa), *Les antiquités gauloises et germaniques dans la culture polonaise*

Early Egypt and the Levant (Chairman: Lech Krzyżaniak)

- Barbara Adams (London), *Early Temples in Egypt: Hierakonpolis and Beyond*
- Ram Gophna (Tel Aviv), *Elusive Anchorage Sites Along the Israel Littoral during the Early Bronze Age*
- Y.Y. Baumgarten (Jerusalem), *Subterranean Systems in the Chalcolithic Period in Southern Israel: were they used as dwellings?*
- Zbigniew E. Szafrański (Warszawa), *Settlement in Egypt in the First Half of the Second Millennium B. C.*
- Marta Guzowska (Warszawa), *Context for Minoan Finds in Cyprus*
- Elżbieta Dubis (Kraków), *Early Bronze Age on Tell el-Umeiri, Jordan*

23rd October 1997

Results of the Latest Archaeological Research
(Chairman: Wiktor A. Daszewski)

- Jan Bouzek (Praha), *The Beirut. Excavations of the Institute for Classical Archaeology, Charles University, in 1996*
- Violetta Pereyra de Fidenza et al. (Buenos Aires), *Tell el-Ghaba: Three Seasons of Excavations in North Sinai*
- Elke Blumenthal (Leipzig), *Gottkönigtum und Statuentypen im Alten Reich*
- Henryk Meyza (Warszawa) - Ewdoksia Papuci -Władyka (Kraków), *Nea Paphos, Cyprus: Pottery from Cistern STR 1/96-97*
- Jolanta Młynarczyk (Warszawa), *Sha 'ar ha-Amakim: A Hellenistic and Roman Site in Lower Galilee*
- Aleksandra Wąsowicz (Warszawa), *Nymphaion - histoire et structure d'une polis grecque. Projet international polono-russo-ukrainien (1993-1997)*
- Sergei Okhotnikov (Odessa), *The Levke Island on Black Sea*
- T.L. Samoilova (Odessa), *Main Sources and Perspectives for Studies Concerning Ancient Tiras*
- Mariusz Mielczarek (Toruń), *Polish-Ukrainian Excavations at Nikonion*
- Evgenia F. Redina (Odessa), *Ancient Settlement and Cemetery at Košary (4th - 3rd centuries B. C.)*

New Studies on Ancient Art and Culture I (Chairman: Michał Gawlikowski)

- Józef Wolski (Kraków), *L' archéologie et l'histoire anciennes: L'Iran a la lumière des nouvelles sources archéologiques*
- Zsolt Kiss (Warszawa), *.Les auriges de Kom el-Dikka*
- Ilona Skupińska-Lovset (Łódź). *Isis Children. Portraits of Boys with Youthplait from Syria*
- Adam Łukaszewicz (Warszawa), *Memnon and Memnonia*

- Günther Schörner (Jena), *Die Pansgrotte von Vari. Ein ländliches Heiligtum in Attika*
- Anna de Vincenz (Jerusalem), *Shuni – Mayumas: a Model of Archaeological Park in Israel*
- Iwona Modrzewska – Pianetti (Warszawa), *Gli scavi polacchi nell'isola di Torcello visti dopo trent'anni*
- Przemysław Nowogórski (Warszawa), *The Iconography of 'Aron ha-Berith in Jewish Art from 2nd to 7th centuries A.D.*
-

New studies on Ancient Art and Culture II
(Chairman: Włodzimierz Godlewski)

- Francine Blondé (Lyon), *Thasos et ses céramiques au IIe s. avant J.- C.*
- Elżbieta Mazurkiewicz – Woźniak (Lublin), *The Augustan Architectonic Complex from Palatine*
- Gérald Finkielsztejn (Jerusalem), *Une fouille de sauvetage d'envergure inhabituelle: la ville byzantine et la nécropole de Kfar Samir*
- Tomasz Waliszewski (Warszawa), *New Researches on the Byzantine Period in Lebanon*
- Barbara Lichocka (Warszawa), *Les monnaies locales et les monnaies impériales à Chypre au IIIe siècle. Le témoignage de Nea Paphos*
- Małgorzata Martens – Czarnecka (Warszawa), *Faras and Dongola. Milestones in Discoveries of the Nubian Painting*
- Ida Ryl-Prejbisz (Warszawa), *Elements of Architectonic Decorations from Old Dongola*
- Bożena Rostkowska (Warszawa), *Lower Nubia and the Institutio Michaelis*
- Bogdan Żurawski (Warszawa), *The Divine Kingdom of Dongola. Some Reconsiderations*

An important supplement to the Symposium was provided by an afternoon cycle of lectures and slide projections on the discoveries made by Polish archaeologists in the Mediterranean. These lectures were addressed to a general audience in Polish at the Arsenal Room of the Czartoryski Museum, and they were numerously attended and attracted a great deal of popular interest. Their programme was as follows:

21st October 1997

- Joachim Śliwa (Kraków), *Excavations at Qasr el-Sagha, Egypt*
- Michał Gawlikowski (Warszawa), *Polish Excavations in Palmyra, Syria*
- Lech Krzyżaniak (Poznań), *Decline of Prehistoric period on the Nile (Egypt and Sudan)*

22nd October 1997

- Jadwiga Lipińska (Warszawa), *Polish Excavations at Deir el-Bahari, Egypt*
- Piotr Bieliński (Warszawa), *On the Tigris and Khabur. Polish Excavations in Upper Mesopotamia, 1984-1997*
- Jan Chochorowski (Kraków), *Tomb of a Scythian Prince at Ryzhanovka, Ukraine*

23rd October 1997

- Wiktor A. Daszewski (Warszawa - Trier), *Nea Paphos - Ancient Capital of Cyprus in the Light of Polish Excavations*
- Karol Myśliwiec (Warszawa), *Fertility Cults and Erotic Art in Ptolemaic Athribis. New Polish Excavations at Tell Atrib, Egypt*
- Włodzimierz Godlewski (Warszawa), *Hermitages, Papyri and Paintings. Polish Excavations at Naqlun, Egypt*

The volume of proceedings from the Symposium, containing the papers on the history of the Cracow centre and on the history of archaeology and collecting, along with a full bibliography of Professor Bieńkowski's work and other commemorative items, has already been published[3]. This volume, its sequel, presents the remainder of the contributions arranged in order of the individual sections. Those contributions whose authors did not submit full versions for publication are represented by short summaries.

Joachim Śliwa

Jagiellonian University of Cracow

---

[3] See the first volume of proceedings, *Archeologia śródziemnomorska w Uniwersytecie Jagiellońskim 1897-1997. Materiały sympozjum naukowego. Kraków, 21-23 października 1997.* Pod redakcją Joachima Śliwy, Kraków 1998, pp. 263.

Early Egypt and the Levant

Barbara Adams
London

Early Temples at Hierakonpolis and Beyond

Introduction

The most well-known temple at Hierakonpolis, the Predynastic capital of Upper Egypt, is that excavated in 1897-9 by James Quibell and Frederick Green (Quibell and Green 1900 and 1902), situated in the south-east corner of the town enclosure of Nekhen. Some people will also be aware of part of another large enclosure with a niched gateway which Walter Fairservis excavated in the town enclosure in the 1970s & 80s (Fairservis 1972, 1983, 1986). Recent publications have also brought more attention to an earlier temple in the Predynastic desert edge settlement at Hierakonpolis (Holmes 1992, Friedman 1990, 1996). This paper attempts to show a continuity from the early temple complex in the desert with those in the city of Nekhen in the alluvium and then extend a legacy beyond the regional context.

Locality 29A

The excavations which the late Michael Hoffman directed at Locality 29A in the Gerzean desert town site at Hierakonpolis in 1985-6 and 1988-9 revealed an unexpected and intriguing complex which has been described as a temple. It certainly bears no relationship to the earlier houses of Locality 29 and, although not completely cleared, it consists of a large, oval courtyard (33 m. long and 14 m. wide) with various surrounding walls and outbuildings. The courtyard was paved four or five times with smoothed clay; one of these floors still bore the imprint of human and animal feet. At the north side of the courtyard, near the unexcavated west end, there are large post holes which may mark a gateway. Smaller postholes seem to connect the large postholes to a mud brick wall and various outbuildings. At the south east end, to which the floor sloped up at a 9° angle, there is a deep hole with rocks inside, which perhaps once supported a freestanding pole, possibly surmounted by the totem of a god, or a large mace head on a pole, such as depicted on an ivory cylinder fragment from the Main Deposit recently conserved in Oxford (Whitehouse 1992). Such an oval walled courtyard structure is shown on the ceremonial mace head of the Protodynastic king Narmer from Hierakonpolis where it encloses three dead gazelles (Quibell & Green 1902). A totem pole surmounted by a bird is also shown on the mace head and a large pot on a fenestrated pot stand, as well as a shrine in the form of the Lower Egyptian *Per-nu*. On the south side of the courtyard there are four even larger post holes (1.7 m. deep) fronting the supposed 13 m. wide temple building which faces the gateway and the courtyard. Hoffman speculated that the post holes were big enough to take columns made of cedars of Lebanon sheathed in bundled reeds. He also produced architectural reconstructions of the complex from different aspects, with the buildings in wood, wattle and daub and mud brick. A three-dimensional model of the ceremonial centre was included in the "First Egyptians" exhibition which he organised in the United States in 1988. Since then, Renée Friedman has taken interpretation further by suggesting a reconstruction of the building fronted with the four large posts as the original *Per-wer* of Upper Egypt, and drawn attention to parallels with the reconstructed southern and northern shrines in the Third Dynasty Step Pyramid complex of Djoser (2688-2649 B.C.) at Saqqara (Friedman 1996).

The use of the complex at Locality 29A has been dated to Naqada IIb-IId (3500-3150 B.C.) on the basis of the ceramic pieces recovered, with some re-use in Naqada IIIa after a period of abandonment, and a Naqada IIIb (Dynasty "0" - Dynasty I, 3150-3000 B.C.) component in a pit at the west. To the east of the large post holes there were traces of a sinusoidal brick wall, which is not only another point of comparison with the scene on the Narmer mace head, but, because of the increase in retaining properties gained with this type of construction, reinforces the interpretation that there had been an intentional placing of sand over the courtyard to create a mound at the end of Naqada III. Just west of the gateway in a severely disturbed and deflated area at the northwestern end of the floor post holes outline a square building, possibly a pavilion, and this maybe associated with a large area of melted and toppled mud bricks, which may be the remains of a platform.

Nekhen Stratigraphy

A chronological continuity with the complex in the desert can be shown through a re-examination of the architectural history of Nekhen. Green was the real archaeologist in the second season of 1898-9, and it is to him that we owe the description of the stratigraphy of the site. This was formulated from sections cut in various locii in the town and temple area working by the method of recording depth in metres below datum level. The results of these sections were then correlated to produce an overall stratification of the site with each stratum being given a descriptive title. It should be stressed that the existence of these strata is not universal over the site, Fairservis confirmed there is variation between the town and the temple and differences in detail in various locations. More detailed study of Green's manuscript notebooks (kept in the Faculty of Oriental Studies at the University of Cambridge) has helped to clarify important points of dissension.

The *First Stratum* was the lowest and was described as the *Old Desert Surface*, noted at 5.0 metres below datum level. Green was hampered by the rising water table at this level, which was to hinder the work of Fairservis and Hoffman at higher levels, but he commented that he was not sure that traces of prehistoric pottery found at this depth were *in situ*, or if they had been washed down by rain. This level was only well observed in a longitudinal sectional trench within the circular revetment and between the two enclosure walls on the S.W. side of the temple. Fortunately, the detail of the excavation of one of these two locii can be checked in Green's notebook entries. The section within the revetment, site no. 220 (Adams 1974b), produced prehistoric pottery at and below 4.9 metres beneath a layer of clean white sand. In Green's notes the sherds are described as "ash jars", and this becomes "rough red prehistoric pottery" in the publication, indicating the straw

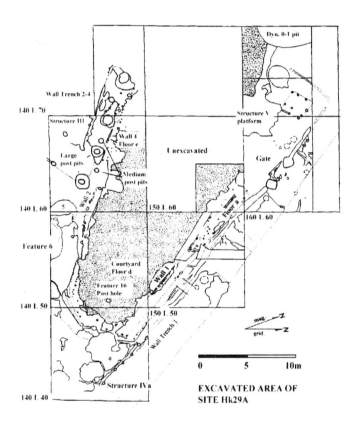

Fig. 1. Plan of Hierakonpolis Locality 29A temple, reversed

tempered ware (R-class) of Naqada II; he also found a few fragments of polished red pottery (P-class) and fragments of a large pottery cist or majur. The coring undertaken by Hany Hamroush under Hoffman's direction in 1984 across Nekhen confirmed Predynastic occupation at a depth of 4 metres below the present surface (Hoffman 1986; Hoffman, Hamroush and Allen 1987).

Green's *Second Stratum* was entitled *Accumulations*, and he saw it as an ill-defined stratum representing the accumulation on the desert surface before any buildings were erected. The circular revetment and the low-lying pavements which he found in various parts of the temple area rested on this stratum at 4.2 to 4.15 metres below datum level. Fairservis and Hoffman identified a yellow clay level in various quadrants which equates with this stratum; the type of artifacts found within it, such as developed fish-shaped palettes, painted pottery and vestigial wavy handle cylinder jars indicate a late Naqada II to Protodynastic (Naqada III) date.

The next and most ubiquitous stratum over the site was Green's *Third Stratum*, the *Charcoal-Discoloured*, which he found underlying the town and temple site at about 4 metres below datum level. The four inch (10 cm) thick stratum, which no doubt indicates an extensive occupation, thinned out on the southwest of the temple where sandstone paving slabs and limestone pillars were found, and it did not occur within the circular revetment. Green says that the artifacts found in this stratum were: "rough red prehistoric and IInd to IIIrd Dynasty pottery"; the stratum also contained flint implements, limestone spindle whorls and inscribed clay sealings. There has been some confusion as to the date of the pottery and the correlation of this stratum with that of the recent work (O'Connor 1992) and convoluted attempts to explain a date range for the stratum which seems to extend from Naqada III/Dynasty I to the Third Dynasty (Williams 1988). The descriptive terms for the pottery can be clarified in Green's manuscript notebooks where the "rough red pre-historic" pottery is described as "coarse red" and is distinguished from the Predynastic ash jars, so it is most likely to be the orange-fired straw tempered pottery of the early First Dynasty. The "IInd and IIIrd Dynasty pottery" is a translation of the the term "Libyan" which Green used in his notebooks to refer to crushed calcium carbonate tempered (hard orange) pottery, which is the regional desert (marl) ware of the Protodynastic to First Dynasty. Green clearly distinguishes this plain hard "stone ware" from the "N.R. (New Race) polished red and painted pottery", which he knew to be prehistoric (Gerzean), although, judging from his sketches, he sometimes used the term to refer to the polished red, carinated 'Meydum' bowls. Thus, there is actually no discrepancy with the rest of the material culture of this stratum and it represents an intensity of Protodynastic (Naqada III) and early First Dynasty occupation.

The next or *Fourth Stratum* of *Dark Earth* defined by Green represents a continuity of occupation 0.6 m above the charcoal-discoloured stratum and 2.75 m below his datum level. He correlated it with the houses in the town area, which, to judge by the sealings, the pottery and other artifacts, date from the First to the Third Dynasty, and notes that these houses seem to have been built on Stratum Three. Fairservis distinguished four levels by floor for his "Archaic period" (= Early Dynastic) strata: (6) through (3) with subdivisions which equate with Green's third and fourth strata. He noted that streak-burnished red wares were part of phases (6a) and (5a) and red-orange carinated ('Meydum') wares were found in levels (5a) and (4a); in other words the early levels date to the First Dynasty and the later levels to the Second and Third Dynasties. This type of information on the evolution of fine ware is readily available from the stratigraphic work of Petrie on the early levels of the temenos of the temple at Abydos, and merely reinforces the

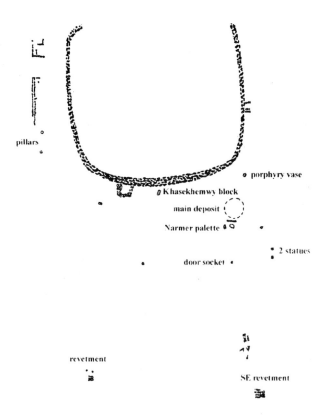

Fig. 2. Early stone structures isolated from the plan of Nekhen (Hierakonpolis)

date range of First to Third Dynasty for the third and fourth strata which was given by Green.

Green did not define a fifth stratum, which he saw as ground prepared for the building of the mud brick temple with layers of thin white sand marking the foundation level of the new temple. Fairservis' level (2) represents the sand deposits, which he noted as being covered with an eroded paving, no more than a brick or two in thickness. Above this ill-defined level, there are pockets of what Fairservis described as "junk", mixed deposits of Graeco-Roman, New Kingdom and Early Dynastic pottery, disturbed by the *sebakhin* and farming activities and deeply penetrated by Halfa grass and animal burrows.

The Temple of Nekhen

It is certain that Hierakonpolis was an extremely important centre during the last phase of prehistory which no doubt contained the shrine of Upper Egypt, the *Per-wer*, in its early temple, perhaps transferred from the desert ceremonial centre at the end of the Gerzean. Like that complex, this shrine is presumed to have been a structure largely built in wood and reed in the form of a tent, perhaps with horns and a tail, as depicted on First Dynasty sealings. or within an enclosure as shown on ivory tags and bone tubes. It probably would have included a portable shrine, such as those found as votive models from early temple deposits at Abydos and Hierakonpolis, to contain the revealed image of the god, the *Repit*, which was set on a mud brick pedestal, of which there is an excavated example at Elephantine (Dreyer 1986). The mixed media in the Locality 29A desert complex demonstrates that the use of wood and reed and mud brick were not separate religious architectural traditions, as has been argued by Barry Kemp. The Protodynastic post hole and trench structure excavated by Hoffman in a quadrant (10N5W) in Nekhen in 1969 is an example of this type of architecture. Continued excavation in 1984 exposed a thick (3 m wide) mud brick wall nearby, and the wattle and daub walls of a rectangular Naqada II-III house.

One of the purposes of Green's detailed examination of the strata was to clarify the building phases in the temple area in a scientific way because, after the publication of photographs and drawings of the important ceremonial artifacts which Quibell had found in the temple, there had already been much scholarly speculation about the date of the Main Deposit, where most of them had been found. The relation of the architecture and the stratigraphy to this 'deposit' was held to be crucial to the date of its deposition. Regardless of Green's efforts, there has continued to be much speculation, although a concensus has been reached on the early date of the objects, and useful comments and suggestions are still being made on the architecture of the early temple.

Green identified the stone work resting on his Second Stratum which he considered to be part of an early temple and marked it on the plan with dark shading. The main stone structure extant at the time of Quibell and Green's work, but no longer observable at the site, was the circular revetment, which stood 2.5 m. high at the time of their excavation. This 4926 m. wide structure can be seen in the centre of the temple plan as an incomplete oval, drawn as if it were constructed over the later mud brick walls of the "citadel", when in fact it was beneath them. Although no contemporary photographs of the large revetment exist, Green located another revetment on the south-east side of the temple which abutted with the later enclosure wall. The dark earth and charcoal discoloured third and fourth strata passed over the revetment and under the enclosure wall, so that the builders of the wall must have cut through it, although the face which abutted onto the wall was well defined, rather as if the later builders had avoided it. A pinhole photograph of this structure has survived in the Petrie Museum archives which clearly shows the stepped stone construction. The circular revetment was composed of rough blocks of sandstone laid in horizontal courses, one block thick, and battered at an angle of $45°$, and it enclosed a mound of desert sand. The lower courses of the revetment rested on the second stratum of Predynastic accumulations and the sand within it was remarkably clear of artifacts. The third and fourth charcoal-discoloured and dark earth strata were missing within the structure, although they abutted its exterior. This would therefore indicate that domestic occupation and rubbish accumulation were avoided in ceremonial areas, which was a pattern followed in later times. At the west of the revetment there were two walls composed of the same stone slabs projecting from its southern face, closed by a cross wall at 10 m. from the top of the revetment. At the end of this 3 m. wide passage there was a circular block of limestone, 1.4 m. in diameter, partly under the wall, with a slight depression on its upper face. The walls of the passage stood on a hard surface of rammed earth, with traces of early brick walls, resting on the charcoal discoloured stratum, and was therefore a later addition to the revetted structure. There were two other parallel walls of rough stone projecting from the east side of the revetment, forming a passage narrower than the one on the south face, but lacking a cross wall at the end. Green suggested that the revetment enclosed an artificial mound which had been constructed at the beginning of the First Dynasty, and this intepretation has even more validity now that comparisons can be made with similar complexes. David O'Connor suggests the rectangular temple enclosure at Nekhen dates to the First Dynasty by comparison with the funerary cult enclosures of Djer and Merytneith at Abydos, which also have an entrance at the north corner and another on the northeast wall near the east corner.

As mentioned, the revetments were not the only stone built structure remaining in the temple area in 1898. In various places in the temple area there were remaining patches of rough stone pavements, most of them were resting on the charcoal-discoloured stratum, except one section in the east part of the enclosure which was at the same depth as the foot of the circular revetment. On the western side of the enclosure there were two parallel rows of rough Nubian sandstone blocks resting on the charcoal-discoloured stratum 3.5 m. below datum level, the inner face of the thick mud brick enclosure wall had been skewed to avoid them, further stone blocks were found further to the northwest at a higher level. There was part of another row of stones resting on the charcoal-discoloured stratum close to a slab of limestone with a rectangular depression in its upper surface near to the Narmer palette and the Main Deposit.

Beside the sandstone pavements, Quibell and Green also found a number of other architectural features, including a number of possible limestone pillars. Two of them were found close to the row of stones on the west side of the enclosure. The largest fragment of these laterally bulging columns of stone was 40 cm. wide and had been broken off at a height of 1.25 m. Both of these pieces of stone were set in sockets supported by rough blocks of sandstone. Protodynastic "coarse red" (straw tempered) and polished red pottery sherds were found between the stones of the larger pillar, and a Protodynastic decorated sherd was found near the base of the smaller pillar. Another slightly smaller pillar (D: 36.0 cm.), broken at 1.1 m., was found near the southern inner enclosure wall. Green had the idea that they may have been the lower, featureless parts of rough block statues of deities, such has had been found in the temple at Koptos by Petrie in 1894. One of these statues had been found in front of the town gateway of Nekhen, where it had been re-used as a door socket (see below). Quibell had found two other pillars the previous season, one close to the revetted passage which projected from the south of the revetment and the other in the area of the New Kingdom temple near the brick pylons.

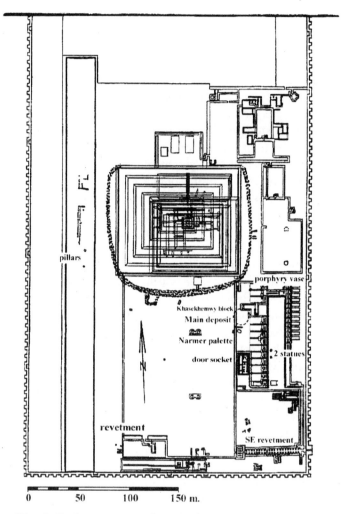

Fig. 3. Early structures from Nekhen transposed over
the Step Pyramid Enclosure

Although the pillars may be dubious contenders for early statues, two life-size statues of limestone were found 2 m. apart near the Main Deposit, erect in the same level. Each of them portray a semi-kneeling man with short, square bottomed wig and false beard wearing a belt with a tassel in front. Behind these statues to the southwest a diorite door socket with a human face projecting from its front was found by Quibell with a limestone door jamb still standing on it at about the level of the base of the revetment. Just behind and level with the base of these statues was a group of small objects including a limestone ape (UC.14998), a fragment of faience, a coarse vase containing spiral faience beads and a disc-shaped bead of obsidian. The door socket stood in a passage way less than a metre wide between two early mud brick walls; near and below it was another group of faience models and a disc mace head, similar to those which were found in the Main Deposit. In his publication of the early temple at Elephantine, Gunter Dreyer (1986) carefully re-analyzed the report by Quibell on the disposition of finds in the Main Deposit and reconstructed the placement of groups which were listed, but not planned, on an enlarged plan of the northeast section of the temple (Dreyer 1986). From this, it can clearly be seen that the deposit relates to the two limestone statues and the door socket, and to finds made under the mud brick walls of the later "citadel", the objects being of the same votive nature and unlike the artifacts found in the rest of the temple area and the town. Furthermore, these finds are linked by the discovery of large stone vessels in various places in this area. One of them, a large fluted vase of black and white porphyry with a relief of Hathor on the rim (UC.16245), was found scattered in fragments in various places including inside an inscribed granite vase of Khasekhemwy and below the footing of the walls of the "citadel" chambers. This and the other large hard stone vessels were obviously part of the early temple furniture and a similar large diorite vessel fragment was found at Locality 29A.

Cult Enclosures and the Step Pyramid Complex

During Fairservis' excavations in 1967, 1969 and 1981 a north-south traverse was made across the town site, and an overall plan of the Early Dynastic structures encountered in the area was made (Fairservis 1986). At one point the 10 m. squares were extended to the east to follow the line of a building complex which leads from a large mud brick niched-facade gateway discovered in 1969. This complex is aligned north-west and south-east at a ten degree variation to the orientation of the northern buildings of the temple area. The niched-facade mud brick gateway, which was interpreted as a palace entrance by Fairservis, has been reconstructed by O'Connor as a large rectangular temple enclosure of the Second Dynasty, based on comparisons with the funerary cult-enclosure of Peribsen at Abydos (O'Connor 1992). The niched gateway, which had a dog burial in a cist on its south side, opens into a small court, to the south and west of which are habitational rooms at a higher level and there are further rooms and courts to the north, one of which contained seven fragments of clay sealings including one with the name of King Qa'a of the First Dynasty. Further into the complex there were diffuse areas of clean sand covering earlier habitational structures which could, as O'Connor postulates, be the deflated remnants of a sand mound like that enclosed by the stepped revetment, and the custom of constructing these sand mounds may have begun in the later stages of use of the Predynastic ceremonial complex in the low desert. Beneath this sand layer there was a series of recessed limestone blocks which rested on sandstone boulders in a curved row across the area, identified by Fairservis as a balustrade. At the south and above the sand covered area was a niched clay platform with post holes in the front projections, backed by series of compartments each containing circular storage silos. This platform faces the niched gate and it is tempting to think of the ceremonial appearance of the king overlooking a courtyard and the oval mound.

The city enclosure wall was probably built, or, if O'Connor is correct about an original First Dynasty rectangular structure, renewed, at the end of the Second Dynasty, or the beginning of the Third Dynasty, according to Green. who noted that the bricks of which it is built are practically the same dimensions as those used for houses in the town area and that some of the houses were built against its inner face. About 2.5 m. in front of the town gateway, which is cut into the northeast enclosure wall, a headless Archaic limestone statue, one and half meters high, was found beneath the level of the stone paved entrance, lying on its left side, with a row of shallow holes which had probably been made later for its use as a door socket. There was a foundation deposit in the northwest angle of the temple enclosure, which, to judge from the published drawings of the pottery, seems to be late Old Kingdom or First Intermediate Period. The mud brick walls of the "citadel" complex over the centre of the revetment and to the east over the Main Deposit were deemed to have been built at the same time as the double enclosure wall of the temple by the excavators, but they could not agree exactly when this took place. Green established that the temple enclosure wall had been erected over the dark earth fourth and charcoal discoloured third strata and therefore postdated the Third Dynasty. The town enclosure walls become part of the temple enclosure walls on the southwest side where the bricks become the larger uniform size (37 x 19 x 11 cm.); the bricks of the town enclosure wall were the same size as those used in the houses (26 x 13 x 7 cm.). Although Green was of the opinion that the town wall was built at the end of the Second Dynasty, or the beginning of the Third Dynasty, he was not so certain about the mud brick structures in the temple. In his manuscript notes he ventured the opinion that they were constructed in the Middle Kingdom, and in the site report he agreed with Quibell that they must have been constructed in the New Kingdom. On the northeast side of the temple enclosure the space between the inner, thicker wall and the outer, thinner wall is paved at two levels, once at the foot of the walls and again on a metre of accumulated earth. Early Dynastic flints and pottery were found between the two pavements and two circular hollows (Site Nos. 110 and 122) with baked mud floors containing numerous quantities of drill points of flint and unfinished beads of steatite, carnelian and obsidian were cut into the outer and inner side of the outermost thinner wall and the lower pavement; the upper pavement passed over them. This would seem to indicate that the outer, thinner wall was an early structure that had been cut into by these *shuna* stores of the Old Kingdom; the inner, thicker wall could of course be as late as the Eighteenth Dynasty.

Obviously interpretation of the early architecture at Nekhen is complex, and some of the complexity may be explained by the fact that the enclosure walls of the temple may have been renewed and altered over a long period of time. If comparisons to a possible First Dynasty temple enclosure, as suggested by O'Connor, are extended to the supposed Second Dynasty temple enclosure in the town site and to the funerary enclosures (*Talbezirke*) of Djer, Peribsen and Khasekhemwy at Abydos, it can be seen that they all share a basic layout. This comprises a rectangular enclosure with an entrance in the north corner, which is niched in the Second Dynasty, and another in the north east wall near the east corner. Slightly off centre of the main axis is a sand mound, contained by a stone or mud brick wall. The loca-

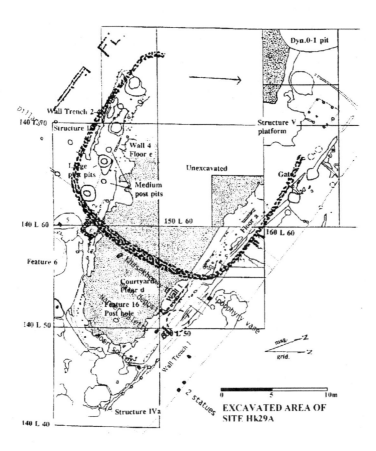

Fig. 4. Early structures from Nekhen transposed over Locality 29A

tion of this mound is similar to that of the stone "mastaba" which is the first phase of the Step Pyramid of Djoser at Saqqara, and O'Connor suggests that this Third Dynasty complex was a copy of the Khasekhemwy enclosure at Abydos, where he has discovered a brickclad mound of sand in the northwest quadrant. He sees the double walled mud brick Fort of Khasekhemwy overlooking the Wadi Abul Suffian at the edge of the cultivation at Hierakonpolis as an aberrant example, lacking an entrance in the north corner, but its niched gateway and recessed panelling on the inner enclosure walls certainly connect it with the Second Dynasty structure in the town enclosure. A ruined mud brick building was found in the centre of the Fort by Garstang (Garstang 1907; Adams 1987) together with two granite blocks, one of which was a column base.

If these comparisons are valid, perhaps the analogy can be extended further, first going forward in time to the Step Pyramid enclosure (plan adapted from F.D. Friedman 1995). The eastern entrance in the panelled enclosure wall leads to a colonnaded processional hall which faces onto an open ceremonial court. To the north (right) of this colonnade is the small Heb-Sed court with a stone platform approached by steps on which it is surmised that the thrones of Upper and Lower Egypt were placed for the ceremony of renewal for the Ka of the king. The Heb-Sed court is lined on each side with chapels for each of the nomes and at the north there are buildings representing the shrines of Upper and Lower Egypt, the House of the South (*Per-wer)* and the House of the North (*Per-nu)*. Extrapolating this layout back to Hierakonpolis, and merging the plans of Nekhen and the Step Pyramid, it can be seen that there is room on the east side of the central mound for a group of buildings. In the case of the temple of Nekhen this area was built over by the mud brick walls of the "citadel", but on this east side there were traces of early stone pavements, two standing statues, a door socket and, most significantly, the votive objects of the Main Deposit. Rather than the idea of "holy rubbish", come upon and re-buried by later builders, which was one of Green's suggestions for the explanation of the Main Deposit which I took up in 1974 (Adams 1974b), it could be that it was contemporary with use of the Early Dynastic temple, and that the objects were buried shortly after their dedication in an area which would correspond to the Heb-Sed court and associated buildings in the Step Pyramid complex. The large *wsht* courtyard to the west has the remains of stone markers between which the king performed the Heb-Sed run. It is curious that in the same relative position in Nekhen there is a area south-east of the revetment, where Green found traces of a temple founded by Tuthmosis III and Hatshepsut of the Eighteenth Dynasty, which seems devoid of early structures, and, although any mud brick structures could have *sebakhed* out, the space does fit well with the emplacement of the *wsht* court at Saqqara. The location of Djoser's tomb of the south corresponds roughly with the south east revetment and other patches of early pavement in Nekhen.

If it is accepted that the early stone walls, pavements, pillars, and Main Deposit and statuary groups east and west of the central revetment are part of an early temple complex at Nekhen, then this layout can also be extrapolated backwards to the ceremonial complex at Locality 29A. First it is necessary to use the same orientation, i.e., river side, or local north, by reversing the plan of Locality 29A. By merging this plan with the plan of Nekhen it can be seen, apart from the obvious comparison between the shape of the oval courtyard and the squarer revetment, that on the south side a line of large post pits, said by Friedman to front the *Per Wer*, is approximately where the stone pillars were found in Nekhen. Contenders for a similar totem pole to that supposed by the deep hole at the south east end of the oval at Locality 29A exist south east of the revetment, or perhaps the site of the revetted passage once held a tall monument. There is also a range of buildings along the north east side in the desert site where a possible pavilion and a platform may have also stood, providing a elevated place where the king could appear in a formal setting with a token palace for his private robing and resting, as shown on the Narmer mace head. As mentioned, the last use of the Locality 29A complex is signified by a pit containing Dynasty "0" - Dynasty I (contemporary with Narmer -

Hor Aha) pottery at the north edge of the excavated area. At this final stage of the life of the desert temple it seems that sand was heaped over the courtyard to create a mound, and then presumably religious activities were concentrated in Nekhen with its own central reveted mound. Obviously, much of this analogy is fanciful, but the comparisons are worth noting from the point of view of the longevity of architectural styles in religious and funerary architecture. There seems to have been some separation of the mound and the courtyard in later complexes, whilst the central mound became a mastaba in the time of Djoser and ultimately, a pyramid. In the true pyramid complexes of the Fourth Dynasty the great enclosed southern area of the royal appearance and the Sed-festival architecture all vanish in favour of a mortuary temple on the east side of the pyramid and a linear architectural sequence leading from it to the Valley Temple.

Bibliography

Adams, B.
1974 a   *Ancient Hierakonpolis.* Aris & Phillips, Warminster.
1974 b   *Ancient Hierakonpolis Supplement.* Aris & Phillips, Warminster.
1987   *The Fort Cemetery at Hierakonpolis.* Kegan Paul International, London and New York.
1996   *Ancient Nekhen.* SIA Publishing, New Malden.

Dreyer, G.
1986   *Elephantine VIII. Der Tempel der Satet. Die Funde der Frühzeit und des Alten Reiches.* AVDAIK 39, Mainz.

Fairservis, W.A. Jr.
1972   "Preliminary Report on the First Two Seasons at Hierakonpolis", *JARCE* 9: 7-27, 67-99.
1983a   *The Hierakonpolis Project No.1: Excavation of the Temple Area on the Kom el Gemuwia Season of 1978.* Occasional Papers in Anthropology, Vassar College, Poughkeepsie, New York.
1986   *The Hierakonpolis Project No.3: Excavation of the Archaic Remains East of the Niched Gate, Season of 1981.* Occasional Papers in Anthropology, Vassar College, Poughkeepsie, New York.

Friedman, R.F.
1990   "Hierakonpolis, Locality 29A", *Bulletin de Liaison du Groupe International d'Étude de la Ceramique Égyptienne*, XIV: 18-25.
1996   "The Ceremonial Centre at Hierakonpolis: Locality 29A" in A.J. Spencer (ed.), *Aspects of Early Egypt*, Proceedings of a Colloquium held at the British Museum in 1993, London: 16-35.

Garstang, J.
1907   "Excavations at Hierakonpolis, at Esna and in Nubia", *ASAE* 8: 132-148.

Hoffman, M.A.
1986   "A Model of Urban Development for the Hierakonpolis Region
               from Predynastic through Old Kingdom Times", *JARCE* 23: 175-
               187.

Hoffman, M.A., Hamroush, H. and Allen, R.
1987   "The Environmental and Evolution of an Early Egyptian Urban
               Center: Archaeological and Geochemical Investigations at
               Hierakonpolis", *Geoarchaeology* 2 (1): 1-13.

Holmes, D.L.
1992   "Chipped Stone-Working Craftsmen, Hierakonpolis and the Rise
               of Civilization in Egypt" in R. Friedman & B. Adams (eds.), *The
               Followers of Horus: Studies Dedicated to Michael Allen Hoffman
               1944-1990*. ESA Publication No. 2, Oxbow Monograph 20: 37-44.

O'Connor, D.
1992   "The Status of Early Egyptian Temples", in R. Friedman and B.
               Adams (eds.), *The Followers of Horus: Studies Dedicated to Mi-
               chael Allen Hoffman 1944-1990*. ESA Publication No. 2, Oxbow
               Monograph 20: 83-98.

Quibell, J.E.
1900   *Hierakonpolis* I. ERA & BSAE 4.

Quibell,J.E. and Green, F.W.
1902   *Hierakonpolis* II. ERA & BSAE 5.

Whitehouse, H.
1992   "The Hierakonpolis Ivories in Oxford. A Progress Report", in R.
               Friedman and B. Adams (eds.), *The Followers of Horus: Studies
               Dedicated to Michael Allen Hoffman 1944-1990*, ESA Publication
               No. 2, Oxbow Monograph 20: 77-82.

Williams B.B.
1988   "Narmer and the Coptos Colossi", *JARCE* XXV: 35-59.

Y.Y. Baumgarten

Omer

Subterranean Systems in the Chalcolithic Period in Southern Israel: Were They Used As Dwellings?

In the fourth millennium BCE, in the Chalcolithic period (Levy 1986; Gonen 1992; Gilead 1988,1994; Joffe & Dessel 1995; Evin 1995) there was a phenomena in Israel of underground structures (Perrot 1984; Gilead 1987; Alon 1989). These systems are located in the southern part of Israel, in the Negev (Fig.1), at such sites as: Tel Sheva[1] (Fig.2), Horvat Beter (Dothan 1959; Rosen & Eldar 1993) (Fig.3), Beer Safad (=Neve Noy) (Eldar & Baumgarten 1985) (Fig.4), Abu Matar (Perrot 1984; Commenge - Pellerin 1987) (Fig.5), Horvat Ashan (Cohen 1976), Abu Hof (Alon 1988, 1991), Shikmim (Levy. Alon. Grigson, Holl, Goldberg. Rowan, & Smith 1991; Levy 1987) (Fig.6).

The entrances to these underground systems are through downward sloping tunnels or paths that lead downwards to open courtyards/patio. From the courtyard/patio one enters the structure through openings or horizontal tunnels in order to reach underground rooms. Often, the shape of the underground rooms is that of a prism and at other times they appear as partial domes. In some cases the system includes a series of rooms connected by tunnels in a chain like fashion. At times the plan of the rooms vary from site to site, at other times the plan changes from one level to the next within the same site. One of the primary characteristics of these systems is that the openings occur in the ceiling of the rooms. Their function, other than use as a passageway, is to provide adequate ventilation. The underground systems were cut into the loess (Bruins 1976). Chalcolithic sites in the Negev also include above ground structures, which are found next to the subterranean systems.

---

[1] Excavations in Tel Sheva took place between 1993-1994 under the direction of the author. The size of the site is 100 dunes; 15 dunes were excavated.

Some of the sites, located in rocky areas, include dwellings in natural or artificial caves. For instance, Arad (Amiran 1978, 4), Tel Masos (Thuesen 1983), Horvat Hor (Govrin 1978), and other sites (Cohen 1986, 7).

The climate in the northern Negev where these sites are distributed is at present semi-arid. The climate is not stable and the amount of rainfall varies from year to year. Excavations of these underground systems have revealed only a small amount of pig bones, an animal that requires substantial amounts of water. This fact is a strong indication that the weather in Chalcolithic period was semi-arid similar to the present day conditions[2].

Other than cultivation and hunting, the herding of sheep and goats formed a major part of the economic base of these sites and was particularly well suited to semi-arid conditions (Alon & Levy 1996).

The phenomenon of underground systems dating to this period and found in similar environmental conditions have been uncovered in areas outside of Israel:
1. Egypt, Maadi (Hoffman 1984 201-201 Fig. 54).
2. Cyprus,Kalvasos-Ayios (Todd 1991 Figs. 1-3).

Since these systems were contemporaneous with above ground structures (Eldar & Baumgarten 1985 139; Gilead 1987), the question arises as to their function (Baumgarten 1986).

There are some answers to this question:
1. Dwellings - this suggestion was raised by Jean Perrot (Perrot 1984) in spite of the fact that no remains have been found on the floors of the underground rooms which would provide evidence for their use as dwellings. It may be argued that several elements, such as lack of ventilation, lighting and difficulty in transversing the systems, would preclude their use as dwellings (Gilead 1987). In fact, modern planners of arid and semi-arid areas have adopted this type of structure for dwellings (Kempe 1988; Golany 1983 b).

In their opinion, and according to tests and experimentation, there are several advantages to subterranean dwelling such as the advantage of natural insulation, which maintains uniform temperatures. We will return to this point later.

2. Storage - (Gophna 1982:89; Alon 198858-59,61-62 1989, 86; Gilead 1987):
A). Animals - the underground systems have not produced animal remains. Moreover, the size of sheep and goats, which was smaller in the Chalcolithic period, would not have been able to transverse the underground passages and tunnels and are traditionally kept in open spaces, their natural habitat.

---

[2] According to Alon and Levy (Alon & Levy 1966) on the basis of plant samples the climate in the Negev was more humid than at present. However, signs of a more humid climate could be produced by other climatological factors:
1)   The region received a small and uniform amount of rainfall for a number of years.
2)   The region received a large amount of rainfall over a limited period of time (ten to twenty years) a condition that would produce the impression of a more humid climate.
It should be recalled that the samples that were found in various sites represent "la longue dure'e".

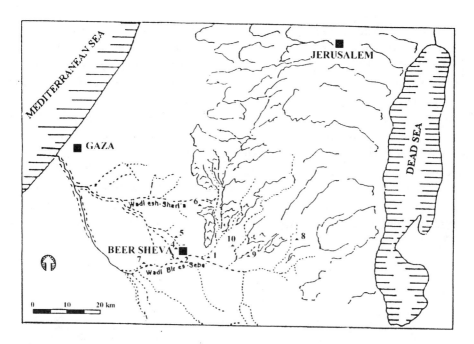

Fig. 1. Subterranean systems in the Israeli Negev
(1-Tel Sheva, 2-Horvat Beter, 3-Beer Safad, 4-Abu Matar, 5-Horvat Ashan, 6-
Abu Hof, 7-Shikhim, 8-Arad, 9-Tel Masos, 10-Horvat Hor)

B) Product - (Gophna 1982 89; Gilead 1987; Alon 1988 86, 1989 58-59,61-62): The underground systems have not produced any evidence of storage containers with the exception of one site, Neve Noy, in which built bins that may have been used for this purpose, were uncovered (Eldar & Baumgarten 1985 137). In addition, the architecture of these systems would have created great difficulties in transferring storage containers from one area to another. In spite of the fact that ivory objects and tools used for working ivory have been uncovered in some systems it appears that the lack of adequate lighting would have made this activity unlikely and would be more suitable above ground. At Tel Sheva, one small side room contained evidence of niches that held small storage jars while the larger room of this system appears to have been used for other purposes. If, in fact, the function of the underground systems were strictly for storage, it would have been unlikely that a small storage room of this type would have been constructed.

3) Refuge - (Kempe 1988 193-195): The underground systems are quite simply constructed with comfortable approaches. They would have been inadequate as refuges since blockage of the entrances would have cut off all ventilation to the inhabitants. If this was the purpose, one would expect greater evidence of the storage in the underground systems.

4) Burial - (Gilead 1987): Only a few systems contained evidence of burials. Excavations of these systems have produced conclusive evidence that a small number were used for this purpose. Burials in these systems were usually those of individuals buried without grave goods. Except in one case in Neve Noy (Eldar & Baumgarten 1985 137) the rooms adjoining that of the burial were found to be empty of any objects. It is probable that burial in these systems represented the last phase of use of the systems. It should be emphasised that use of only one room for an individual burial in these complicated, multi-room underground systems would have been unlikely considering the overall investment of labour in their construction. Cave burials are common in the Chalcolithic period and have been uncovered in sites such as Hadera, Azor and Peqi'in. However, these burial caves contained evidence of multiple burials and ossuraries (Perrot & Ladiray 1980; Levy 1986 96-99; Gal 1977).

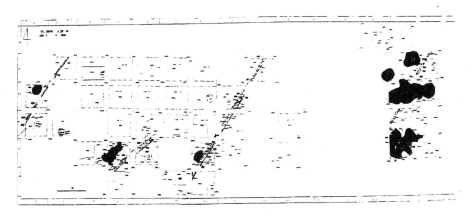

Fig. 2. Tel Sheva, area C (Black areas = subterranean systems)

In view of the points raised here, it is likely that the underground systems were used for domestic dwellings, particularly when one considers the environment, climate and the advantages of the use of earth for insulation.

There are two possible means of testing this hypothesis, in view of the lack of archaeological evidence that would otherwise clarify the function of the underground systems.

1. Comparison with function of modern systems of such type that would contain parallels with the Chalcolithic examples.

A) If one considers that the type of dwelling constructed in the harshest climatic conditions on the planet - the igloo (Forde 1964 117-121; Rapoport 1969 96) is based on the insulation of natural material with warmth provided by body heat and a small oil lamp, the size and shape of these structures are parallel to the type of

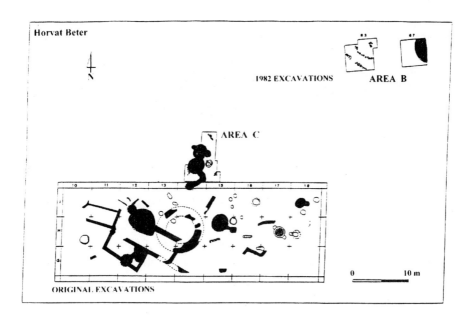

Fig. 3. Horvat Beter (Black areas = subterranean systems)

underground rooms found at Tel Sheva and may have functioned in a similar manner.

B) In China's Jiangs province, thousand of people have lived for centuries in underground systems cut into loessy soil:

"Home for Z, Y and their three young children is a cave, but such a living quarters have their advantages. The front is a large opening with a door and wooden-framed windows covered by translucent oil-paper to admit light. Inside are rooms that are cool in summer and easy to keep warm in winter (...). The (...) home is one of many carved in rows up a hillside to form a kind of vertical village. Such earthen cave dwellings, long used in this region of steep but easy excavated hills (...). Using hand tools, a family can carve a warm, dry and even airy home, 3 by 5.5 meters, in just a few month" (van Tulleken 1985 24-25,100)

From the testimony of people who are living in such dwellings we can read that:
"People in our part of the country prefer living in caves. This is largely because our loessial soil makes cave building easy and the result is a nicer and better insulated dwelling then an ordinary house. I must have built a good cave in my day. My father taught me how to build them (...). There are two kinds of caves: earth ones and a stone ones. The earth caves are dug into the hillside. The first thing to do is to find a place with right kind of soil, hard yellow loessial soil (...). You don't need many people to build an earthen cave. An ordinary cave of normal size 18-19 chi (9.6- 10 m.) long 9-10 chi (4.8-5.3 m.) high and 8-9 chi (4.2-4.8 m.) wide (...) takes about

Neve Noy

Fig. 4. Beer Safad (= Neve Noy), (Black areas = subterranean systems)

forty work-days. A house of the same size the same or a little less' but it isn't so practical and costs more to heat. At first, caves are slightly damp, but they dry out after three or five months (...). People prefer, as I said, to live in caves, because they are warmer in winter and cooler in summer; But earth caves don't last well, and they can also be dangerous. Even if the soil is of good quality, an earth cave seldom last more than two or three generations." (Myrdal 1965 12-14)

Also in China's Shanxi, Kansu, Shenxi, and Yan'an provinces this type of dwelling is widespread and it appears that at least ten million Chinese live in underground systems (van Tullken 1985 24-25).

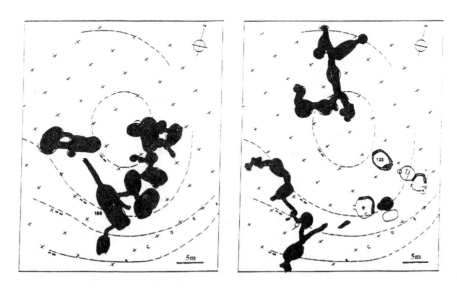

Fig. 5. Abu Matar (Black areas = subterranean systems)

C) In Tunis' Matamata region, underground dwellings exist which contain rooms with specific functions: living rooms, storage rooms and animal shelters. One these structures is used today as a hotel (Kempe 1988 249; Edwards 1980 212-21`3; Golany 1983b, 10-13). Concerning these structures it is said:

" Cave and earth dwellings (of) the world (all) over keep warm in winter and cool in summer, a fact certainly appreciated by the Berbers. They are mainly farmers, herding flocks and cultivating some wheat and barley (...). Water is the major problem and the meagre rainfall - some 8 to 12 inches per year in the hills - is conserved by dams to feed the *oueds*, river beds that are usually dry, which then irrigate terraces built on the same level ... " (Rapoport 1969 90 Fig.4.3 Kempe 1988 134-140).

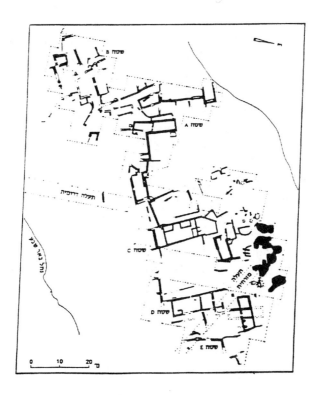

Fig. 6. Shikmim (Black areas = subterranean systems)

An account of this way of life would appear to exactly describe a Chalcolithic site in the Negev. However, the proportions of the living rooms and passages are larger than those of the Negev structures.

In the last two countries, China and Tunis, the soil is loess and the climatic conditions are similar to Israel's Negev region.

2. Experiments and tests concern the feasibility of dwelling underground.

Dwellings constructed aboveground are exposed to radiation and overheating whereas underground dwellings experience uniform temperatures (Etzion & Faiman 1983; Kaplan 1983; Rapoport 1969 90; Forester & Mulligan 1988).

In Israel, experiments have taken place, using earth as a building material at Sede Boqer. An experimental underground dwelling was constructed out of loess (Kaplan 1983; Etzion & Faiman 1983; Golany 1983b, 42; Pearlmutter, Evyatar & Etzion 1993, 11). The experiment showed conclusive evidence of energy conservation. Experimental dwellings that have been built by environmentalists in the United States revealed a near fifty-percent in energy conservation and similar results have been found concerning underground dwellings (Forester & Mulligan 1988).

We should bear in mind that from a long time before the Chalcolithic period man has been capable of producing fire. On the other hand, only in modern times has it been possible to cool dwellings by the use of electric air conditioners. The underground systems were used as dwellings during hot months and took advantage of the feature of constant temperatures and passive air conditioning.

Underground dwellings have enjoyed widespread use throughout human history (Kempe 1988; Golany 1983b) and are also widespread in modern times. At least ten million Chinese and 10,000 Native Americans benefit from the advantages of this type of dwelling (Forester & Mulligan 1988 12).

In spite of the obvious advantages of dwelling underground, such as: constant uniform temperatures, the conservation of energy, sheltering from wind and dust (as was proved experimentally); and in spite of their use in China and elsewhere, this type of dwelling has barely been used in modern construction in the Middle East and North America (Golany 1983a, 13, Fig.1-2).

It appears that the reluctance of living underground, and the lack of awareness of the advantages of this type of dwelling, are due to our way of thinking as people accustomed to living above ground (Golany 1983), and to the our cultural background but not to the facts.

REFERENCES

Alon D., 1988, The Spatial Distribution of Chalcolitic Settlement in the Southern Shefela, in: Stern E. & Urman D. (eds.) *Man and Environment in the Southern Shefela*, 84-88 (Hebrew)

Alon D., 1989, The Patriarchs stories and the Chalcolitic Period, *Alpayim* 1, 55-77 (Hebrew)

Alon D., 1991, Horvat Abu Hof, *Daroma* 1, 2-13 (Hebrew)

Alon D., Levy T.E., 1996, Demographic and Climate Problems during the Chalcolithic Period in the 1996 Northern Negev: Case Studiesfrom Gilat and Shiqmim, *Eretz - Israel* 25, 41-44 (Hebrew)

Amiran R., 1978, *Early Arad*, The Chalcolitic settlement and Early Bronze city, Jerusalem

Baumgarten Y., 1986, New Aspects of Chalcolitic Bir es-Safadi in the Light of 1982 Excavations. *Michmanim* 3, 31-36 (Hebrew, English Summary)

Bruins H., 1976, *Origins, Nature and Stratigraphy of Paleosols in the Loessial Deposit of Western Negev*. MSD. Department of Geology. Hebrew University, Jerusalem

Cohen R., 1976, Horvat 'Ashan , *Hadashot Arciologiot* 69-70, 49-50 (Hebrew)

Cohen R., 1986, *The Settlement of the Central Negev*. Jerusalem (Unpublished Ph. D. dissertation), (Hebrew)

Commenge - Pellerin C., 1987, *La poterie d'Abu Matar et de l'audai Zoumeili (Beersheva) au IVe millenaire avant l'ere chretienne* (CRFJ 3) Jerusalem

Commenge - Pellerin C., 1990, *La poterie de Safadi (Beersheva) au IVe millenaire avant l'ere chretienne* (CRFJ 5), Jerusalem

Dothan M., 1959, Excavations at Horvat Beter (Beersheva). *Atiqot* 2 (ES), 1-42

Edwards M., (Harvey D.A. Photographer) 1980, Tunisia: Sea, Sand, Success, *National Geographic*, 157, 184-217

Eldar E., Baumgarten Y., 1985, Neve Noy, a Chalcolithic Site of the Beer-Sheava Culture, *Biblical Archaelogist* 48, 134-139

Etzion I., Faiman D., 1983, The Solar Adobe House at Sede Boqer, *Alef Alef* 4/5, 25-26

Evin J., 1995, Possibilité et necessité de la calibration des datations C-14 de l'archéologie du Proche-Orient , *Paleorient* 21, 15-16

Forde D. C., 1964, *Habitat , Economy and Society* , London. (Methuen & Co Ltd)

Forester P., Mulligan 1988, Coming to Ground, *The Geographical Magazine* 60: 10, 12-19

Gilead I., 1987, A New Look at Chalcolitic Beer –Sheava, *Biblical Archaelogist* 50, 110-117

Gilead I., 1988, The Chalcolitic Period in the Levant, *Journal of World Prehistory* 2, 397-441

Gilead I., 1994, The History of the Chalcolitic Settlement in the Nahal Beer Sheva Area: The Radiocarbon Aspect, *Bulletin of the American Schools of Oriental Reaserch* (BASOR) 291, 1-13

Golany G. S., 1983a, Urban Form Design for Arid Regios, in: *Design For Arid Regions*. Golany G. S (ed.), New York (Van Nostrand Reinhold Company)

Golany G. S., 1983b, *Earth-Sheltered Habitat*, New York (Van Nostrand Reinhold Company)

Gonen R., 1992, The Chalcolithic Period, in: *The Archaeology of Ancient Israel*, New Haven.

Gophna R., 1982, The Chalcolitic Period, in: Ephal I. (ed.) *The History of Eretz Israel*. Vol. 1, 76-94, Jerusalem

Govrin Y., Horvat Hor, 1987, A Dwelling Cave from the Chalcolithic Period in the Northern Negev, *Mitekufat Haeven* 20, 119*-127*

Hoffman M. A., 1984, *Egypt Before the Pharaohs*, London (Ark Paperbacks)

Joffe A. H., Dessel J. P., 1995, Redefining Chronology and Terminology for the Chalcolitic of Southern Levant, *Current Anthropology* 36:3, 507-518

Kaplan M., 1983, Earth Building in Israel, *Alef Alef*, 4/5, 22-24

Kempe D., 1988, *Living Underground. A History of Cave and Cliff Dwelling*, London (The Herbert Press)

Levy T. E., 1986, The Chalcolithic Period, *Biblical Archaeologist* 49, 82-108

Levy T. E. (ed.), 1987, *Shiqmim* I (BAR Int. Series 356), Oxford

Levy T. E., Alon D., Grigson C., Holl A., Goldberg P., Rowan Y., Smith P., 1991, Subterranean Negev Settlement in the Negev Desert ca. 4500-3700 b.c., *National Geographic Research and Exploration* 7, 394-414

Myrdal J., 1965, *Report from a Chinese Village*, New York (Vintage Books)

Pearlmutter D.. Evyatar E., Etzion Y., 1993, Monitoring the Thermal Performance of an Insulataed Earth-sheltered Structre: A Hot-arid Zone Case Study. *Architectural Science Review* 36, 3-12

Perrot J., 1984, Structures d'habitat, mode de vie et environnement. Les villages souterrains des pasteurs de Beersheva dans le sud d'Israel, au IVe millenaiire avant l'ere chretienne, *Paleorient* 10:1, 75-96

Perrot J., 1955, The Excavations at Tell Abu Matar near Beersheba, *IEJ* 5, 17-40, 73-84, 164-186

Ladiray D., Perrot J., 1980, *Tombes a ossuaires de la region cotiere palestinienne au IVe millenaire avant l'ere chretienne.* Memoires et Travaux du CRFJ. Association Paleorient, Paris

Rosen S., Eldar I., 1993, Horvat Beter, Revisited: The 1982 Salvage Excavations, *Atiqot* 22, 13-27

Thuesen I., 1983, A Chalcolithic Subterranean Dwelling, In: *Ergebnisse Der Ausgrabungen auf der Hirbet El-msas (Tel Masos) 1972-1975*, Wiesbaden, 114-122 (Otto Harrassowitz)

Todd I. A., 1991, The Vasilikos Valley and the Chalcolitic Period in Cyprus, *BASOR* 282-283, 3-16

Van Tullken K. (ed.), 1985, *China*, Amsterdam (Time-Life Books)

Zbigniew E. Szafrański
Warsaw

Settlement in Egypt in the First Half of the Second Millennium BC
Summary

The so-called town problem has been investigated with application of different methods. They based very often on only one criteria, for example that of philological, juridical, economic, social, geographic, etc. nature. The discussion has resulted in extremely, sometimes opposite, options. Egypt was once described as a „*civilisation without cities*".

B.J. Kemp has pointed to archaeological excavations, and to results of analysis of archaeological settlement material, as one more source of information in studies on a town problem in ancient Egypt. Archaeological investigation became then a *conditio sine qua non* of researches on this subject. New projects of researches at such sites as Elephantine, El-Amarna and Tell el-Dab'a inaugurated a new subdiscipline within Egyptology, called „settlement archaeology".

Urban layouts of Egyptian town and town elements are the subject of this paper. Description of the collected materials consists of the following elements:

1. Description of site and covered area
2. Stratigraphy of settlement
3. Town elements
4. Settlement archaeological material.

Pottery (4.1) and finds (4.2), among them tools (4.2.1), have been analysed in order to estimate function of settlement elements. Written sources, if not mentioned earlier (§ 1), were discussed at this point.

A town or settlement consisted of several topographical elements (§ 3). In this study twelve main elements have been proposed in order to describe a given urban layout. They were arranged in the following scheme:

1. Enclosure walls.
2. Administrative building (buildings). Two types of buildings were discussed:
    2.1. palace (palaces), and/or
    2.2. command building.

3. Temple (temples).

4. Chapels or/and sanctuaries.

5. Dwellings.

To take the description more clearly and for further analysis, dwellings (these characteristic elements of urban layout) have been described as:

    5.1. house types, and

    5.2. house units.

6. Storage installations.

7. Industrial and economic installations.

8. Open areas.

9. Gardens.

10. Tombs or cemeteries; their relation to settlement.

11. Streets.

12. Water-conduits.

Analysis of relations between the above described elements has provided conclusions as to their function within urban layout. A final conclusion has depended on condition of preserved materials, excavated area, quality and quantity of sources, etc. Type of town or settlement, however, was not always clear, but types of urban layouts should be more broadly defined. „City" is not understood in a most narrow sense and this feature of urbanism was characteristic of Egyptian civilisation.

Marta Guzowska

Warsaw

Contexts for Minoan finds in Cyprus
Summary

The variety of products which were traded across the Mediterranean in the Late Bronze Age is amazing. Most of them cannot be traced today in archaeological contexts but we learn from occasionally preserved written sources, like the Egyptian story of Wenamun about timber, jars full of gold and silver, clothing of byssus, Egyptian linen, veils and other fabrics, oxhide ingots, ropes, food lentils, fish and various other perishables.

In theory all closed vessels of Cretan manufacture imported in the eastern Mediterranean may have been used to transport organic products, most probably thick liquids and ointments, and the presence of Minoan pottery in foreign context may thus suggest that such an exchange took place. In fact however, among Minoan vessels imported in Cyprus we find only two types which undoubtedly were used in transporting perishables across the Mediterranean - stirrup jars were most likely containing thin, pourable oil products, and large, wide mouthed vessels like pithoid jars and jugs may have contained thick oil substances of various types referred to in Linear B as *we-a-re-pe*, seeds, dried fruits, grain or resins. Most - if not all - Minoan pots from Cyprus couldn't however be used as containers in overseas exchange. They were themselves objects of trade, sold abroad as attractive table- and houseware of much finer quality than the local Cypriot pottery. As such they must have been much appreciated by their owners - it may possibly be proved by contexts in which Minoan vessels are found in Cyprus. Indeed ordinary transport vessels are usually found in contexts suggesting their smaller value for their Cypriot owners when compared to the fine, decorated pottery.

Results of the latest archaeological research

Jan Bouzek

Praha

Charles University of Prague excavations in Beirut, Martyrs Square

Preliminary report

Following the invitation of the Beirut UNESCO Quarters and the Directorate of Antiquities of Lebanon, a six weeks excavation season was conducted in spring 1996 in the city centre of Beirut, on the Martyrs Square, in the sector called Bey 69, Sondage A.[1] The 30 x 10 m sector offered to us was situated on the western side of the square (Fig. 1). The excavations were enabled by the support given by the UNESCO, which covered the main parts of the expenses, while several smaller contributions by private persons helped to cover the rest.[2]

---

[1] Cf. J. Bouzek, Bey 69, sondage A: preliminary report. *Bulletin d'archéologie et d'architecture Libanaises 1 1996*, 135-147. Besides the undersigned who was the bearer of the excavation permit, Prof. Radislav Hošek, epigraphist, Prof. Petr Charvát, orientalist who worked on Medieaval Glazed Ware, Mgr.Jiří Musil, who acted as the vice-director of the excavations, Mgr. Jana Kupková and three of our students: Pavel Titz, Alice Hayerová and Martin Trefný participated.

[2] We would like to thank for the support of our mission to the Department of Antiquities, Dr. Camil Asmar and Mrs. Renata Oteli Tarawzi, to the UNESCO Beirut Headquarters, whose financial support covered the main part of the expenses, most notably to Mr. Bensalah and Mr. Joe Kreidi, and to our colleagues of other missions for their friendly support: Prof. Hans Curvers and his colleagues from the Dutch mission working under the Solidaire project, whose support was indispensable, Dr. Christine Aubert from the Institut francaise d'archéologie du Proche Orient, Prof. Helga Seeden from the American University of Beirut, Prof. Muntaha Saghiyé from the Lebanese University. Prof. J.W. Hayes kindly checked much of our Roman pottery classifications and advised us in this field, and our Lebanese assistant Omaya Faraldine. At the end, our gratitude goes especially to our ambassador in Beirut, Dr.Petr Skalník, who initiated our mission and prepared, in collaboration with other members of our embassy, the main framework for our participation in the project.

The excavation was divided into three 10 by 10 m square, supervised by Mgr. Musil, Mgr. Kupková and M. Trefný, A. Hayerová was in charge of the pottery finds. The site revealed a very complicated stratigraphy. Already the upper layers contained fragments of Early Roman pottery (Eastern Sigillata A, a few fragments of Italic sigillata and one fragment of an Italic lamp), several sherds of Hellenistic Black-Glazed ware, and also one Black-Glazed lip fragment of cup and one fragmentary wheel-turned lamp of c. 300 B.C. Most of them belong to classes which also have turned up in the lower layers on the spot, and came to their secondary position mainly through the pilage or excavations for the 17th and 19th century foundations. It must be remembered that all building activities here not only destroyed earlier foundations, but reused remains of them several times: even the latest 19th century pillar bases rested partly on remaining fragments of earlier stone foundations. Fig. 2 gives the generalized picture of the architectonic development of the area.

1. The earliest finds

Though several chipped stone blades dating from the Middle Bronze Age were uncovered, the site was long under the sea level, as marked by limestone beach rock, and only in the Hellenistic times it became part of the city.

The few walls using river stones for foundations date the sherds from their foundation trenches to the early Roman period; these stones may have been reused, as was observed elsewhere in the area, from some Phoenician-Persian building. But we found none in our sector. The earliest finds from our sector dating from c. 300 and early 3rd century B.C. are extremely rare and scattered: they cannot bear witness to an intense occupation of this area.

2. Hellenistic city

The Hellenistic technique of foundations was fine: the outer faces of the foundation walls were made straight, and the interior carefully composed as a mosaic. The walls built on these foundations are of well dressed stone blocks joined without mortar.

The pottery from the foundation deposits in our area dates the Hippodamean planning of the new quarter of the Hellenistic city of Berytus in the second half of the third century B.C., before 200 B.C., when the city was still under the Ptolemies, before it came to the Seleucids. The early deposits contain Hellenistic pottery from late third to early second century B.C. Some of these deposits may perhaps be connected with the report of the destruction of Beirut in 145 B.C. by Tryphon. But only in one place in square 2 we found traces of burning underlying later construction on identical foundation wall, and generally the repairs and new construction followed the earlier system of main walls. There is hardly any reason to

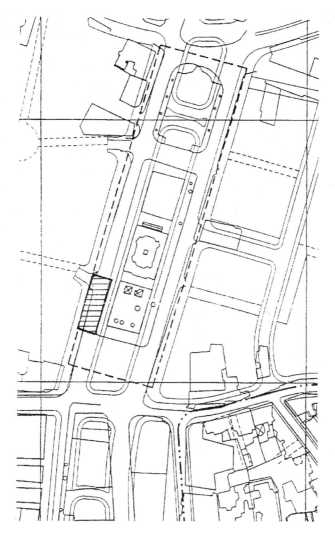

Fig. 1. Beirut, Martyrs Square, with our sector of Charles University
excavations (Bey 62, Sondage A) marked by hatching (J. Musil)

believe that the changing of political power would be connected with change of
town-planning whose general rules were identical in all parts of the Hellenistic
world.

In squares 2 and 3 we found the perforated limestone rocks of an ancient
shoreline running c. NW - SE. The pits dug into the virgin yellow sedimentary soil
here between the rocks contained Hellenistic and some very early Roman pottery
fragments. We know from many parts of the Mediterranean that the sea level there
was lower in Hellenistic times than it is now. Perhaps this sinking of sea level
encouraged the Hellenistic planners to use this rather low area of a shallow ravine,

where the abundance of water flowing in winter months from the hills southwards necessitated a well-functioning system of drainage to include this area in the enlarged city plan.

As other areas excavated in the centre of Beirut, also our sondage has shown traces of participation of overseas trade links since the earliest times recorded. Attic Black-Glazed pottery and lamps from early 3rd century B.C. are among the earliest documents of this kind, but they only come from secondary deposits.

Megarian bowls (Figs. 4: 1-4 and Fig. 5: 1), West Slope (Fig. 3) and late Black-Glazed pottery were imported from the Aegean (Ephesus, Pergamon and other centres in southern Ionia, even from Athens), from northern Syria (Fig. 3: 4) and Palestine. The West Slope fragments found seem to be Attic and Pergamene, the Lagynos Ware items probably Syrian. Several terracotta figurines found in fragments (standing male in cloak, sitting woman) are of types designed in West Anatolian workshops and are either imports or close local imitations of types from this area.

Transport amphorae from Rhodes and Kos are well attested (the former even with stamped handles) and they were followed by Italic (Dressel 1-2) imports. The Aegean wares of Hellenistic Beirut show a composition similar to that found in Delos, an interesting parallel to the epigraphical testimony of a presence of merchants from Berytus at Delos.

Of the earliest Roman tablewares, Cypriot Red Slip is represented and Eastern Sigillata A (probably made in North Syria) is common here (since their earliest stage in late second century B.C)., but other early red wares from the Aegean are also present. Their exact identification has to be confirmed by scientific analyses, but Aegean (Pergamene?) and Italic fragments seem to be repressented, even in small quantities only. Several crusted and corrroded coins, which could not be identified before conservation seem to date from the Hellenistic period.

3. Berytus Colonia

The Italic Augustean sigillata and Early Roman picture lamps seem to mark the beginnings of the Roman colonia: fragments of Italic amphorae of Dressel I-II types seem to go with them. Some of the less high quality Red-Glazed Ware fragments seem to be either local or coming from the vicinity of Beirut, as did some of their Black-Glazed predecessors of similar character.

Some deposits of the first century B.C. pottery may perhaps be connected with the smaller troubles during the civil war between Antonius and Octavianus, and with rebuildings of the city, when Berytus Colonia was founded shortly after the battle of Actium: other innovations may perhaps have been connected also with the Herodian building activities in Berytus described by Josephus Flavius.

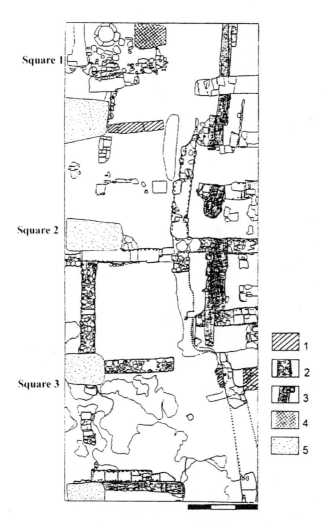

Fig. 2. Our sector of excavations (Bey 62, sondage A). 1 Hellenistic walls, 2 Early Roman walls, 3 Byzantine drains, 4 Byzantine walls and floors, 5 Late Ottoman pillars of a vaulting (J. Musil)

Some blown glass can be connected with the remains the earliest Roman colony. East Mediterranean amphorae are more common than Italic imports. Local items are the most common, Palestinian and Egyptian imports rare.

A close relation between the Hellenistic and Early Roman cities of Beirut in their planning was observed in other sectors excavated in the centre of the Lebanon's capital, and it seems that the originally Hellenistic foundations were also used again when reconstructing the Early Roman city of Berytus Colonia. Of destroyed Roman (and perhaps also Hellenistic) water conduits we found only fragments of clay water pipes.

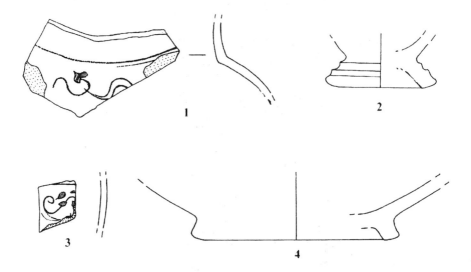

Fig. 3. Examples of West Slope and Black Glazed wares, Early to Middle Hellenistic. 1 WS amphora fragment with incised lines and red ivy leaves, from deposit 3203 D, rather Attic than Pergamene, 2 foot of the same fabric, also from deposit 3203, 3 WS fragment with incised lines and small leaves in red, probably Pergamene, from deposit 2704, 4 local Syrian bowl, interior poor glaze, outside unglazed, ochre clay, from deposit 3203 (A. Waldhauserová)

4. Middle Roman Period

The missing of larger pottery deposits of the second and third century A.D. has been observed also by other excavators and explained by them as a testimony of stability, when houses were kept tidy, the refuse brought out of the city, and the building activity connected with the rule of Septimius Severus and his wife Iulia Domna did not affect our insula in particular.

The Middle Roman material is scarce, as in other excavated sectors, and only later 3rd - 4th century again shows more intense imports of finer well-datable tableware. The Cypriot class is represented, besides some African Ware and several other eastern classes

5. Late Roman / Early Byzantine Period

Only the Late Roman city brought substantial changes of urbanistic planning and building system to our sector. Foundations of small stones just thrown unarranged in the foundation trench and using much soft mortar of whitish colour are typical for Late Roman to Early Byzantine constructions. They are often crossing remains of earlier walls built of large dressed blocks on subterranean rubble foundations, whose stones were carefully laid into the foundation trench: the lowest layer of Hellenistic and Early Roman walls is usually broader than the next courses, and no mortar is used.

In square 3, we found a deposit of Late Roman/Early Byzantine pottery on a floor of a house for whose foundations much white mortar had been used, and which has been largely demolished when it served as a quarry for later use of its stones. It seems that the main deposit with several transport amphorae (one of them found in situ) was left buried at the time of the earthquake in 551 A.D., but some fragments of later amphoras (among them imports from Egypt) show that the area, or the partly restored building, was used even later, and probably only abandoned in the Umayad period.

In the other two squares, there are only small Late Roman deposits left by later activities, but the walls preserved there show several construction phases of that period, two of them apparently preceding the earthquake, and one following it. In squares 1-2 we uncovered remains of several drains running mainly S-N, but with some branches also directed W-E. The drain system shows several phases. All drains are built of stone, without bricks and most of them (those of the main phase, not any more the replacements) had their bottoms plastered. In one place we found a small basin for cleaning.

The drains and the foundation walls all date from the Late Roman period: few fragments of cemented floors are just above them, and also fragments of marble tiles and marble revetments (of white grey and "black" marble, all apparently of NW Anatolian origin) and of mosaics, of which white limestone tesserae could still be found. A few tesserae still joined together by mortar were found overlying the drain 1514: the much destroyed wall on which it was lying, however, blocked just this drain, so it has been replaced by another drain running parallel, but without a cemented bottom.

One fragmentary mosaic with scale pattern was uncovered in the northern extension of our square 1, and fragments of drums and Ionic bases of small columns were overlying the ruins above the level where we started our excavations.

Another larger Byzantine floor has only been preserved in our square 3. In other places, the floors were either destroyed by later Mediaeval pilage, or were lying above the level we started our excavations.

Late Roman to early Byzantine layers show amphorae imported from various East Mediterranean centres, besides those from Lebanon, and also fine tableware from these areas. Also some fragments of Byzantine glass have been found.

7. An abandoned area: between Byzantine nad Mamlouk periods

During the Mediaeval period, our area was only a modest periphery of the town for many generations, without any new buildings constructed here. Traces of the pilage of the ruins and of seasonal floodings, which caused decomposition of bricks and mortar used in the upper parts of the ruins of Late Roman/Byzantine buildings (of whose walls many bigger stones were taken away for further use elsewhere), and traces of fire (in clay and in burnt decomposed bricks), are all witnesses of destruction and of centuries of abandonment of this part of the present centre of Beirut.

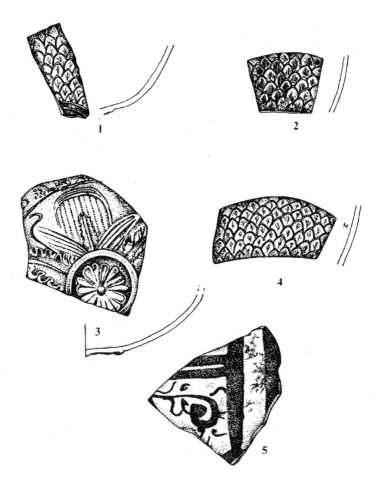

Fig. 4. Examples of Megarian bowls, Attic with imbrications (1-2, 4, from deposits 3005 and 3010) and Ephesian (3, Workshop *A dans carré*, from deposit 3010). 5 Mediaeval (Abside) fragment painted under the glaze (A. Waldhauserová)

A few fragents of Early Islamic glass vessels, some of them apparently of misblown items, suggest the existence of a glass workshop situated not far from our sondage, though its traces are much more modest than those found further northwards in the sector excavated by the French Institute (C. Aubert).

Mediaeval pottery fragments in our upper layers are single items which came here either with the 17th century levelling, or were brought here earlier between the 7th and 16th centuries. This group included Mediaeval glazed pottery of different classes, several bowls with sgraffito decoration and Abbaside vases painted under the glaze (fig. 4: 5), besides a few eastern imports and a few fragments perhaps dating of the Crussaders period.

The Umayad period seems to be still represented in the southernmost part of our sondage, where there seems to have been rather a slow decaying than a rapid end of the quarter, but fairly restricted number of Mediaeval pottery types, mainly provenant from the 16th century levelling layers, document only modest activities in this area, which seems to be abandoned, as were frequently other cities and their quarters lying close to the sea in all parts of the Merditerranean at that time, because of the frequent piracy.

The only iron object worth of mentioning seems is a heavily corroded fragment of a large arrowhead used for crossbow: its similarity to items known from Europe may suggest that it may have come from the period of the Crusaders.

8. The pottery workshops of 15th-16th century A.D.

The misfired fragments of black- and brown-glazed, and of unglazed pottery dating roughly to the transition from the Mamlouk to the Ottoman period (c. 15th - 16th century) show that pottery workshops existed near the area. This is also attested by clay cones and sticks used to separate the pots from each other when firing them in the kiln, all abundant in the Fakhr ed-Din levelling deposits. The winds blowing from the sea may have been useful for pottery kilns.

9. The gardens of Fakhr ed-Din

The forelast construction period ascertained is represented by garden arrangements with well-like constructions (probably big flower-pots) in our square 1, built with all probability by Fakhr ed-Din in early 17th century. For these gardens lying in the vicinity of his palace (which was probably situated below the present opera building), the area was levelled: the deposits connected with this arrangement contain large amounts of misfired fragments from potter's kilns of the 15th-16th century mentioned above, besides earlier pottery in secondary positions. 17th century constructions are of roughly dressed stones and brown mortar.

10. Between Fakhr ed-Din and the 19th century

No building activity could be ascertained here between the 16th and 19th centuries, but perhaps some constructions with shallow foundation may have escaped our notice due to the fact that all upper layers above the lavel of the pillar bases of the 19th century arcades had already been removed before we started our excavations here. Also only one Ottoman tobacco pipe has been found.

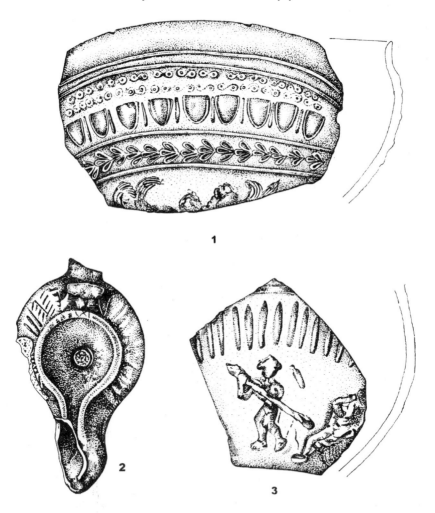

Fig. 5. 1 and 3 Megarian bowl fragments. 1 Ephesus, Workshop *A dans carré* (from deposit 3005), 2 local bowl, satyr and maenad (from deposit 3010). 2 Lamp of the Ephesian type, probably import from Ephesus (A. Waldhauserová)

11. The modern city and the civil war

The uppermost construction in our sector was the foundations of a Late Ottoman souk of the 19th century A.D., similar to those lying more to the west of the Place of Martyrs. According to the information availablee to us, jewellers and money-changing offices were situated here, besides one famous shop selling sweets. The bases of pillars of the vaulted construction of foundations could be ascertained at the western edge of the strip we were excavating, and in several places also some fragments of the collapsed vaulting could be traced, notably in our sector 3. This large construction also affected changes in the earlier layers around the pillars, for which pits were dug. The pillars was at a distance c. 6 m from each other, reasonable for the c. 3 m high vaulting, traces of which could still be seen where unearthed by the baggers along the parking place west of our sector.

The use of identical pinkish mortar connects this building both with the now demolished canal, which ran across our sondage from south to north, and with the cellars of the Saint George church of the Maronites. These buildings were forming the western edge of the Martyrs Square until the civil war.

Conclusion

Our rescue excavation was part of the restoration project of the destroyed city centre, and the area is now used for subterranean garages. Though only a modest slice of evidence for the history of the Lebanese capital, our sondage could confirm that this part of the Martyrs Square had a story similar to other sectors of the inner city: flourishing occupation starting in Hellenistic times and continuing up to the end of Classical Antiquity, then long abandonment, reuse as gardens in the 17th century, and reintegration in the modern town in the 19th century, of which it became the centre, now emerging from its last ruins caused by the civil war. Let's its reconstruction bring anew fresh life here, as we all hope.

Violeta Pereyra, Eduardo Crivelli, Silvia Lupo,
Silvana Fantechi and Andrea Zingarelli
Buenos Aires

TELL EL-GHABA:
THREE SEASONS OF EXCAVATION IN NORTH SINAI

INTRODUCTION

The "North Sinai Archaeological Salvage Project", an international cooperation plan for the preservation of archaeological resources, was launched by the S(upreme) C(ouncil) of A(ntiquities) of Egypt as an answer to the impact of the "Northern Sinai Agricultural Development Project". In this context, the Argentine Archaeological Mission, under the direction of Perla Fuscaldo, started work at Tell el-Ghaba in 1995, financed mainly by the National Council for Scientific Research and the University of Buenos Aires, but also by private sponsors.

THE AREA

The regional settlement system was conditioned by the coastal plain and the active freshwater course. The coastline prograded and lacked good harbors. The Pelusiac branch of the Nile featured a changing course along its existence, until it ceased to flow around the 7th century AD (Sneh and Weissbrod, 1973). Thus, the colonization of the easternmost part of the Delta was oriented not only by the ancient Egyptian policy toward the Levant, but also by the processes of silting up of the Nile branches and the seaward advance of the Mediterranean shoreline. The distribution of the reported archaeological sites seems to follow these processes: Pharaonic sites are south of the Flandrian coast line and scattered around both the Western and the Eastern lagoons, while the later ones are found in the Post-Pelusiac plain (Chartier-Raymond and Traunecker, 1993:46-50).

The major sites enclose important evidences of the Greek and Roman Periods (4th BC - 4th AD): Pelusium, a famous harbor linked with the Levantine trade, Tell Abu-Seifah, and Tell el-Herr. The last one also comprises occupation levels dated from Persian to Byzantine periods. Pelusium, frequently mentioned in classical sources, was identified at the mouth of the defunct Pelusiac branch and seems to be the largest site in the area. It is already mentioned by Herodotus (III, 10), who reports that Psammetichus III was defeated by Cambyses nearby.

Being the only land bridge between Egypt and the Levant, North Sinai was crossed by troops, trade expeditions, herders and invaders and, as ancient sources show, from the end of the IIIrd millennium BC, Egyptian rulers established frontier outposts and fortresses along the coastal road to Palestine to give support to garrisons, supplies for royal messengers or soldiers and security for traders. This road is already mentioned in Egyptian texts from the Middle Kingdom referring to *inbw hk3* (the Ruler's Wall) and to *w3t hr*. This last toponym, meaning "Horus Way", may refer to a road, a fortress or an area in north Sinai.

Several settlements flourished at least from the New Kingdom. Thus, in a relief of Seti I in Karnak, several forts, associated to wells, lay along the military road to Pi-Canaan, which begins close to a fresh water course ("the frontier canal" - Kitchen 1992:8-) that flows into the sea.

The drying of the Pelusiac branch turned what was the eastern border of the Delta into stark desert, peopled by nomad herders. Nevertheless, the importance of North Sinai as a land bridge continues until now.

THE SITE

A littoral fringe of c. 200-500 m between the sea coast and two lagoons (that are depressions of c. 1 m under the sea level) was formed during the Flandrian transgression (c. 6.000 BC). A deposit of pumice stone, that points out to an ancient sea edge, was discovered near Hebua I (Chartier-Raymond -Traunecker, 1993:61). The ancient coastal and flood plain is covered by more recent dune systems

Tell el-Ghaba is located on the "Sand tongue" of the flat coastal plain of North Sinai. The place is a low, sandy elevation jutting as a triangular peninsula into the Eastern Lagoon, a marshy depression which surrounds the site by the east, south and west. In Pharaonic times, the lagoon was probably fed by the Pelusiac branch, and the sea shore was closer than today (Marcolongo, 1992:24).

As its modern Arab name indicates, Tell el-Ghaba is sparsely covered by tamarisks and other bushes. Several sand dunes, up to 4 m higher than the surrounding terrain and fixed by bushes, strongly suggest that deflation has been very active, sweeping away the upper levels of the site.

The strategic position of Tell el-Ghaba where an ancient road to Palestine crosses the Sinaitic frontier of Egypt perhaps explains that it had been settled during several historical periods. In effect, it was occupied at least from the Saite Period, but artifacts found in the periphery suggest occupations from other periods (see below). There are hints that the site was a frontier post of some importance. It was perhaps linked with two nearby sites: Tell el-Hebua and Tell el-Kedua. The former was identified as an Egyptian New Kingdom stronghold (Abd el-Maksoud, 1986 and 1989); the second was a fortified place in the Persian period (Oren, 1982).

The utilization of North Sinai archaeological sites for military goals has continued until very recent times, and Tell el-Ghaba was not an exception: an Israeli division was situated there during the occupation of Sinai, from which some archaeological disturbance resulted.

FORMER INVESTIGATIONS

Research at Tell el-Ghaba began with the rescue project. The French Mission of Lille University, directed by Dominique Valbelle, performed prospections at a regional scale in which course, between 1990-1992, Tell el-Ghaba was surveyed. The published plan of the site and the field notes and drawings (which were kindly sent to us by the French Mission) represented the most specific information available before our first campaign.

After these preliminary operations by the French Mission, Nabil Sherif (from the SCA) dug some squares in 1992. Unfortunately, until now it has not been possible for us to read Sherif's report or to examine the archaeological materials recovered during this season. In 1995, the Argentine Mission cleaned the area and surveyed a building uncovered by the Egyptian team.

The reconnaissances suggest that Tell el-Ghaba comprises occupations mainly from the Saite and Persian periods (7th - 4th centuries BC), including public and private buildings, living and industrial areas, and burials.

SURVEY AND EXCAVATIONS OF THE ARGENTINE MISSION

INTRODUCTION

Objectives of the Argentine Mission are manifold. Principally, they concern paleoenvironment, chronology, composition of the population, economy, organization of the settlement, setting of the site in the network of national and international relationships, beliefs, and burial practices. Available ecological, archaeological and documentary data were intertwined in what seemed the most plausible *a priori* model, which is contrasted against the evidence and subsequently reformulated. Three field seasons (1995, 1996 and 1997) were carried out at Tell el-

Ghaba, under the organization of Project Vice-Director V. Pereyra. E. Crivelli was Field Director.

RECORDING SYSTEM

The layout of the excavation consists a of a 5 m by 5 m-square grid, oriented toward the cardinal points. The basic recording system consists of both chronological and systematic, graphic and textual documents:

	CHRONOLOGICAL	SYSTEMATIC
TEXTUAL	Journal Photography Record	Locus Sheet Floor/Surface Sheet Wall Sheet Installation Sheet Burial Sheet Carbon-14 Sheet Operation Sheet
GRAPHIC	Top Plans Sections	

Following Harris' proposal (Harris 1979), stratigraphic control is kept all the time along the excavation and not confined to sections.

FIELD WORK

Generalities

Field work began in September 1995 in the southeast side of site, in a level surface clear of dunes and seemingly not much affected by clandestine excavations (Area I).

As knowledge of the local stratigraphy was deemed a priority for the first season, five squares were vertically excavated under the supervision of two or three members of the Mission. Since we wanted many sections, 50 cm balks were left at each side of each square. Two units were dug until sterile sediment, one of them reaching groundwater at 1.75 m from surface.

Once the topographic survey of the site was completed by the architect and stakes set in, a systematic, aligned surface sampling was performed. All archaeological material was collected in an area of 2 x 2 meters at each 50 x 50 meters intersection. This sampling resulted informative in deflated areas, but failed where the surface was covered by recent dunes, confirming that geomorphic setting takes precedence to sampling design (see Brookes, Levine and Dennell 1982:299). In consequence, a second, rather opportunistic surface sampling, by small areas and transects across deflated areas, was carried out as a complement.

For the 1996 season, with an increased crew and impending risk of bulldozing in parts of the site, it was accorded that the dig should progress in at least two fronts, with intensive excavation in some areas and exploratory, quicker work in other parts of it. Decisions concerning target areas were taken according differing, explicit tactics and priorities.

In accordance with this plan, two series of operations were conducted:

a. In the area opened in 1995, several balks were dug away, in order to connect loci and structures: then, four additional squares were opened, to continue exposing two structures identified in 1995.

b. Considering the strategic position of Tell el-Ghaba in a corridor along a frontier area, it was deemed highly possible the existence of some substantial defensive structure, as a fortification and/or a town wall. Since the aim was to intercept a linear feature, continuous trenches were considered more adequate than test pits. Four slit (1 meter wide) trenches were planned, starting from a roughly central point of the site in Area II (stake AZ BA 70 71), towards the four cardinal points. They would be dug until the first feature was found and, for better control, they would be excavated in segments 20 meters long. Each trench would be called an Operation and would be given a number. The conditional tenses in the preceding sentences indicate that this plan was carried out only in part, since soon after it was launched, a substantial structure was spotted and we turned to horizontal excavation to expose it as much as possible.

In the present report, Area I and Area II are treated separately.

Area I

The sequence will be summarized in chronological order.

1. Sterile soil is greenish, very plastic clay, quite similar to the one forming the bottom of the Oriental Lagoon. The first feature built in Area I is Building A, excavated only in part because it extends outside the opened squares and later features were built over it. It measured at least 4 x 2 meters. Two foundation trenches, L[ocus]101 and L102, each geminating at the bottom, were found, running at right angles (NNE - SSW and WNW - ESE); we expect to find at least two additional ones. They received the walls of what should have been a flimsy building, which we found thoroughly burned. Oxidation runs along the foundation trenches and spreads to at least part of the floor (L44), an additional indication that the building materials were light and opposed no obstacle to the flames (a smoldering fire should have carbonized the interior).

2. After the destruction of Building A, a small cooking pit (L37), 30 cm wide at mouth and 20 cm deep, was dug. It suggests that at the time, this was an open area. In the very carbonaceous fill of the pit, some scraps of bone were found, and two freshwater mussel shells remained at the bottom.

3. Building B is a later, larger, complex mudbrick building. Exposed still only in part, it measured not less than 14 m x 8 m and enclosed at least five rooms and a magazine. It covered Building A, but kept its orientation, a first hint of continuity in the internal organization of the settlement across different episodes of occupation. No foundation trenches were dug; instead, for each wall, one course of (mostly) headers was disposed as a base and then, stretchers (with some headers) were added.

Up to now, two ovens, L13 and L176, have been found in Building B. Considering the hot, dry climate of north Sinai, the enclosed areas in which they have been built may well have been open courtyards. Oven L13 was built of mud and some reused mudbricks. Two big jars were lying on the top of the fire area. Oven L176 was constructed forming part of wall L179. A fragment of a big plate was found on the burned area.

The magazine (L84) may be called a cellar, since the floor was at a somewhat lower level than the first course of the walls. Inside, several pots were found *in situ*.

4. Structure B was subject to some rebuilding or reuse: new courses of mudbricks were added to wall L23; curiously enough, a hearth had been lit on top of the old wall and was found sandwiched between the two series of bricks.

Later human activity at the site, perhaps united to deflation (see below), seriously damaged Building B, to the point that only patches of possible floors have been found up to now: L17-18 and L98. A golden bead of both longitudinal and radial symmetry, made of small spheres, was found in L17.

5. What seems to be a cooking and industrial area was partly uncovered south of Building B, with center in a hearth or oven (L186) associated to a bricked area (L201). The stratified fill of L186, comprising charcoal, burned earth and many bones (mainly of fish), points to a cooking place; but it may have been for industrial use as well, as suggested by abounding bits of faience slag found in the surroundings and into a channel connecting the fire feature with the depressed area to the north.

6. A later human activity, that prevents us from getting a better knowledge of Building B, left many long and narrow furrows crisscrossing roughly at right angles, very difficult to interpret for the time being. They may be the foundation trenches of flimsy structures; nevertheless, no traces of reeds or of other light building materials have been noted at the bottom of these furrows. Determining which are contemporary would help to isolate possible trenches of single buildings; but the upper parts have been eroded away, so that it is not possible to order them in a relative stratigraphy.

7. After an important unconformity just referred to, a thick, dark, carbonaceous, salt-capped layer (L1) covered at least a large part of the site, filling the mentioned furrows and other depressions. The contact of L1 with the eroded surface of underlying loci is frequently of carbonization or oxidation, that is, of combustion, and along with big sherds, pulverized pottery is common. As a whole, the evidence suggests a violent, destructive episode, or a series of such episodes, that put an end to a period of the history of Tell el-Ghaba as a formal settlement, at least in this part

of the site and, as we will see, in Area II. Although faunal remains and even small finds occur along with the pottery in large quantities in L1, only one mudbrick wall (L1029) was identified up to now resting on it, as if most human presence had been limited to highly mobile people or to squatters. In short, the erosion and the formation of L1 are the stratigraphic expression of an extensive ruin of the site, in which both natural causes and a conflagration took part. The abundance of fish (mainly catfish; see below) in L1 suggests that when it was deposited, the Pelusiac branch was still active.

8. A new unconformity separates L1 from the modern topsoil, a sandy fill almost without archaeological material.

Area II

The first operation was the digging of the north slit trench from stake AZ BA 70 71 until the high dunes that made it impossible to reach archaeologically fertile sediments in so narrow an exposure. Several features were found at different points, but no clear fortification wall was identified. When the west slit trench was opened, a thick mudbrick wall was intersected less than 1 m from the stake chosen as starting point. Further work proved that it belonged to some kind of public building (Structure C). First, it was exposed in accordance with the general grid of the site, and then, out of celerity, by area excavation. Remains of a dump left by the Israeli army still covers part of the building, and the deep track of a tank runs across the mudbricks.

The building is a square of some 22 m x 22 m, disposed NNE-SSW and formed by an external wall 2.90 m thick and four internal walls around 1.70-1.80 m thick. They crisscross at right angles leaving rectangular spaces between them, which we will call "casemates" without giving to the term, for the time being, a functional meaning (for a discussion of comparable features see Oren 1984:9-13.). The size of the bricks is quite variable, but 40 x 20 x 10 cm can be given as an average.

Given that neither doors nor floor were recognized, it seems that only the foundations remain. Although the casemates are good sediment traps, they were also affected by erosion. The stratigraphic test pits dug into the casemates revealing trenches running roughly WNW-ESE, parallel to the sides of the building, which may have been dug in order to place the scaffolding for the masons that erected the building. No floors associated to Structure C were identified into the casemates, which probably were just voids in the building and not living spaces; but erosion would perhaps have swept them if they existed.

The simplicity, symmetry and massiveness of Structure C, along with the thick walls separated by casemates, make it possible that we are dealing with a fortification. More excavation is necessary to know if it is a functional unit of a wider military structure.

As judged in the field, pottery from the fill of the casemates does not differ significantly from that associated to Building B.

It should be noted that Buildings A, B and C share the same orientation. This consistency across time, area of site and function gives an impression of urban control exerted by an official hand.

As the exploration of Area II by test trenches (dug, as always, until the first features appeared) progressed, an extended burial (L1006) and another building (Structure D) were found. The body of burial L1006 had been placed into an oval pit (L1012), resting on the back, oriented toward SW (245°). The right arm was along the side and the left arm was slightly flexed, the hand resting on the pelvis. Orbits perhaps had been directed toward zenith (and the face was eroded away in the past). There were no grave goods. Since the burial pit was dug into L1001 (equivalent to the destruction layer L1 of Area I), this tomb is later (perhaps much later) than Building C.

As for Structure D, its excavation is just beginning. Two phases of construction were identified, and it seems to have been a public building, since its walls are 2.20 m thick. Mudbricks are 40 cm long by 20 cm wide.

ADDITIONAL SAMPLING

Both in Area I and Area II, samples were extracted for pollen analysis. At the Mission House, the fill of several pots and samples taken from some loci were floated. Whenever adequate, charcoal was collected for anthracological analysis. This sampling points to a better knowledge of the past environment of Tell el-Ghaba and of the organic resources exploited by its ancient settlers. Also, several charcoal samples for ^{14}C dating were collected.

Planned operations at Tell el-Ghaba include the digging of test pits according to a systematic, aligned scheme.

POTTERY

Two Laboratory Seasons were carried out at the Argentine Mission House at Qantarah on September-November 1995, and October-November 1996 under the direction of P. Fuscaldo. The processed material (Area I) amounts to about 50 % of the pottery sample, so our conclusions can only be preliminary.

To classify the fabrics, the Vienna System was adopted as a starting point, in the knowledge that additional types are still to be defined.

Diagnostic feature sherds were separated according to their morphology, fabric and technology for statistics purposes. Body sherds were separated by fabrics and measured, and then discarded at the site. Special Egyptian and imported vessels, and sherds were inventoried.

Most Egyptian fabrics belong to Nile silt clays group. Marls, far scarcer, are limited to variants Marl F from the border of the Eastern Delta and Marl A4 from Upper Egypt. Eastern Lagoon and mixed fabrics await additional study.

More than 1100 imported samples were analyzed and classified in 35 different groups. The rest of them, at least 800, remains to be standardized for they differ from the other groups. The classification of Egyptian pottery was performed with a manual lens 20x and the imported pottery were analyzed with a trinocular lens 100x.

The morphology of the Egyptian ceramic material suggests a domestic function for Area I, in accordance with architectural evidence. Domestic vessels of Egyptian pottery are numerous, and most of them are open shapes (mainly bowls). In general, dishes are made of Nile B2 and Nile C2 fabrics. There are also many Nile C2 and Nile B2 baker trays for bread, very widespread type which has changed very little along the Egyptian history. Most closed shapes are jars made of Nile B2 and Nile E.

1st. millennium Nile B2 fabrics were harder, more compact and better fired than the 2nd. millennium ones. In Nile B2, surface smoothing is common, and red and white slip may also occur. Nile C2, well represented in trays, is usually very coarse in surface and break.

Imported pottery points to commercial links with the Levant, Cyprus, and other East Mediterranean areas during Iron Age II. It amounts to 25 % in Area I and 10 % in Area II. Cypriot-Phoenician imports include "Black-on-Red II" (IV) perfume flasks and compact marl coated juggles with painted circles and horizontal bands. This kind of pottery has been found in several East Mediterranean sites and was exported to Egypt during centuries 10th to 6th BC.

Torpedo jars are well known in Egypt and widespread through all the Levant. In Egypt, they have been found, among other sites in Tell el-Maskhuta, Mendes, Tell el-Herr and Tell el-Ghaba. According to their fabrics, those found at Tell el-Ghaba come from Phoenicia, Palestine and Cyprus, and almost all of them would date to the Early Saite Period, judging from Paice's (1986-1987).

By comparison with pottery from other sites (Aston, 1996), some Egyptian and imported vessels, and sherds from Tell el-Ghaba can be dated to the 8th - 7th centuries BC. But the sporadic appearance of New Kingdom fabrics (Nile B2/E) in Area I must be further analyzed. Moreover, occasional stray surface finds of sherds with fabrics or shapes seemingly from Roman, Coptic and Islamic times suggest a wide chronological span for the occupations of the site.

Some quantitative information is provided in the following concerning L17, a floor of Building B.

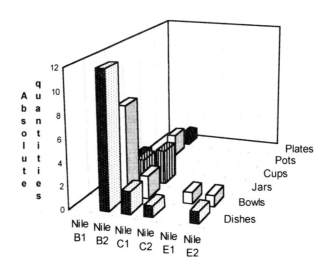

Fig. 2. Tell el Ghaba, Locus 17. Fabrics and shapes of Nile clay pottery

Fig. 2 shows the relationship between fabrics and shapes (these, according to rims). Note that Nile B2 is the most common fabric.

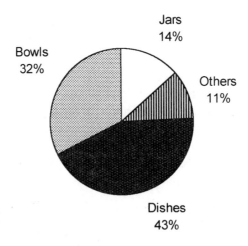

Fig. 3. Tell el-Ghaba. Locus 17. Shapes in Nile clay pottery

Fig. 3 shows that open shapes predominate.

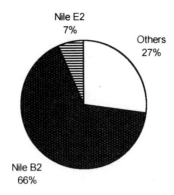

Fig. 4. Tell el-Ghaba, Locus 17. Percentage of fabrics in plain sherds

Fig. 4 shows again the predominance of Nile B2.

SMALL FINDS

Most small finds from Tell el-Ghaba are amulets, the commonest being the udjat-eyes. The simpler type, made of faience, is the most recurrent in both Area I and Area II.

As a rule, udjat-eyes are made of faience, but a few of them are made of stone, including one of carnelian.

Quadruple udjat-eyes (of which two faience specimens were found) are known from 22nd-25th Dyn. (Müller-Winckler, 1987:98, 146) and 7th century BC (Aston, 1996:28).

Among the fragmentary pottery figurines found, there are two schematic representations of an equid, one of them with the rider's legs (for comparison, see Holland, 1977: fig. 8.2); one fragmentary plaque with the legs of a nude woman or goddess, and a very well made baboon head.

Bes is the god more frequently portrayed in Tell el-Ghaba: he appears in small amulets, in a limestone statue (head and torso of which have been preserved) and a bronze figurine. There is also a double-faced Bes statuette, an uncommon representation (for a parallel dating from 25th Dyn., see Shoske - Wildung, 1992:109-110 and fig. 77).

Two faience figurines were found into a small cache test pit in casemate L1023 (Building C). One of them, in very good condition, is a baboon, a kind of representation of Toth that was common during the 1st millennium BC. The other is a double-pipes player, the head being the only part preserved. It is quite akin to a statuette found in Tell el-Far'ah in Palestine, dated to the 10th century by Chambon (1986:75 and pl. 63.6). A specimen from Naukratis, not so similar to the one from Tell el-Ghaba, was dated by De Salvia (1989:90-92; fig.5) to centuries 7th - 6th BC.

Another group of finds is represented by beads, mostly made of faience, many of pottery and a few of stone or metal (one in gold). The most frequent type of faience bead has a flat circular shape. There are a few bead in quartz. One necklace was recovered complete, consisting of 4 faience udjats and 152 pierced conical shells.

Seal amulets of Tell el-Ghaba comprise one button seal, one rectangular plaque and a few number of scarabs and one scaraboid. They are made of stone or faience; some of them bear hieroglyphic inscriptions.

The button seal is frog-shaped and the base has an inscription.

The plaque, in stone, features a short, finely carved inscription on each side.

Tueris is shown on the back of the scaraboid. In its base, as well as in the base of a scarab, the group *Mn-hpr-r`* is very well preserved.

Moreover, samples of magic and cryptic thematic compositions were identified in the Tell el-Ghaba scarabs: one is a very well known Bes composition (see Matouk, 1976: 249, Reisner, 1958: pl. IV.12,667), and the other includes the representation of a sphinx (see Newberry, 1907: pl. VI-VII).

SUBSISTENCE

Organic preservation is not very good at Tell el-Ghaba, as a result, among other factors, of a saline water table oscillating near the surface. With this limitation in mind, some field observations are advanced concerning the food quest.

We have still little information concerning agricultural practices at the site. Analysis of flotation samples has not begun yet.

Fish remains, burnt in a high proportion, are exceedingly abundant in the whole excavated area, indicating that they were a major contribution to the diet and, by implication, that the site was close to a Nile branch or canal. Most of the identified bones belong to the silurid *Clarias* sp. ('catfish', Arabic 'armut' or 'karmuut'), whose preferences are shallow, muddy waters (Brewer and Friedman 1989:60). Its very high representation in the archaeological record is, at least in part, an effect of its anatomic structure: cranial roof elements are resistant and easily identifiable even as small fragments (Brewer and Friedman 1989:1). But its economic importance is out of question: catfish can be taken by hand in the mudflats bordering river branches and canals (Brewer and Friedman 1989:61; Gaillard *et al.* 1923:50-56), making it an easy prey even for women and boys and prompting occasional catches without fishing tackle. Moreover, its meat is highly appreciated still nowadays.

The fill preserved some natural molds of fish, an additional resource of identification.

As we have seen, freshwater mussel shells were occasionally cooked in small pits.

Bovid, ovicaprid, equid and bird bones are rather scarce. This could be taken as an indication that fish was the main source of protein; but cleaning practices may have affect the distribution of the bigger remains far more than that of the smaller ones (as the fish bones). If the rubbish was taken out of the living areas, we can expect clusterings of bigger mammal bones at Tell el-Ghaba. In ancient Egypt, specialized middens are uncommon (Dixon 1972); but old houses served as dumps.

Nets were used for fishing, as indicated by several weights made by folding short lead bars (see Petrie 1890, plate XVIII and Bates 1917:259 and fig. 205). Moreover, the Nile and its artificial canals were extremely productive, allowing collective catches without tackle, as Petrie saw in 1886 near Tell Defenneh (Petrie n.d. 67).

Silurid fish are a dependable, ubiquitous and rather sedentary resource which would hardly be supplied by a central administration. The strong dependence on them suggested by our sample can be taken as an indication that at least in the main, the settlement was not provisioned by the government.

PRELIMINARY CONCLUSIONS

Tell el Ghaba, in the crossing between a frontier and an international road, seems to have been a seat of Egyptian state control during the Iron Age II. Along with a public area, there are private dwellings, perhaps of an élite, judging from the golden bead recovered. Faience slag may be an indication of industrial activities at the site.

An important destruction event, which is still to be dated accurately, affected at least a major part of the site.

Imported pottery suggests intensive trade with the Eastern Mediterranean ports.

Popular religion, as expressed by the recovered amulets, was specially concerned with fertility, good luck and the averting of dangerous influences. Minor gods, as Bes, are the most frequently portrayed.

Major protein intake at Tell el-Ghaba seems to have came from fish, and mainly from catfish. It was, then, at least partially, a self-sustaining community.

BIBLIOGRAPHY

Abd el-Maksoud, M. 1989. Excavations on "The Ways of Horus". Tell Heboua North Sinai (1986-1987). In *Proceedings of Colloquium The Archaeology, Geography and History of the Egyptian Delta in Pharaonic Times, Wadham College, 29-31 August, 1988. Oxford. Discùssions in Egyptology*, Special number 1: 173-92.

Abd el-Maksoud, M. 1992. Project de sauvatage des sites antiques du Nord-Sinaï. *Discussions in Egyptology* 24: 7-12.

Arnold, D. & J. Bourriau. 1993. *An introduction to ancient Egyptian pottery.* Philipp von Zabern. Mainz am Rhein.

Aston, D. 1996. *Egyptian pottery of the Late New Kingdom and the Third Intermediate Period (twelfth-seventh centuries BC). Tentative footsteps in a forbidding terrain.* Studien zur Archäologie und Geschichte Altägyptens, Band 13. Heidelberg: Orient.

Bates, O. 1917. Ancient Egyptian fishing. *Harvard African Studies* 1: 199-272.

Bietak, M. 1975. *Tell el-Dab'a. II.* Wien: Osterreichische Akademie der Wissenschaften.

Brewer, D. & R. Friedman. 1989. *Fish and fishing in ancient Egypt.* Wiltshire: Aris & Phillips.

Brookes, Y., L. Levine & R. Dennell 1982. Alluvial sequence in central west Iran and implications for archaeological survey. *Journal of Field Archaeology* 9 (3): 285-99.

Chartier-Raymond, M. & C. Traunecker. 1993. Reconnaissance archéologique à la pointe orientale du Delta. Campagne 1992. Note annexe de Françoise Brien-Poitevin, in *Cahier de Recherches de l'Institut de Papyrologie et d'Egyptologie de Lille [CRIPEL]* 15: 45-71.

De Salvia, F. 1989. The Cypriots in the Saite Nile Delta: The Cypriot-Egyptian religious syncretism, *Proceeding of Colloquium The Archaeology, Geography and History of the Egyptian Delta in Pharaonic Times. Wadham College 29-31 August, 1988.* Oxford. Discussion in Egyptology, Special number 1: 81-118.

Dixon, D. M. 1972. The disposal of certain personal, household and town waste in ancient Egypt. In P. Ucko, R. Tringham & G. Dimbleby (eds.), *Man, settlement and urbanism* pp. 647-50. Cambridge: Schenkman.

Gaillard, C., V. Loret & Ch. Kuentz.1923. Recherches sur les poissons représentés dans quelques tombeaux égyptiens de l'Ancien Empire. In *Mémoires de l'Institut Française de Archéologie Orientale [MIFAO]* 51: 1-136. Cairo.

Gardiner, A. 1947. *Ancient Egyptian Onomastica.* London: Oxford University Press.

Gardiner, A. 1920. The Ancient Military Road Between Egypt and Palestine. *Journal of Egyptian Archaeology [JEA]* 6: 99-116.

Harris,E. 1979. *Principles of Archaeological Stratigraphy.* London: Academic Press.

Holland, T. A. 1977. A study of Palestinian Iron Age baked clay figurines, with special reference to Jerusalem: Cave 1. *Levant* 9: 121-55

Kitchen, K. A. 1993. *Ramesside Inscriptions,* Translated and Annotated. Translations I. Oxford: Blackwell.

Marcolongo, B. 1992. Évolution du paléo-environnement dans la partie orientale du Delta du Nil depuis la transgression flandrienne (8000 BP) par rapport aux modèles de peuplement anciens. *Cahier de Recherches de l'Institut de Papyrologie et d'Egyptologie de Lille [CRIPEL]* 14: 23-31.

Matouk, F. S. 1976. *Corpus du Scarabée Egyptien.* Beirut:

Müller-Winckler   C. 1987. *Die Ägyptischen Objekt-Amulette.* Fribourg: Universitätsverlag Fribourg; Göttingen:Wanderhoeck & Ruprecht.

Newberry, P. E. 1907. *Scarab-shapes seals. Catalogue général des antiquités Égyptiennes du Musée du Cairo, Nos. 36001 - 37521.* London: Service des Antiquités de l'Egypte.

Oren, E. 1984. Migdol: a new fortress on the edge of the eastern Nile Delta. *Bulletin of the American School of Oriental Research [BASOR]* 256: 7-44.

_____. 1987. The Horus Way. In A. F. Rainey (ed.), *Egypt, Israel and Sinai. Archaeological and Historical Relationships in the Biblical Period:* 69-119. Jerusalem: Tel Aviv University.

_____ 1985. Northern Sinai. In E. Stern & J. Aviram (eds.), *The New Enclyclopedia of Archaeological Excavations in the Holy Land,* 4: 1387-1396. Jerusalem: Israel Exploration Society.

Paice, P. 1986-1987. A preliminary analysis of some elements of the Saite and Persian period pottery at Tell el-Maskhuta. *Bulletin of the Egyptological Seminar[BES]* 8: 95-107.

Petrie, W. M. F. 1890. *Kahun, Gurob, and Hawara.* London: Kegan Paul, Trench, Trubner & Co.

_____ n.d. *Seventy years in archaeology.* London: Sampson Low, Marston & Co.

Reisner, G. A. 1958. *Amulets, Vol. 2. Catalogue général des antiquités Égyptiennes du Musée du Caire.* London: Services des Antiquités de l'Egypte.

Shaffei, A. B. 1946. Historical notes on the Pelusiac branch, the Red Sea Canal and the road to the Exodus. In *Société Royale de Géographie d'Égypte* 21: 231-287.

Shoske S. & D. Wildung. 1992. *Gott und Götter im Alten Ägypten.* Mainz am Rhein: Philipp von Zabern.

Sneh, A. & T. Weissbrod. 1973. Nile Delta: The Defunct Pelusiac Branch Identified. In *Science* 180: 59-61.

Valbelle, D., F. Le Saout, M. Chartier-Raymond, M. Abd el-Samie, C. Traunecker., G. Wagner; J.-Y. Carrez-Maratray & P Zignani. Reconaissance archéologique à la pointe orientale du Delta. Rapport préliminaire sur les saisons 1990 et 1991. In *Cahier de Recherches de l'Institut de Papyrologie et d'Egyptologie de Lille [CRIPEL]* 14: 11-22.

van den Brink, E. C. M. 1993. Settlement patterns in the Northeastern Nile Delta during the fourth-second millennia B.C. In L. Krzyżaniak, M. Kobusiewicz & J. Alexander (eds.), *Environmental Change and Human Culture in the Nile Basin and Northern Africa until the second Millennium B.C:* 279-305. Poznań: Archaeological Museum.

Henryk Meyza, Ewdoksia Papuci-Władyka
Warsaw, Cracow

Nea Paphos, Cyprus: Pottery from cistern STR 1/96-97

Nea Paphos is at present a site of large development project of an "Archaeological Park". Polish Mission, trying to keep pace with changes, has extended its activities to define the area immediately related to structures which were at least partly uncovered during previous excavation[1]. One of the areas tested was the southwestern corner of the insula preceding construction of the palace and destroyed by southeastern corner of the Villa of Theseus (VT). As expected, corner of two streets (A' and 9, according to J. Młynarczyk[2]) was found, with N-S street 9 blocked when VT was built. Within that corner a well plastered cistern appeared (Fig. 1). Its excavation, begun in 1996 has been finished at the end of September 1997.[3]

The structures above cistern were extensively disturbed, first most probably on occasion of street blocking in 2nd c. AD when street surfaces and many related structures were removed, and later in 7th century, when a pit was hollowed reaching down below the top of the eastern street curb.[4] During the first disturbance[5] most of the wellhead

---

[1] Recent collected bibliography of the site excavated by Polish Mission in *Cypr w badaniach polskich*, ed. W.A. Daszewski and H. Meyza, Warsaw 1998, p. 131-138. On structures preceding Villa of Theseus - south of it: W.A. Daszewski, Z. Sztetyłło, La région de Maloutena avant la construction de la Villa de Thésée, RDAC 1987, p. 199; E. Papuci-Władyka, Nea Paphos. Studia nad ceramiką hellenistyczną z polskich wykopalisk, Kraków 1995 (=Papuci-Władyka), p. 15-22. Later reports by W.A. Daszewski in Polish Archaeology in Mediterranean (=PAM) - the last is: *Nea Paphos. Excavations 1997*, PAM IX, 1998, p. 119-129.

[2] J. Młynarczyk, Remarks on the Town Plan of Hellenistic Nea Paphos, Πρακτικά Β' Διεθνούς Κυπρολογικού Συνεδρίου, Α', Nicosia 1985, p. 320, Ill. 2; id., Nea Paphos in the Hellenistic Period, Nea Paphos III, Warsaw 1990, p. 166f, 173f, Fig. 16, 21; St. Medeksza, w: Cypr w badaniach polskich, Warszawa 1998, fig. 3.

[3] W.A. Daszewski, Nea Paphos: Excavations 1996, PAM VIII, Reports 1996, 1997, p. 118-120; id., Nea Paphos: Excavations 1997..., p. 125; E. Papuci-Władyka, The Cistern South of the Villa of Theseus, PAM IX, Reports 1997, Warsaw 1998, p. 130-135.

[4] Fragments of Cypriot Red Slip Ware Hayes' form 9, 11B and African Red Slip high ring base as in form Hayes 86. At higher level a coin of Heraclius was found (inv. 748) in what seems to be a homogeneous fill.

(apart from one block to SW, 54 cm high) was dismantled, but the cistern itself must have been filled before that. The stony layer including one of the removed wellhead sections did not penetrate below ca. 30 cm above top of preserved cylindrical shaft. We may conclude therefore that the fill of the cistern is intact from top.

Cistern entrance was circular (0.65 m in diameter). Below, a vertical, cylindrical shaft leads to conical to pear-shaped reservoir with almost flat floor, 1.75 m wide at 3.42-3.48 m from the edge of shaft and a narrow blind offshot 2.25 m long, which goes north-eastward and slightly upwards. Walls of the cistern are plastered. The coating has fallen off in some places revealing greenish-gray clay deposits lying under calcarenite crust. At present it is impossible to date the moment in which the cistern itself has been hollowed. Its construction is evidently related to the wall separating it from the E-W street to the south. The remaining wellhead stone is leaning against it (Fig. 1). It has evidently been finished and used, though it is not easy to explain the purpose of the short "corridor". The conical or pear shaped section is a standard shape, particularly so in the local geological conditions. The walls started to cave in when the cistern fell out of use.

Top part of the shaft was filled with loose light brown soil with some fist-to-head sized stones, quite probably deposited at the time of destruction, which seems to have hit Paphos before the middle of the 2nd c. AD.[6] The shaft seems to have been reused as a bin. On its sides traces of fire are still visible. It has been probably desinsected by fumigation. Within its upper part two practically intact vessels were found: a kitchen pot and a plate of Eastern Sigillata A Hf 29 plate used as a lid (Fig. 2 A-B). These may be interpreted as remains of kitchen use dating to the times of Augustus or early Tiberius. The sigillata type seems to be well dated by its presence, among other contexts, in early Tiberian well in Corinth and a deposit closed by floor in Sibaris.[7] Hayes suggests that

---

[5]Best dating is offered by a fragment of Cypriot Sigillata Hayes' form 40 imbedded in plaster fragment and found between the moved wellhead stone and the south wall.

[6]I. Nicolau, Paphos II. The Coins from the House of Dionysos, Nicosia 1990, p. 2, 144-146; J.W. Hayes. Paphos III. Hellenistic and Roman Pottery, Nicosia 1991 (=Hayes, Paphos III), p. 202-206, 212; W.A. Daszewski, Z. Sztetyłło, op.cit., p. 199; W.A. Daszewski, Nea Paphos 1995, PAM VII, p. 95f; id., Nea Paphos. Excavations 1996, PAM VIII, p. 117f - the similarity of destruction deposits on both sites, ranging between last quarter of 1st and 1st quarter of 2nd c. suggests contemporaneity of events, which led to all these destructions.

[7]K. Slane Wright, A Tiberian Pottery Deposit from Corinth, Hesperia 49, 1980, p. 145, n. 20f, Fig. 3, Pl. 28; F. Daddi in: P.G. Guzzo, Sibari: Scavi al Parco del Cavallo, III Supp., NotSc 1970, p. 439, 471; P.M. Kenrick, Excavations at Sidi Khrebish, Benghazi III.1: The Fine Pottery, Supp. Libya Antiqua V, Tripoli 1985, p. 233 thinks that Hayes' dating is too early and that the type cannot be earlier than form 28. The earliest occurrence seems to be in the well RR/K/60 at Knossos - but the date is itself only by assemblage contents, without clear sealing of the deposit - BSA 66, 1971, p. 252, n. 4, fig. 3. Hayes' dating probably results from typological considerations - f. 29 is a development of f. 28 and there are examples transitional to f. 28 - intermediate date would fit best. Contextual data are decisive, however. At Anafa the form (type TA 20) is infrequent, one piece has been found in ROM 1A stratum, cf. K. Warner Slane, The Fine Wares, in: Tel Anafa II,i, The Hellenistic and Roman Pottery (ed. Sh.C. Herbert), JRA Supp 10, Ann Arbor 1997 (= Anafa II.1), p. 304, Pls. 15, 40, which would put the initial date to ca. 20 BC, earlier than TA 22 = Hayes' form 28.

pieces with offset at bottom close to base ring as in our example are later in series. The cooking pot belongs to class which may equally well be Late Hellenistic as 2nd c. AD.[8]

Under the pot with a lid made of ESA plate Hf 29 the fill was greyish-brown, loose, with small clumps and this extended down to a layer of clean greyish quite compact soil closed on top and bottom by loose layers with numerous fist-to-headsized stones. Within this clean stratum a coin, most probably of Cleopatra VII was found at depth of 163 cm (inv. 749). Stratigraphically, these levels could belong to a later phase fill, while strata below could form the main fill consisiting of intercalated layers of greyish and brown soil with some burnt matter and some large stones. The deposits under the shaft were compact, while those close to the walls were loose and contained more pottery, usually crushed into medium size sherds.

Large amounts of broken pottery were found, but in many cases mendable enough to restore complete section, and in some cases whole vessel. Besides - coins, amphora stamps and lamps are here briefly refered to and used for dating.[9] We have been able to prepare preliminary presentation of some groups of finds only. The study of pottery included more evident joining pieces. We do not doubt, that further effort in mending and ware classification will produce many more restorable and characteristic pieces. Nevertheless, having selected a series of over 80 more or less completely mended vessels, we have found this series representative enough to present a preliminary report. A short announcement on this group of pottery was made already in spring 1997 during the International Conference devoted to Hellenistic Pottery at Khania, Crete by Meyza[10] and here corrections of some of the statements made then are presented.

The limit between upper and lower fill is not a clear-cut one either. A preliminary study of joining fragments shows that there may exist a discontinuity at the level of a loose, reddish-brown soil clearly separated from underlying greyish soil with some charcoals and little pottery at 2.40/2.70 m. Joins above and below between quite widely separated lots make care in dividing possible fill phases necessary and do not permit at a present moment any final conclusions. Between that discrimination and the stratigraphic division described above there are distinct levels with traces of burning. Anyway, an attempt to interpret this fill as an Augustan earthquake debris dump, as this cistern has been presented at Khania, seems now to have been premature. A negative statement may however be still supported that this is not a primary dump with deposits slowly accumulating over centuries. There was no time for analysis of the pottery found to describe thoroughly dispersion of datable fragments. Therefore the only way this preliminary communication can be arranged is by typology.

It is worthwhile however to set a frame for dating. The above mentioned coin struck probably by Cleopatra VII seems to be the latest object in upper fill (both defined by

[8] e.g. Hayes, Paphos III, Fig. 29:5, probably from W.2 or W.8, cf. p. 214.
[9] Preliminary identification of those is the work or has profited from support of other members of the team: Daszewski who has identified coins, Sztetyłło who has commented upon amphora stamps, and Młynarczyk who has kindly helped in classification and dating of lamps.
[10] H. Meyza, Early Eastern Sigillata A from Paphos, Cyprus, Ε΄ Επιστημονική Συνάντηση για την Ελληνιστική Κεραμική, Χανιά 6-13 Απριλίου 1997, in print.

stratigraphy and by pottery joins). The lower part of fill has probably been thrown in at one time. The best proof is provided by coin finds: coins of Ptolemy X Alexander I ruling 107-88 BC, with Cleopatra III until 101 and later with Cleopatra Berenice, have been found from layers both at 211 cm from preserved shaft edge (inv. 750) and from the layer at very bottom - clayey deposit - (inv. 798 and 799) at 348 cm. In the lower deposit occur also stamped amphora handles dating to the Vth period of Rhodian amphorae (eg. AR 7 of Midas and AR 10/97 of Aristanax) i.e. according to traditional dating 146-108 BC.[11] Found chiefly in the loose part of lower fill at 326-338 cm, a mending Knidian amphora, most probably of the duoviri but with almost obliterated stamps belongs to this period as well. Latest lamps seem to be produced in Cyprus with a "couvette centrale",[12] while moulded kite-form grey ware lamp with Erotes found in the lower strata belongs to the end of 2nd or beginning of the 1st century BC, and may also be contemporary with the coins.[13] Other two lamps of that type earlier version with a pair of embracing lovers were found in the upper deposit. The dominating lamp types however are: the sub-Rhodian wheelmade form, which seems to be produced in Cyprus in the 1st half of the 2nd century BC and imported or imitated in Cyprus lamps with depressed globular body of an earlier standard (3rd c. BC).[14]

Presence of conspicuous ESA both in top deposit and in lower one suggests that there is no large difference, in both parts occur form 22 cups on foot, which seem to be one of the latest ESA forms apart from the Augustan/Tiberian plate in the bin.

Sequence of presentation follows frequence of occurrence in the main groups: table ware and domestic use vessels. Among table wares Colour Coated Ware[15] - the characteristic Cypriot Hellenistic pottery class is the most numerous. Ubiquitous small sized plates with various rims and incurved rim bowls are commonest. Among plates those with rolled or knobbed rims (fig. 2 C-D) are most frequent. There are close analogies in the deposits of the House of Dionysos, as e.g. a plate from ΓΝ[16] dated to the end of 2nd century or even later in 1st century BC, or plates from E and Λ, dated to ca. 40-10 BC.[17] Similar vessels have also been found in Polish excavations in e.g. "pithos"

[11]NP IV, p. 79, nos 140f. (Μίδας); and idem, p. 22, no 22 (Αρισταναξ); cf. G. Finkielsztejn, Les amphores importées en Palestine à l'époque hellénistique et la chronologie basse des eponymes Rhodiens, Ε´ Επιστημονική Συνάντηση για την Ελληνιστική Κεραμική, Χανιά 6-13 Απριλίου 1997, in print, who suggests 145-109 BC for V period.

[12]J. Młynarczyk, Hellenistic Terracotta Lamps from Nea Paphos, RDAC 1978, p. 243f, 252, Fig. 3, Pl. LVIII.

[13]J. Młynarczyk, Alexandrian and Alexandria-Influenced Mould-Made Lamps of the Hellenistic Period, BAR S 677, Oxford 1997, p. 36-39, Fig. 26-28; this lamp seems to be late in series Dc2 or more probably D Prime, similar to Delian examples: Délos XXVI, p. 87, no 4144 in particular. A lamp found in a tomb close to Famagusta: BCH 90, 1966, p. 336, fig. 90 was also found with coins of Ptolemy X - but the context has been dismissed as insecure by both Bailey (BMC Lamps I, p. 208) and Młynarczyk, op. cit., p. 36.

[14]Th. Oziol, Lampes, in: Kition-Bamboula IV, Les niveaux hellénistiques, ed. J.F. Salles, Paris 1993, p. 300, no 667, Fig. 243.

[15]Hayes, Paphos III, p. 26ff; Papuci-Władyka, p. 47ff.

[16]Hayes, Paphos III, fig. 45: 2, p. 122.

[17]As above, Fig. 53: 10, 11, p. 148 and Fig. 53: 37, 38, p. 152.

from room 96 of Villa of Theseus or burnt layer in the cistern found in corridor 50 of the Villa,[18] both dated to the 2nd half and the end of 2nd century BC. There are also plates with tapering rim[19] (fig. 2 E), narrow overhanging rim[20] (fig. 2 G) and drooping rim (fig. 2 F).[21]

As in all other Hellenistic deposits from Nea Paphos incurved rim bowls dominate over other bowl forms. Eighteen out of twenty best preserved bowls belong to this type. Outcurved rim bowls were much less popular. The first type may be subdivided into: a) bowls close to hemispherical with clearly incurved rim (Fig. 3 A); b) with straight rim (Fig. 3 B); c) conical (Fig. 3 C); d) thick-walled with fat bottom (Fig. 3 D). Three sub-groups listed first are also present in AΛ deposit of the House of Dionysos, dated to 110-100 BC.[22] A bowl of the last sub-group occurs in the Well 20 in the House of Dionysos.[23]

Outcurved-rim bowls have flaring wall and small flanged rim (Fig. 3 E)[24] or a rim without a flange (Fig. 3 F). The latter variety occurs in cistern W/73 (deposit K) from Polish excavations.[25]

Open forms besides plates and bowls are also represented by kyathos (Fig. 4 A) with looped handle, which should be dated to the 2nd half of 2nd c. by analogies from the House of Dionysos,[26] like the objects discussed before.

In the cistern occurred also various well preserved jugs. Olpe - slender jugs derived from forms known in Classical Greece and Cyprus - were most numerous (3 pieces). At Paphos they are best represented in the Late Hellenistic phase of the House of Dionysos deposits of Wells 11 and 21, Room L etc. and the secondary Hellenistic and Roman deposits in Polish excavations.[27] Fragment Fig. 4 B has an inset base, typical for olpe, while bases of fragments Fig. 4 C and 4 D are more articulated. There were diverse small jugs and juglets: sagging body with simple splaying rim (Fig. 4 E),[28] narrow necked jug (Fig. 4 F),[29] and a spouted jug (Fig. 4 G).[30] Large jug (Fig. 4 H) can be classified

---

[18]Papuci-Władyka, Pl. 54: 46, 407, p. 214f., Pl. 56: 432, p. 223.

[19]Hayes, Paphos III, Fig. 48: 55, p. 135, deposit AΛ, dated to about 110-100 BC.

[20]As above, Fig. 15: 3, Cistern 3, p. 120, dated to 2nd c. BC.

[21]As above, Fig. 48: 56, p. 136 deposit AΛ.

[22]As above, Fig. 49, p. 136.

[23]As above, Fig. 59: 5, 6 (upper), p. 168.

[24]As above, Fig. 15: 15, p. 30 (Fig. 15: 11 is the earlier version of this type).

[25]Papuci-Władyka, Pl. 44: 329, p. 192, 2nd century BC., another example comes from the Trial Pit excavated in 1993 (TP 1/93.8); see also Hayes, Paphos III, Fig. 43: ΓΞ 14-15, p. 110, about middle of 2nd century BC.

[26]Hayes, Paphos III, Fig. 45:5, p. 122 (deposit ΓN, "which runs into 2nd century at a higer level"), Fig. 56: 44, 46, p. 159; Well 11, 150-140/30 BC; Fig. 47:79, p. 157, deposit AΛ, 110-100 BC.

[27]Hayes, Paphos III, Fig. 16: 8-10, p. 28 and 160; Fig. 58: 5, p. 163, end of 2nd c. BC; Fig. 55: 30, 151 (dated: "pre-25 B.C.", p. 149). Papuci-Władyka, Nea Pafos, Pl. 10: 67, 68.

[28]Hayes, Paphos III, Fig. 58: 49, Well 11, p. 160.

[29]As above, Fig. 54: 28, Room Λ, p. 160.

[30]Westholm, SCE IV: 3, Fig. 23: 17; Hayes, Paphos III, Fig. 50: BZ: 25, p. 145 (ca. 100 to early 1st c. BC).

together with a group of round-mouthed jugs of Hayes,[31] though its lip seems to belong to later class than examples cited from the House of Dionysos.

Another class of table ware present among finds in this cistern is the Plain White. As is the case in other contexts dug by the Polish Mission, it is not very often found. A thin-walled jug (Fig. 5 A), preserved only in part, may be used here as an example. Small juglet with a loop handle, without slip, may be classified as Coarse Ware.

Lagynoi are represented both by plain, slipped only examples (Fig. 5 B) and fragments of painted ones. Among the latter, those produced most probably in Cyprus are frequent, as well as ones imported probably from Asia Minor, e.g. beautiful fragment with partly preserved dolphin, made of light brown clay with large amount of micaceous impurities.

Another group of fine ware vessels consists of unguentaria. Most of over a dozen of balsamaria found in the cistern were spindle shaped. Pieces Fig. 5 C and 5 D belong to a group "fusiform in plain buff ware (local?)" defined by J.W. Hayes,[32] dated to the end of 2nd c. BC. The Piece Fig 5 E belongs, on the other hand, to a group of fusiform red slipped balsamaria, first recognized in pottery from Polish excavations and dated as the preceding ones.[33]

Imported relief mouldmade bowls - so called Megarian Bowls are also fairly numerous. No locally made bowls as defined by P. Puppo and produced near Nicosia were found here.[34] As the available evidence from the House of Dionysos and our excavations suggests - they did not reach western part of the island. Here exclusively imported bowls are found, mostly from Ephesian workshops (formerly called "Delian"). Three of these were better preserved. The first, Fig. 6 A, was produced in a workshop of Apollonios identified by A. Laumonier on basis of Delian finds[35] and carries a retrograde relief signature *AΠOΛ* on its bottom. Ornaments of rounded scales on lower parts of wall[36] and two types of rosettes occurring in two bands above[37] found on our bowl are present on other bowls made in this workshop. Another bowl preserved almost intact/complete belongs to dark gray coated group (Fig. 6 B) and her bottom has a regular cross in relief. Similar motif occurs on bowls produced by Philo workshop.[38] Another piece, Fig. 6 C is decorated on lower wall by pattern of double-outlined lozenges. Similar pattern is known from the workshop of Heraios.[39] All of these should be dated in second half of second century BC or beginning of the next century.

---

[31]Hayes, Paphos III, Fig. 16: 3-5, p. 31.

[32]Hayes, Paphos III, p. 70, nos 28-29, Pl. 15: 6, 7, Fig. 1: 28, both from AΛ deposit dated to 110-100 BC.

[33]Papuci-Władyka, Nea Pafos, p. 68, cat. 440, 441, p. 224f, Pl. 2 and Fig. 57.

[34]P. Puppo, La ceramica megarese a Cipro: ritrovamenti ed individuazione di officine, (in:) Ε Συνάντηση.... (ab. Note 10) (in print).

[35]A. Laumonier, EAD XXXI, 1: La céramiques hellénistiques à reliefs. Ateliers "Ioniens", Paris 1977, pp. 223 ff, Pl. 50-51, 133.

[36]Laumonier, op.cit., Pl. 50: 209, 210, 299, p. 226: IIIᵉ serie-écailles, 1 - grandes écailles arrondiés.

[37]Laumonier, op.cit., Pl. 50: 3124, 1273, 373, p. 226, 224; Pl. 50: 5382, p. 227.

[38]Laumonier, op.cit., Pl. 58: 5393+5351, p. 257, Pl. 58: 4482, p. 259; Pl. 60: 4957, p. 262.

[39]Laumonier, op.cit., Pl. 72: 4006, 4001, 4002, 4036,4030, 4035, 4019, 4037, 9154, p. 307, series VII, group a.

Last but not least: there is quite a number of relatively well preserved Eastern Sigillata A. Generally only plates and bowls are represented. The former belong to Hayes' form 2A - one base (Fig. 7 A)[40], form 4A plates - two out of three pieces complete (fig 7 B-C)[41], one deep dish form 5A (Fig. 7 D)[42] and a wide rim of plate form 6 (Fig. 7 E).[43] Plate forms or variants present all belong to pre-Augustan phase of ware development. K. Warner Slane argues for earlier dating of some of these forms. Our group cannot supply decisive data, since as she points out rightly, closed contexts of "Agora style" - i.e. cisterns, wells, etc. have to be dated each by itself.[44] Nevertheless it may seem that her dating of the end of production of some forms may be due to overinterpretation. Rapid abandonment of types does not have to be the general rule and though we should differentiate between production and use timespans, it is risky to expect usage time of

---

[40]Base diameter 8.7 cm, comparable to Hayes, Paphos III, ΟΔ 1663, ΑΛ:16, Fig. 46, p. 132; EAA Atl II. Tav I:4, p. 14. N.B. rim diameter ca. 25 cm is, in this last paper, the discrimination point between variants A and B, so ΟΔ 1663 with D: 26.2 should belong rather to B. It is a type TA 13a or (less probably) TA 13b in Tel Anafa classification, though type TA 12 cannot be excluded according to K. Warner Slane, cf. Anafa II.1, p. 283-288 and n. 118 in particular, see also p. 271, n. 65. Dating advocated there for types TA 12 and TA 13a is 2nd half of 2nd c. BC (160/140-100/95 BC). Type TA 13b (approximately corresponding to Hayes' f. 3) is probably according to her more long-lived (p. 286, n. 130).

[41]Two larger and better preserved pieces are similar to one from Antikythera wreck with almost vertical rim - an early feature according to J.W. Hayes cf. EAA Atl II, p. 15; H.S. Robinson, The Early Roman Pottery, in: G. Weinberg et al., The Antikythera Shipwreck Reconsidered, Transactions of the American Philosophical Society, Philadelphia 1965, p. 28f, Fig. 1, no 4, Fig. 4, No 5 = V. Mitsopoulos-Leon, Gefässe der Ostsigillata A von einem gesunkenen Schiff aus dem Golf von Antalya, Germania 53, 1973, p. 111f. Abb. 4: 1, 4. Illustrated piece was found high in the fill, while an intact one was found in lower deposit, cf. Khania Acts: H. Meyza, (ab. note 10), Fig. 9. There is difference in support surface, concave in the latter and flat in the former. In Anafa classification both belong to type TA 13c, dated widely between end of 2nd and end of 1st c. BC - all our examples exhibit concavity between bottom of floor and base, seen by Warner Slane as an early attribute. Profile of two larger plates has closest counterparts in FW 69 and FW 73 from HELL 2B or 2C, Anafa II.1, p. 288-290, Pl. 7, while the third one is more similar to FW 83, ibid, p. 291, Pl. 9, from HELL 2C+. This would mean that both on ground of Hayes' and Anafa systems the plates should be dated in the first half of 1st c. BC.

[42]This seems somewhat later than Hayes, Paphos III, ΟΔ 747, BZ:6, Fig. 50, p. 143, but earlier than Samaria III. Fig. 73: 16, p. 309, 315 from Vault Cistern 2. K. Warner Slane suggests a date contemporary with TA 13, c for beginning of this form (type TA 14, a in her classification), Anafa II.1, p. 297-299, n. 151, Pl. 13. Our example is most similar to FW 131 from ROM 1A "Herodian" (20 BC - post 5 BC/ante AD 44 [probably ca. AD 15]) level.

[43]The form is popular already in the beginning of 1st c. BC: Hayes, Paphos III, p. 133, ΑΛ: 22 (ΟΔ 5215), 23 (ΟΔ 2800) and table, Fig. 46. Other plates of this form were found at Polish excavations - E. Papuci - Władyka, Ελληνιστική κεραμική απο την πολωνική νασκαφή στην Πάφο της Κύπρου, Δεξαμενή W/73, in: Γ Συνάντηση για την Ελληνιστική Κεραμική, Μυτιλήνη 27-30 Μαρτίου 1994, Athens 1994, p. 266, no 219, Fig. on p. 217; id, Nea Pafos, nos 114 (HA3/86, p. 119, Tabl. 18), 348 (W/73, p. 197, Tabl. 46) - black slipped. Late examples are found at Samaria "Herodian levels" and in Well 6 of the House of Dionysos - Samaria III, p. 294, Fig. 66: 5 cf. EAA Atl II, p. 17; Hayes, Paphos III, p. 35, 172, OD 596, Fig. 17: 5. This is form TA 12 in Tel Anafa, cf. note 38. K. Warner Slane "does not think likely that ... continued to be manufactured to the first quarter of the first century BCE, let alone into the late first century ...", Anafa II.1, p. 284.

[44]Anafa II.1, p. 257, see also Meyza, in print (ab. note 10).

more than say 10 years in average for fragile pottery. The real problem is the post-depositional history and the interpretation constraints.[45]

The same pre-Augustan date may be suggested for bowls. There were several hemispherical footed cups of form 22 both with concave and flat support surface of foot - one of the smaller with concave resting surface is found in upper fill (Fig. 8 A-D).[46] All these cups are deep and narrow but comparison with those found in House of Dionysos would suggest that all should be dated to 2nd half of 1st cent. BC., while Tel Anafa classification would place two complete examples in early 1st c. or in Herodian phase. The base rouletted inside should be late 2nd to 1st quarter of 1st c. BC.[47] Another, larger sized is similar to the piece from the House of Dionysos AΛ: 27, though without rouletting.[48]There were quite numerous bowls with round bottom, preserved almost complete. These were: mastoid profiled bowl form 17B rim (Fig. 8 E),[49] two hemispherical to ovoid bowls form 18 (Fig. 8 F and 9 A)[50] and hemispherical vertically gouged bowl form 19B (Fig. 9 B).[51] This example is unusual (late?), as it is devoid of grooves framing the gouging above and below. There are only thin lines scratched below.

---

[45]Clear statement of method used to separate post-depositon history from prolonged use and to assess production timespan is not made but stress on interpretation makes evident that these problems were thoroughly studied - cf. Anafa II.1, p. 259 n. 22, p. 263 n. 47 - example: p. 260 and n. 29, p. 284 n. 119. It is less obvious whether interpretation was made with enough caution not to press the data too far to fit preconceived production history.

[46]Hayes, EAA Atl II, p. 23f, Tav. III: 10; id., Paphos III, p. 34, three different varieties are present: with rouletted bottom but flat resting surface, clearly hemispherical bowl and light foot but thick bottom like Room Λ: 8, and the illustrated piece with bottom like Room E: 6. It seems that there was no very clear line of development.

[47]Anafa II.1, p. 310, there are no really close analogies: type TA 25, a - FW 179 from HELL 2A for the base (without concave resting surface), type TA 25, b - perhaps FW 200, found on surface, for the illustrated piece (this time it is the Anafa cup which has flat resting surface), FW 198? found in ROM 1B or later for the other cup - idem, p. 312, Pl 19.

[48]Hayes, Paphos III, OΔ 1657, Fig. 47, AΛ: 27, p. 34, 134; id, Atl II, p. 23, Tav, III: 11. At Anafa a large sized cup with equally low foot has been found in HELL 2A stratum and classified together with small ones as type TA 25, a: FW 182 - cf. Anafa II.1, p. 311, Pl. 17 (the resting surface is flat).

[49]Hayes treats this as one of the earliest forms together with the fish plate (form 1), Hayes, Paphos III, p. 33 - latest ones are regarded as residual, cp. G.A. Reisner, Cl. Stanley Fischer, D. Gordon Lyon, Harvard Excavations at Samaria 1908/1910, Cambridge Mass. 1924, p. 306, Fig. 185.9 a, from Vault Cistern 2. Data from Anafa suggest the opposite, only 1 piece has been found below HELL 2C, while most of sherd were found in ROM 1A - cf. Anafa II.1, p. 314 f, Pl. 21 (type TA 26). This cannot be the final proof either, since in other cases Warner Slane argues that occurrences in ROM layers are mostly on secondary bed - ibid p. 263, n. 46, 47, p. 286, n. 127.

[50]At Anafa this form is almost not present. The only piece of type TA 27b was found in ROM 1B layer - cf. Anafa II.1, p. 317, Pl. 21 (FW 228) - therefore Paphos context - AΛ, dated to ca 100 BC is decisive, cf. Paphos p. 133f (nos 29, 30), Fig. 47 supported by Antioch finds.

[51]Hayes, EAA Atl II, p. 22 bases dating on a variant Paphos piece from Well 10 - id., Paphos III, p. 166, Fig. 17: 8, OΔ 1229, but fill accumulation in this well continues until August and the bowl has no depth recorded. It seems therefore that Anafa dating of type TA 27a (1 piece below HELL 1C, more in destruction of LHSB (9 or more), and numerous (over 23) in ROM 1B - secondary?, should be treated as reference - 100-20 BC or later. Cf. Anafa II.1, p. 315f, Pl. 21.

Unprecedented as fully preserved in ESA is a pine-cone relief bowl form 24 (Fig. 9 C)[52]. Body of these vessels varies. Some contain very tiny mica, other minute reddish grains of haematite. Nevertheless they seem homogeneous when compared with evident imitations - this time of form 23, with flaky slip and small dark grits (Fig. 9 D), which may be locally made (?).

The bulk of sherds belong to amphorae: mostly Rhodian with few Knidian and local (e.g. Kourion fragments). Some remarks were made on amphora stamps and two better preserved vessels but to mend larger amount of transport amphorae much more time than available would have to be spent.

Kitchen cooking ware was plentiful, but little was mended, since the thin walled pots break into small sherds which are difficult to attribute to single vessel. Apart from little broken cooking pots (Fig. 9 E) and casseroles, a colander (Fig. 9 F) could be easily selected for mending thanks to its perforated bottom. It has a counterpart in the House of Dionysos, where a similar piece was found in the deposit AΛ, dated to about 110-100 BC.[53] The deformed misfired pot was another case of distinctive sherds. This is evidently a misfired piece, which suggests that a pottery workshop must have been situated not far away. A brazier attachment is also related to kitchen wares. It is decorated with satyr mask with a wreath of vine and belongs to Conze's class IIA.[54] In the House of Dionysos there is only one fragmentary similar object, probably belonging to this class.[55]

Large amount of transport amphorae and cooking wares defines character of the collection: redeposited domestic dump of unusable pottery and minor objects - gem fragment, beads, small glass pendent. It is characteristic that there are no terracottas and relatively little stone in the fill. There are some ashes, but not really enough to suggest fire debris, inevitable if an earthquake were to be the cause of deposition.

---

[52]Pine cone pattern on relief bowls occurs in mastoid shape on "Ionian bowls"- cf. Laumonier, op.cit. p. 200. 222, 478, Pl. 44, 111, 132-134, belonging to Monogram Workshop, Petite Rose Spiralée Workshop, Geometric group; - in the Levant eg. R. Rosenthal-Heginbottom, Moldmade Relief Bowls from Tel Dor, Israel - A Preliminary Report, in: Hellenistic and Roman Pottery in the Eastern Mediterranean. Advances in Scientific Studies, Acts of the II Nieborów Pottery Workshop, ed. By H. Meyza and J. Młynarczyk, Warsaw 1995, p. 372, no 69, Pl. 8: 3 of grey ware. The motif itself is known in ESA - cf. Hama III:2, p. 150, Fig. 57, form 20: 112, 113; Tarsus I, Fig. 142 H. The ware of our piece may not belong to ESA, but final check can be done only by chemical analysis. A very close fragment, though with more inclusions is Milet V.1, p. 78, no M 652, Taf. 47.

[53]Hayes, Paphos III, Fig. 34: 100, p. 139.

[54]A. Conze, Griechische Kohlenbecken, JdI V, 1890, p. 122: Class IIA.

[55]Hayes, Paphos III, p. 75, no 1, Ware I (presumed Cypriot), Fig. 26.

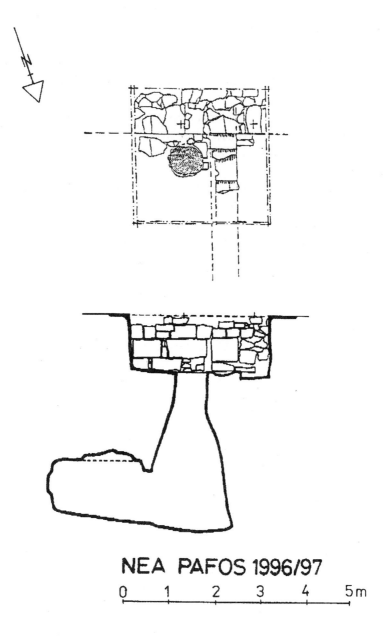

NEA PAFOS 1996/97

0 1 2 3 4 5m

Fig. 1. Nea Paphos 1996-97, South of Villa Theseus. The bottle-shaped cistern, plan and section

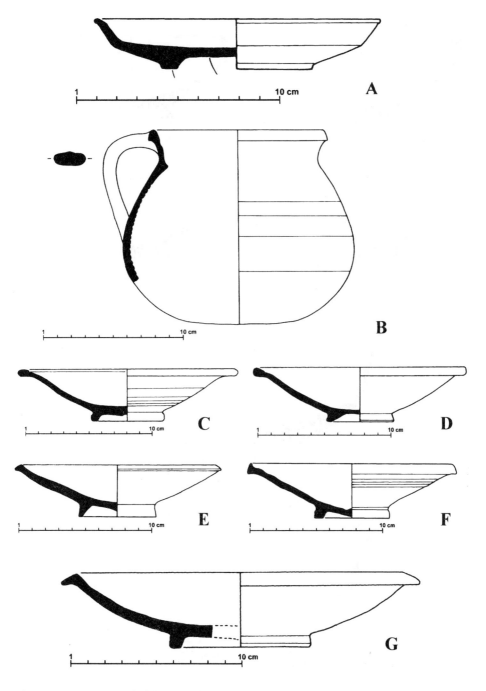

Fig. 2. A - Eastern Sigillata A plate Hayes form 29 used as a lid for the kitchen
pot B. C-G – Colour Coated Ware dishes with different rims

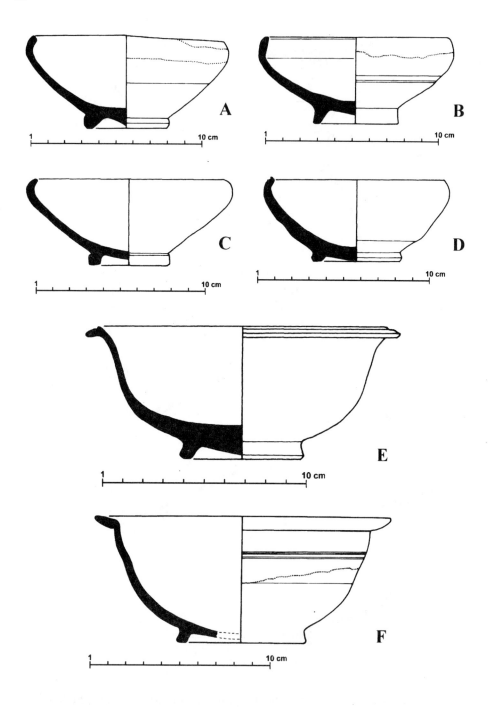

Fig. 3. A-D – Colour Coated Ware incurved rim bowls, E-F – bowls with outcurved rim of the same category

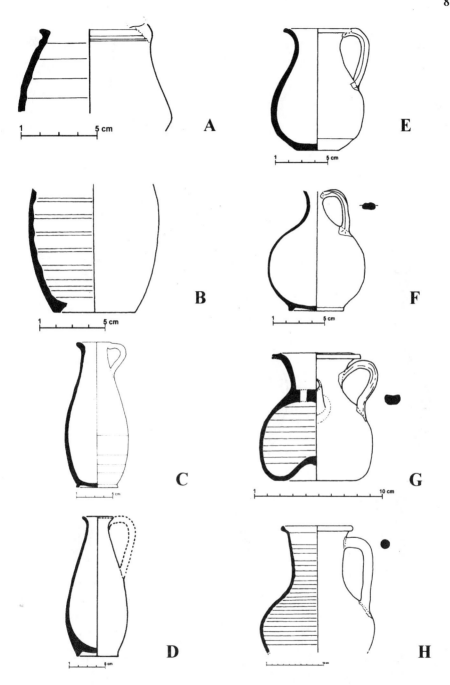

Fig. 4. A – Colour Coated Ware kyathos, B-D – Olpai with various bottoms, Colour Coated Ware, E-H – Different jugs, Colour Coated Ware

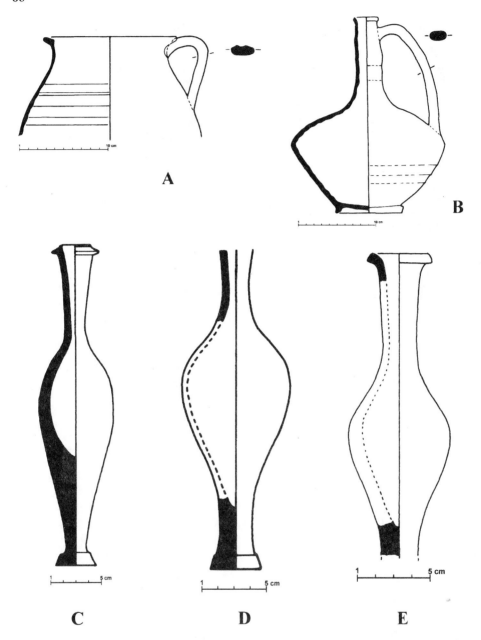

Fig. 5. A – Big jug, Plain White Ware, B – Lagynos with carinated body of Plain White Ware, C-E – Fusiform unguentaria

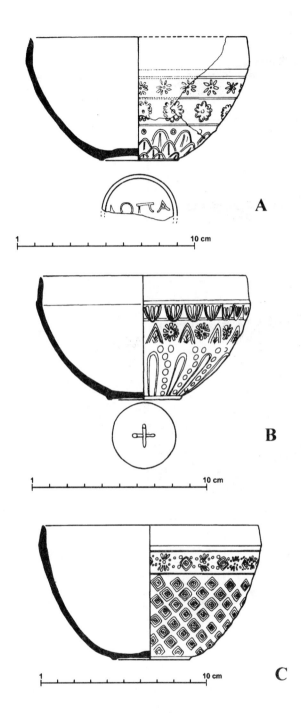

Fig. 6. A – Relief bowls from Ionian Workshops

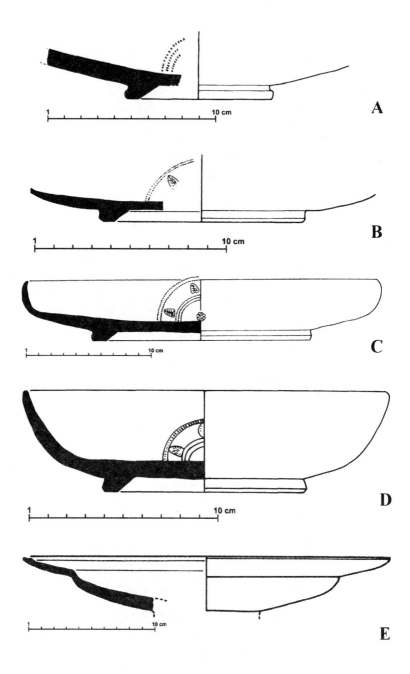

Fig. 7. A-E – Eastern Sigillata A plates

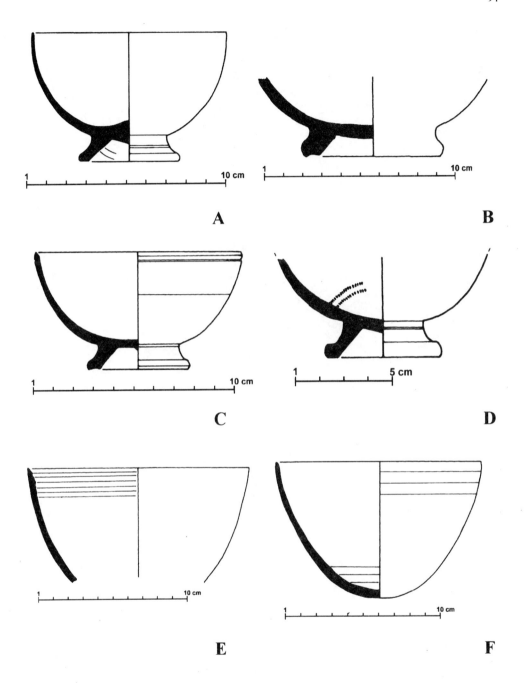

Fig. 8. A-D – Eastern Sigillata A bowls, E-F – Eastern Sigillata A hemispherical bowls

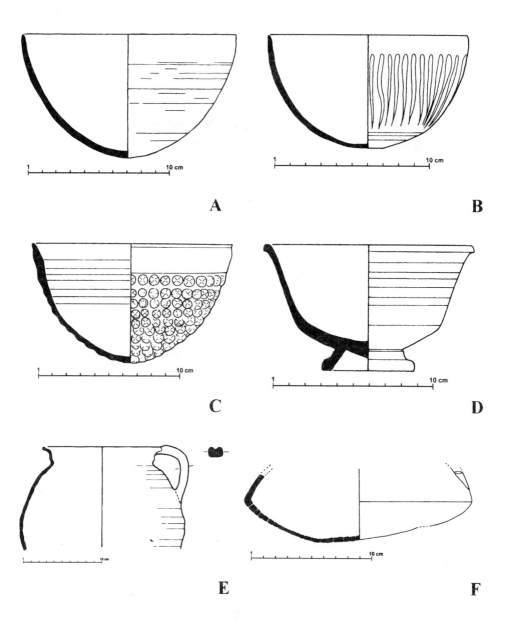

Fig. 9. A-C – Eastern Sigillata A hemispherical bowls, D – Bowl, imitation
(local?) of Eastern Sigillata A Ware, E – Kitchen Ware, cooking pot,
F – Kitchen Ware, partly preserved colander

Jolanta Młynarczyk

Warsaw

Sha'ar ha-Amakim:
a Hellenistic and Roman Site in Lower Galilee

The archaeological site of Sha'ar ha-Amakim is located within the kibbutz of the same name, some 15 km to the east of Haifa. It occupies the western slope of a limestone hill rising to a height of 100 m above sea level and 80 m above the fields which extend westwards to the nearby Kishon river[1]. In antiquity, this site enjoyed an excellent strategic position, guarding the northern exit of a narrow pass which leads from the Jezreel Valley to the plain of Akko (Zebulun Valley), between the hillocks of Lower Galilee and the steep slopes of Mt. Carmel (Fig. 1). This passage was actually part of an international route, Via Maris, which skirted Carmel on the east to run north-northwest via Akko to Phoenicia and beyond. Between Galilee and Phoenicia, the site of Sha'ar ha-Amakim stood literally at the crossroads of political and cultural influences. Occupied continuously from at least the Persian period (6th-4th centuries B.C.) up to the early 4th century A.D., as attested by pottery and coins, it has been excavated since 1984 by Prof. Arthur Segal on behalf of the Department of Archaeology, University of Haifa, in co-operation with Mr Yehuda Naor, a member of kibbutz Sha'ar ha-Amakim, and (since 1993) with the author[2]. The present paper is an attempt at a summary of the key results of the excavations carried out so far[3].

---

[1] My warm thanks go to Ms Iwona Zych, Warsaw, for revising the English of this paper.

[2] I would like to thank Prof. Arthur Segal for entrusting me with the publication of pottery from this site, and Mr Yehuda Naor for his unfailing assistance during my stay in the kibbutz.

[3] Cf. earlier reports: A. Segal and Y. Naor, Four Seasons of Excavations at an Hellenistic Site in the Area of Kibbutz Sha'ar ha-Amakim, *The Eastern Frontier of the Roman Empire*, ed. by D.H. French and C.S. Lightfoot, Oxford 1989 (henceforth: Segal and Naor 1989), 421-435; id.id., Sha'ar ha-Amaqim, *The New Encyclopedia of Archaeological Excavations in the Holy Land*, ed. by E. Stern *et al.*, Jerusalem 1993 (henceforth: Segal and Naor 1993), 1339-1340.

The current work focuses around a tower-like structure of dressed limestone, preserved to a height of 2-3 courses[4]. Founded on bedrock, it is roughly square, measuring 12.30 m from north to south and 13.20 m from east to west, and divided into five rectangular compartments (Fig. 2). An additional wall, just about 1.50 m high, built of alternating headers and stretchers, ran parallel to the tower walls on all four sides; its purpose was to restrict enemy approach[5]. The outer face of this screen wall is ca. 4.50 m away from the tower on three sides except for the east, where it is divided into two separate sections (W 139 and W 142, Fig. 2), the southern one (W 142) exceeding this distance by 2 m. A gap 1.30 m wide between the two sections provided indirect and controlled access to the building which, obviously, might have served both as a watch tower and a small fortress.

An underground water-supply system was also found, entirely cut in the rock. A rectangular shaft about 4 m deep, ending in nine steps, leads from inside the tower to a tunnel, ca. 15 m long and 2 m high, gently sloping in a west-southwest direction. Shortly before the blind end is reached, there is a short extension with a few steps leading down to a bell-shaped chamber, cistern D (maximum diameter 7.5 m, 5 m high, cf. Fig. 3) at the bottom of which there probably was a source of fresh water, either a spring or a water-bearing layer of bedrock. Both the tunnel and the spring cistern have their walls covered with waterproof plaster. It appears that this water system had three successive phases[6].

Since the east side of the entrance shaft is of masonry, unlike the other three sides which were cut in the rock, it is clear that the original entrance to the tunnel was further east, perhaps open to the public[7]. This was cut off by a wall only when the tower was built and a vertical shaft made so that exclusive access to fresh water was from inside the tower. In the third, final phase, a circular opening was made in the roof of the water chamber which became an ordinary collector for rainwater. This must have occurred when the natural water source ran dry, but not before the tower as a defensive structure had been abandoned, for the cutting of an opening through the cistern's roof made it necessary to dismantle the southwestern corner of the screen wall.

That the structure is of Hellenistic date has been apparent from the outset; the very building technique of both the tower and the screen wall is proof enough[8]. A coin of Demetrius II Nikator (minted in 129-125 B.C.), found on the seventh step at

---

[4] For construction details of this building, see Segal and Naor 1989, 422-428; also Segal and Naor 1993, 1340.

[5] The same defensive element in the Herodian fortress of Antonia in Jerusalem is mentioned by Josephus, *BJ* 5, 240.

[6] See discussion of this watersystem by Segal and Naor 1989, 428-430, and id.id. 1993, 1340.

[7] For a comparable (albeit on a much larger scale) underground water system from an earlier period, see the Iron Age Gibeon, J.B. Pritchard, Gibeon, *The New Encyclopedia* (cit., n. 3 supra), 511-512. For other early watersystems in Palestine, see Y. Shiloh, Undergroud Water Systems in the Iron Age, in: A. Kempinski and R. Reich (eds), *The Architecture of Ancient Israel*, Jerusalem 1992, 275-293.

[8] Segal and Naor 1989, 426, 428.

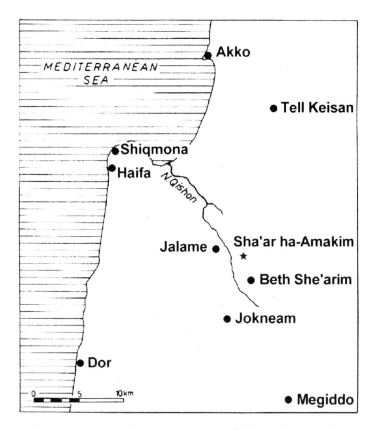

Fig. 1. Map showing the situation of Sha'ar ha-Amakim

the bottom of the shaft, suggests that the water chamber was accessible from the tower towards the end of the 2nd century B.C. What was, however, the stratigraphical context of the tower?

To the north and west of this impressive structure, walls of other buildings have been discovered, apparently pertaining to various periods (Fig. 2). Wherever the stratigraphy could be recorded (e.g. in the sectors O-B and F to the south-west and north of the tower respectively), as many as four to five habitation levels were distinguished (e.g. Fig. 4). The sloping bedrock makes it difficult sometimes to attribute particular floors and walls in individual sectors to specific stratigraphical units. A detailed study of the pottery finds can help to overcome this difficulty, resulting in a step by step reconstruction of the site's development in antiquity.

The earliest pottery found in quantity belongs to the Persian period, 5th-4th century B.C.[9] but, in striking contrast with settlements in the coastal zone (like Tel

---

[9] As a matter of fact, a number of potsherds found in secondary deposits can push the beginnings of the settlement as far back as the IA and LBA, perhaps even the MBA.

Dor, Tell Keisan, Akko), Attic imports are virtually absent from the site. It was probably a modest rural settlement at the time, perhaps with some purple-dyeing industry to judge by the finds of *murex* shells. During the 3rd century B.C., however, imported tableware becomes relatively frequent, and is accompanied by a dozen coins of Ptolemy II Philadelphus (285-246 B.C.), the earliest coinage so far

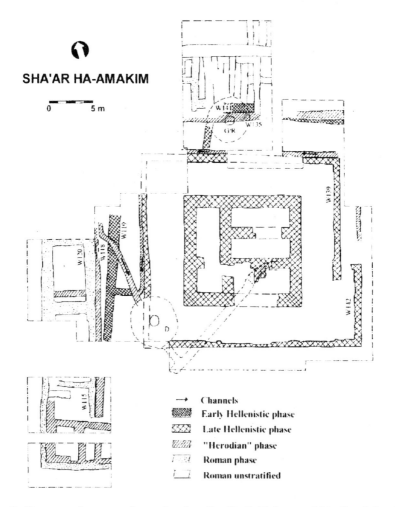

Fig. 2. Excavated area, schematic plan (by R. Stidsing and M. Burdajewicz)

attested at the site[10], suggesting that the settlement had already gained some importance. This new development can be connected plausibly with the economic exploitation of the Syro-Palestinian lands by Philadelphus. It should be kept in mind that not far to the north there was Beth Anath, a vineyard-rich *dorea* of Apollonios,

---

[10] I am very grateful to Mr. Yehuda Naor for information on all the numismatic finds from Sha'ar ha-Amakim; for their identification, see Segal and Naor 1989, 430-431, 434-435, n. 4.

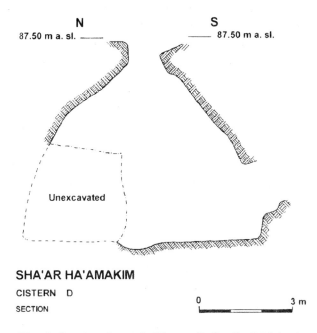

N

87.50 m a. sl. ——

S

—— 87.50 m a. sl.

Unexcavated

SHA'AR HA'AMAKIM

CISTERN   D

SECTION

0   3 m

Fig. 3. Section through Cistern D (by R. Stidsing)

a mighty *dioiketes* of this king[11]. Since the bedrock is fairly close to the surface, virtually no distinction can be made between the Persian-period and the Early Hellenistic strata, both of which can only be referred to the lowermost floor (where preserved), set directly above the bedrock (cf. Fig. 4, layer 11). The earliest remains of the settlement certainly include a few circular vats (perhaps dyeing vats?)[12], ca. 0.85-0.90 m in diameter and 0.70 m in depth, cut in the bedrock here and there, as well as a small enclosure of stones found below a later wall, W 115 (cf. Fig. 2) of the western building.

Apart from the tower itself, only a few walls made of unhewn stones (Fig. 2: W 119, 141) can be dated confidently to the Hellenistic period, in connection with early floors recorded to the west, south-west and north of the tower. Abutting the south face of W 141, there was the opening of a rock-cut underground chamber (Cistern G/R). Devoid of a waterproof plaster coating and only 3.5 m deep, this bell-shaped chamber of slightly oval plan (Fig. 5), is either an unfinished cistern or a wine

---

[11] Cf. P.W. Pestman *et al.*, *A Guide to the Zenon Archive.* Papyrologica Lugduno-Batava XXI A,B, Leiden 1981, A: 264, B: 481 and Map II.

[12] For similar, but smaller, rock-cut dyeing vats attributed to the 8th-7th centuries B.C. at a Judean site, see Z. Yeivin and G. Edelstein, Excavations at Tirat Yehuda, *Atiqot* VI (1970), Hebrew Series, 6* and 59, fig. 3.

98

cellar[13]; its location obviously marks the courtyard of a house (corresponding to layer 10, Fig. 4). After the building in question had been destroyed and before the next architectural phase had begun, the cistern was filled with building stones and household remains bearing traces of fire: pottery, bronze and glass jewelery, iron and stone implements, pieces of a clay oven, charred wood, lots of animal bones and some seeds. This was clearly a one-time fill without any evidence of gradual accumulation. The pottery assemblage[14] comprised a dozen local wine jars, several round-bottomed jugs for bringing and storing water, a Graeco-Italic amphora and a few Rhodian ones, many cooking pots, imported elegant tableware and its local counterparts (for selection of the pottery, see Fig. 6). In particular, the imported vessels help to set the date of this fill around the mid-second century B.C. We should bear in mind that precisely in 150-145 B.C., this part of Syro-Palestine was the stage for an intervention mounted by Ptolemy VI in the strggle between Alexander Balas and Demetrius II, two rivals to the Seleucid throne[15], although the destruction of the house in question was not necessarily caused by war.

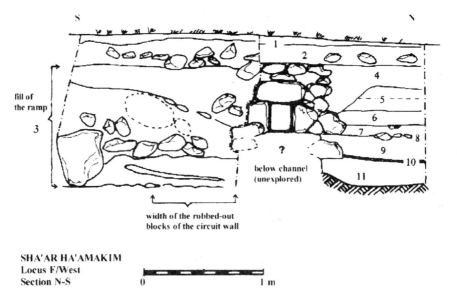

Fig. 4. Sector F, western section, showing the east-west drain, floors 2, 5, 8 and 10, and contaminated remains of Persian and Hellenistic habitation levels in layer 11 (by J. Młynarczyk)

---

[13] Numerous rock-cut wine cellars of a fairly similar shape, but smaller than our "Cistern" G/R, were cut at Gibeon in the 8th-7th centuries B.C.: Pritchard, loc. cit.

[14] Discussed in detail J. Młynarczyk, Pottery from the Hellenistic Cistern at Sha'ar ha-Amakim. *Acts of the 5th International Meeting on Hellenistic Pottery, Chania 1997* (in print).

[15] I Macc. 10, 51-58 and 11, 1-19); cf. C. Préaux, *Le monde hellénistique. La Grèce et l' Orient (323-146 av.J.-C.)*, Paris 1978, I, 173.

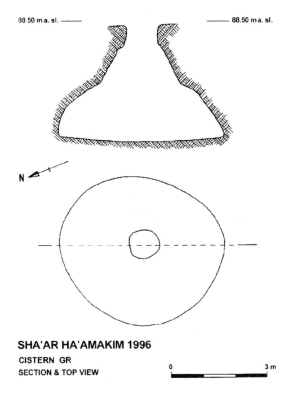

88.50 m a. sl. ———   ——— 88.50 m a. sl.

N

SHA'AR HA'AMAKIM 1996
CISTERN GR
SECTION & TOP VIEW

0   3 m

Fig. 5. Cistern G/R: plan and section (by R. Stidsing)

Initially, it was suggested that the tower had been built in the late 3rd or early 2nd century B.C.[16] At present, it seems more plausible, in view of the stratigraphical evidence, to connect its construction with the date of the sealing of cistern G/R around the mid-2nd century B.C. The tower was built on bedrock, apparently in a roughly levelled destruction layer of earlier walls such as W 119 and W 141 (for the latter, see layer 9, Fig. 4) the orientation of which slightly but clearly differs from that of the tower (Fig. 2). As we remember, the tunnel leading to cistern D appears to have been in use towards the last quarter of the 2nd century B.C., and it seems reasonable to consider the tower as having been built by one of the Seleucid kings in the second half (third quarter?) of the 2nd century B.C. Nevertheless, since the site is exactly on the border between the territory of Ptolemais and that of the Hasmonean realm as enlarged by Aristoboulus I (104-103 B.C.)[17], another possibility is that its construction might date from the early years of this king's successor, Alexander Jannaeus.

---

[16] Segal and Naor 1989, 432; id.id. 1993, 1340.
[17] Cf. H.-P. Kuhnen, *Nordwest-Palästina in hellenistisch-römischer Zeit. Bauten und Gräber im Karmelgebiet*, Weinheim 1987, 10, fig. 2.

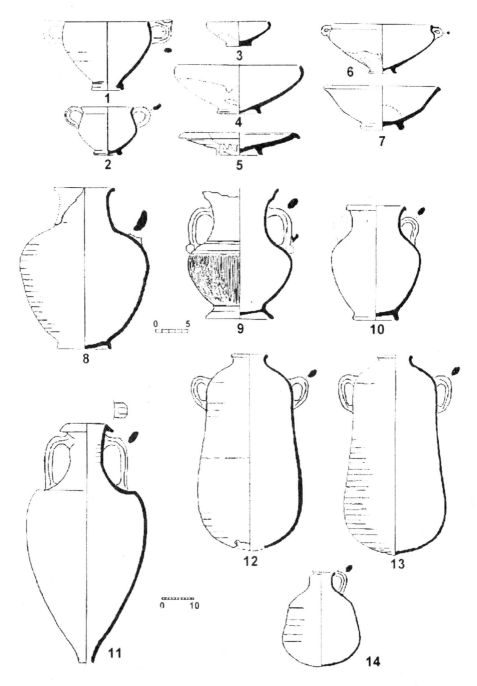

Fig. 6. Selection of pottery from cistern G/R. Pottery registration numbers in order: 907.4, 908.1, 885.1, 887.2, 907.2, 883.2, 883.3, 907.9, 886.1, 907.12, 887.1, 889.7 890.8, 889.1 (by M. Burdajewicz)

A sequence of floors recorded to the north of the tower (Fig. 4) helps in following further site development. After the southwestern corner of the tower's screen wall had been dismantled in order to pierce the roof of ancient cistern D, and when the channels were built to feed it with rainwater (Fig. 2), the rest of this wall was still standing, as indicated by one of the channels; it was built leaning against the outer face of this wall and consequently followed its course. On the north, a new east-west wall was built (W 135) across the blocked mouth of the earlier cistern G/R. Thus, a space 3.50 m wide was left between the northern screen wall of the tower and the building with narrow compartments, undoubtedly a storehouse. No stratigraphical research has actually been conducted inside the latter, but the wall building technique suggests two or even three construction phases.

In the same period, another building (cf. W 118, Fig. 2) was constructed parallel to the west side of the tower, at a distance of 5 m from its outer wall. A channel removing rainwater to cistern D was made along the eastern face of this building and across a pavement of small stones upon lime mortar, which had covered the levelled Hellenistic wall W 119 (Fig. 7), and corresponded to layer 5 on the north (Fig. 4); the two channels met shortly before emptying into the cistern. The evidence of stratified pottery groups and a coin of Herod the Great found in a section of this pavement connected with the western drain date this phase to the end of the 1st century B.C. Moreover, the rectangular arrangement of buildings around the old tower in the centre is no doubt indicative of a consistent architectural program. The data may support a tentative identification of Sha'ar ha-Amakim with Gaba Hippeon, a place where Herod the Great settled the veterans from his cavalry forces[18], as first proposed by Prof. Beniamin Mazar in the mid-1930s[19]. Actually, our site not only was situated exactly on the border between Herod's realm and the territory of Ptolemais, but also combined strategic importance with access to fertile land on the eastern bank of the Kishon river (cf. Fig. 1).

The next phase began when the three lowermost courses of the tower's walls became a substructure for a platform. It was made by throwing the blocks into the spaces between the exterior and interior walls, and filling minor gaps with rubble and earth. Before that, however, some dressed blocks, especially those from the outer ("screen") wall, were extracted (cf. layer 3, Fig. 4) to be re-used in other buildings (cf. "Roman phase", Fig. 2). The channels, after having been inspected, remained in use, but a new floor was made of a thick layer of lime mortar at a level corresponding to the top of the platform, elevated some 40-50 cm above the Herodian floors (Fig. 4: layers 2 and 5 respectively; see also Fig. 7). It seems that the layout of the northern and western buildings remained basically the same, but a number of new walls constructed (e.g. W 120, W 115, Fig. 2). The northern

---

[18] Joseph. BJ III, 36; AJ XV, 294.

[19] B. Mazar, Beth She'arim I, Jerusalem 1973, 8 and 11, n. 55. Cf. Segal and Naor 1993, 1339. For a different view, identifying Gaba Hippeon with the modern Tel Abu Shoshah, see Z. Safrai, The Economy of Roman Palestine, London and New York 1994, 91 and 157, fig. 36.

building apparently continued to serve as a storehouse, while the western one, only 6 m wide, with a single row of rooms, might have housed workshops and kitchens. According to A. Segal, the central platform might have served as a platform under a wooden structure, perhaps a tower once again[20]. Nevertheless, there is another possibility, that of a vast courtyard surrounded by buildings, of which only the western and northern ones have so far been uncovered. A similar plan is featured by the Nabataean and Roman fortress Sha'ar Ramon in the Negev, on the road from Petra to Gaza[21].

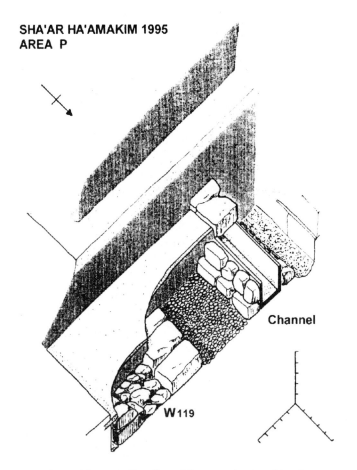

SHA'AR HA'AMAKIM 1995
AREA P

Channel

W 119

Isometric reconstruction of the superimposed levels

Fig. 7. Sector P: three successive floors to the east of W 120
(by M. Burdajewicz)

---

[20] Segal and Naor 1989, 433.
[21] A.Sussman (ed.), *Excavations and Surveys in Israel 1982*, I, 87-88.

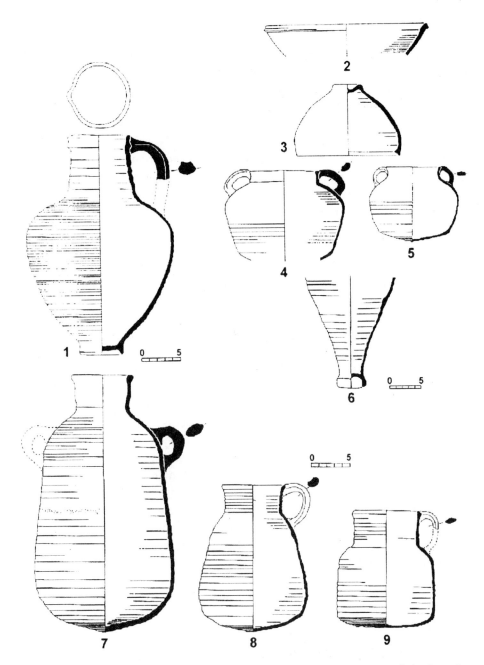

Fig. 8. Selection of pottery from cistern D. Pottery registration numbers in order:
735.1, 720.5, 728.8, 742.1, 728.9, 744.2, 744.1, 709.4, 735.5
(by M. Burdajewicz)

What historical event might have inspired the re-arrangement of the site at Sha'ar ha-Amakim? The pottery from some sealed layers and a coin of Tiberius with a countermark of Caligula, found embedded in a lime mortar floor inside the western building, date the beginning of this habitation phase to the mid-1st century A.D. or slightly later. Actually, this may have corresponded to the years of the First Jewish Revolt. If we accept the identification of Sha'ar ha-Amakim with Gaba Hippeon, we find an explicit mention by Josephus Flavius about Gaba (doubtlessly the same place) as garrisoned by the Romans in A.D. 66[22]. Was the new role, that of a military station, perhaps the reason for removing the remains of the old tower, constructing a massive platform and reinforcing the surrounding buildings at Sha'ar ha-Amakim? The Roman presence during the First Revolt and shortly afterwards is also suggested by a number of silver coins, specifically, 6 coins of Nero, 1 of Vitelius, 3 of Vespasian.

No architectural remains of a later period have been identified thus far, perhaps because the site apparently served as a source of building stone in modern times, specifically for an Arab village, el-Kharitiyye, which existed here before the kibbutz was founded in 1935. We can rely on the pottery and numismatic evidence alone. Their analysis suggests a period of decline following the revolt of Bar Kochba (A.D. 132-135). On the contrary, the 3rd century, especially its first half, seems to have been a period of new prosperity, perhaps in connection with the *floruit* of neighbouring Beth Shearim (cf. Fig. 1), then the seat of the Sanhedrin and the central Jewish necropolis[23]. This period is represented at Sha'ar ha-Amakim by a number of coins and domestic pottery, first of all, many local jars for liquids (water? olive oil? wine?). The old cistern D continued to be used up to the first half of the 4th century as proved by pottery found in a silty layer on its bottom. It comprised a number of shapes (for selection of the pottery, see Fig. 8) comparable to those known from Beth Shearim and Jalame, a Late Roman glass factory some three kilometres to the west[24]. This final date is confirmed by a coin of Constantine the Great, the latest dated find at the site. Probably, the settlement at Sha'ar ha-Amakim was abandoned when the neighbouring Beth Shearim, and many other Galilean cities, were destroyed during the putting down of the Jewish rebellion against Gallus Caesar in A.D. 351[25].

---

[22] *Vit.* 115-118.

[23] Mazar, op. cit., 4-5. Cf. also N. Avigad and B. Mazar, Beth She'arim, *The New Encyclopedia* (cit., n. 3 supra), 248, and N. Avigad, *Beth She'arim* III, Jerusalem 1976.

[24] On pottery finds from Jalame, see B.L. Johnson, The Pottery, in *Excavation at Jalame, Site of a Glass Factory in Late Roman Palestine*, ed. by G. Davidson-Weinberg, Columbia 1988, 137-226.

[25] Avigad and Mazar, loc. cit.

Aleksandra Wąsowicz

Varsovie

"NYMPHAION - histoire et structure d'une polis grecque." Projet international polono-russo-ucrainien avec une collaboration française (1993 - 1997)

Dans le livre VII de sa "Géographie", Strabon écrivait: "L'intervalle entre Théodosie et Panticapée mesure 530 stades environ (soit 98 km). C'est un territoire (*chora*) qui produit partout des céréales; on y trouve de gros villages (*komai*) et une ville dénommée Nymphaion dont le port est excellent (*polis eulimenos*)." [VII,4,4. Les Belles Lettres].

La région de la Crimée signalée dans cette source, appelée la péninsule de Kertch, est une plaine steppique ponctuée de petits reliefs de terrain et coupée de lits d'anciens cours d'eau à sec (de torrents en périodes de crue, sans doute) (Fig. 1). A quelques endroits on remarque encore, moins nets qu'au XIXe siècle, des tracés d'anciens vallums. Des kourganes, isolés ou disposés en rangées ou en groupes, viennent y rompre la monotonie de la steppe. A en juger par la densité du peuplement dans l'Antiquité ainsi que par des témoignages d'auteurs antiques, la contrée était autrefois beaucoup plus verte qu'elle ne l'est à l'heure actuelle, plus riche en cultures céréalières, vergers et vignes. Si important dans l'histoire de la colonisation grecque et dans l'évolution du cabotage, le tracé littoral était à cet endroit différent de celui que l'on observe aujourd'hui.

Nymphaion était situé sur la rive occidentale du détroit de Kertch (l'antique Bosphore Cimmérien), à 17 km au sud de Kertch (l'antique Panticapée), à proximité de l'actuel village Eltigen-Geroevka, entre deux lacs aujourd'hui desséchés: le Čurubaš au nord et le Tobečik au sud. Dans l'Antiquité, les deux lacs n'étaient sans doute que des baies ou des lagunes (question discutable).

Les sources écrites n'apportent que de modestes informations sur Nymphaion; on n'y trouve ni la date de la fondation de cette colonie ni même le nom de la métropole. Les témoignages archéologiques, dont, pour l'essentiel, la céramique, permettent de situer la création de Nymphaion dans le deuxième quart du VIe siècle av. J.-C. Il s'agirait bien d'une colonie ionienne.

La ville était situé sur un vaste plateau relativement régulier, à 24 m d'altitude, et s'étendait sur environ 9 ha (une partie d'agglométarion est actuellement inondée). Des deux côtés, les versants nord-est et sud-est du plateau étaient munis d'importantes fortifications, déjà partiellement dégagées. La limite occidentale de la cité, sans doute celle avec la porte principale, n'a pas encore été située avec précision.

L'emplacement de l'ancien port prête aussi à de nombreuses discussions, et ceci à cause des changemements du niveau de la mer et de la forme du littoral. Certains chercheurs situent le port au nord de la ville, d'autres le localisent plutôt du côté sud.

Les fouilles de la ville, menées par le Musée de l'Ermitage de St. Pétersbourg, continuent depuis 1939. La mission fut dirigée, dans l'ordre chronologique, par M. Chudjak, V. Skundova et N. Grač. Actuellement, la direction des fouilles est assurée par Mme Olga Sokolova. Jusqu'à présent, les travaux se sont concentrés, pour l'essentiel, sur la partie sud-est de la cité s'ouvrant sur le détroit de Kertch (Fig. 2).

En 1993, on a mis sur pied le projet international de recherche intitulé "NYMPHAION - histoire et structure d'une polis grecque". Les participants à ce projet sont: du côté ucrainien, le Musée Archéologique de Kertch et, à partir de 1994, le Commité National de Protection de Monuments Historiques avec le siège à Simferopol; du côté russe, le Musée de l'Ermitage de St. Pétersbourg; du côté polonais, l'Académie Polonaise des Sciences de Varsovie, l'Institut d'Archéologie de l'Université de Varsovie et, depuis 1995, le CNRS de Nantes. L'objectif du projet est d'étudier l'ensemble de l'histoire d'un état grec (polis) choisi, dans son aspect matériel, économique, culturel, politique et religieux. Le projet prévoit l'application de diverses méthodes de recherche (prospection, fouilles, recherches géophysiques, archéologie sous-marine, images aériennes et images par satellite) et l'étude la plus complète de sources (sources archéologiques, écrites, épigraphiques, numismatiques, paléobotaniques et autres). Bref, ce qui nous intéresse, ce sont aussi bien la ville que la chora, aussi bien l'art que la culture matérielle, les recherches dans le terrain que l'édition de sources et la publication d'études sur Nymphaion présentées régulièrement à l'occasion de tables rondes annuelles (quatre rencontres de travail ont déjà eu lieu en Pologne).

Il y a lieu de se poser la question de savoir pourquoi ce projet et pourquoi Nymphaion au centre de notre intérêt. Or, premièrement, Nymphaion est une colonie relativement petite, et il semble qu'il sera beaucoup plus réel d'embrasser l'ensemble de sa problématique que si c'était le cas, par exemple, d'Olbia ou de Massalia. Deuxièmement, aussi bien l'étendue de la ville antique que celle de la nécropole et de la chora n'ont pas encore été détruites par l'aménagement et les constructions modernes. Troisièmement, les découvertes faites par les archéologues russes sur l'emplacement de la ville antique et de sa nécropole ont été fort intéressantes et permettent d'espérer la réponse à de nombreuses questions concernant différents aspects de cette colonie. Et enfin, ce qui est très important, en 1992, la directrice du Musée de Kertch, dans les compétences duquel se trouve tout ce territoire, Mme Eleonora Jakovenko nous a proposé une collaboration.

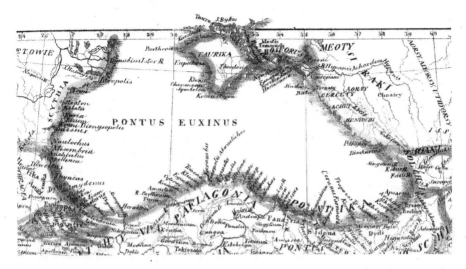

Fig. 1. Principales colonies grecques sur la mer Noire. J. Lelewel, Atlas do historii i geografii starożytnej, Warszawa 1828, p. X.

Les fouilles systématiques menées sur l'emplacement de la ville depuis près de cinquante ans ont apporté de nombreuses données relatives à l'aménagement de cet établissement. Ainsi, il me semble que l'agglomération ne connaissait pas de plan régulier du type hippodaméen. En effet, les constructions mises au jour dans certains secteurs attestent plutôt d'une disposition libre de différentes structures. Au IVe siècle av. J.-C., la ville fut ceinte d'un mur solide en pierres. Nous n'avons par contre aucune information concernant l'aspect des fortifications urbaines d'avant cette période. Dans l'enceinte de la ville, on a découvert quelques pressoirs à vin dont un date de la fin du Ve s. av. J.-C. Il serait donc le plus ancien de toutes les installations de ce type dans le monde colonial grec. Il est important de rappeler que la vigne figure au revers des monnaies de Nymphaion émises dans le dernier quart du Ve siècle.

Quatre structures mises au jour à Nymphaion sont interprétées par les archéologues russes comme des vestiges de sanctuaires. Il s'agit d'un nombre surprenant pour une colonie relativement petite. Ce qui est caractéristique dans cette situation, c'est que les constructions considérées comme sanctuaires ne se trouvent pas réunies à un endroit, par exemple dans l'enceinte d'un temenos ou à proximité de l'agora comme - rappelons-le - à Olbia ou à Histria, mais qu'elles sont dispersées à différents endroits de la ville.

A proximité de la limite occidentale de la ville, à une très petite distance des murs d'enceinte, sur une terrasse dominant le détroit de Kertch, parmi des rochers, tout près d'une source était situé le sanctuaire des divinités chtoniennes. On y a découvert de petites constructions, retravaillées à plusieurs reprises entre le VIe et le IIIe siècle, qui s'appuyaient sur le rocher.

Dans la partie centrale de la ville, la plus haute, ont été découverts deux autres présumés sanctuaires existant depuis le VIe siècle. Une de ces structures mérite une attention toute particulière. Il s'agit en effet d'une construction allongée, très originale, aux dimensions 5 x 14,3 m, et possédant une abside. Ce type de construction est très rarement attesté aux bords de la mer Noire (l'unique analogue que je puisse évoquer provient de l'île Berezan). S'appuyant sur les résultats des confrontations avec les sanctuaires de Thèbes et de Samothrace. M. Chudjak pensait qu'il s'agissait d'un sanctuaire des Kabires.

Parmi les découvertes les plus sensationnelles de Nymphaion, on compte une grande construction de parade, reposant sur un haut soubassement, située à proximité de la limite sud de la ville (secteur M, fouilles en cours). Des fragments de colonnes, de pilastres, de corniches, d'escaliers et d'autres détails architecturaux indiquent qu'il s'agit d'un édifice monumental, à plusieurs étages, datant des IVe-IIIe siècles. De nombreuses fresques portant des graffiti, qui servaient autrefois de décor à l'intérieur des salles, indiquent le caractère tout à fait particulier de cette construction. Des milliers de menus fragments de stucs couverts de dessins et d'inscriptions sont déjà restaurés par l'atelier de restauration du Musée de l'Ermitage. On y trouve des dédicaces en l'honneur de différentes divinités, parmi lesquelles des formules consarcées à Aphrodite et à Apollon, des voeux de bon voyage, des notices relatives aux dettes, une oeuvre poétique de la plume d'un poète local, un registre de noms, des noms isolés, y compris le nom d'un des rois bosphorans - Pairisades, ce qui constitue un important critère de datation. Les représentations de nombreux vaisseaux, y compris celle d'un grand bateau portant le nom d'Isis, sont déjà connues des spécialistes grâce aux publications préliminaires de N. Grač.

De précieuses informations relatives non seulement à des traditions sépulcrales mais aussi à des relations sociales et ethniques sont fournies par de nombreuses nécropoles de Nymphaion. Parmi les nécropoles particulièrement intéressantes, on compte les riches nécropoles à kourgans, lesquelles exigeront sans doute une nouvelle interprétation quant à la question ethnique. Les rites funéraires ainsi que le mobilier mis au jour dans ces sépultures attestent de nombreux contacts gréco-scythes.

Avec la mise sur pied du projet commun NYMPHAION nous nous sommes penchés sur le problème de la chora de cette colonie grecque. En nous basant, premièrement, sur des analogies observées entre Nymphaion et les autres colonies grecques et, deuxièmement, sur l'analyse de la configuration du terrain, nous avons admis, a priori, que la chora était naturellement délimité par le lac Čurubaš au nord, par le détroit de Kertch à l'est et par le lac Tobečik au sud. Il se dessine ainsi une sorte de micro-région fermée, une étendue d'environ 70 ha appartenant à Nymphaion, délimitée de façon naturelle et facile à contrôler. La limite occidentale de la chora ne peut être déterminée qu'en termes d'hypothèse. Elle pouvait bien correspondre à la ligne nord-sud reliant les extrémités occidentales des deux lacs. On ne peut pas non plus exclure l'hypothèse selon laquelle cette limite était différente à différents moment de l'histoire (Fig. 3).

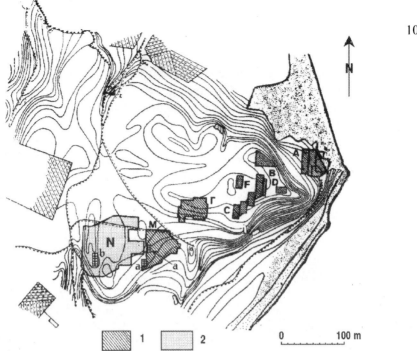

Fig. 2. Plan de Nymphaion: 1- fouilles russes, 2 – superficie des travaux
géophysiques

Le territoire correspondant, à notre avis, à la chora de Nymphaion n'a été que
très sommairement étudié. Certaines traces d'aménagement aux environs du lac
Čurubaš ont été déjà constatées au XIXe siècle. Puis, en 1940, V. Gajdukevič a
publié les vestiges de villages antiques et de parcelles-champs environnants, de
forme irrégulière, qu'il avait lui-même découverts dans cette région. Dans les années
1956-1957 (prospection) et 1963-1964 (fouilles), à Čurubaš, Geroevka et Ogonki,
T. Kruglikova a constaté l'existence de restes de villages à l'habitat dispersé. Toutes
ces découvertes n'ont connu que des publications sommaires, si bien qu'aujourd'hui il
est difficile de les localiser dans le tarrain. Elles constituent néanmoins un argument
important en faveur de la thèse sur l'existence, dans l'entourage de la ville de
Nymphaion, de traces d'un aménagement systématique et planifié remontant à
l'Antiquité.

Depuis les années 90, des fouilles systématiques sont menées à quelques endroits
de la chora, à savoir: sur le littoral du détroit de Kertch, au sud du village de
Geroevka. Il s'agit là de villages composés de quelques maisons, mais étendus sur
quelques kilomètres, avec une couche archéologique datant du VIe s. av. J.-C.
jusqu'au Moyen Age.

En 1993 et 1994, dans le cadre de notre projet, une première prospection a été
menée sur tout le territoire compris entre les lacs Čurubaš et Tobečik.

En 1995-1997, on a mené des travaux polono-ucrainiens visant à établir la Carte
Archéologique de Nymphaion (les travaux menés avec autorisation de V. Zin'ko du
Comité de Protection des Monuments de la Crimée). L'obectif de ce projet est de
déterminer les limites de la chora et d'étudier sa structure et sa chronologie.

Face à l'absence de modèles de référence dans les études d'archéologie antique de la mer Noire, nous avons décidé d'adopter, après modification, la méthode utilisée dans la préparation de la Carte Archéologique de la Pologne.

Notre travail part d'une carte russe à échelle 1 : 25000, dressée dans les années 70, et d'une autre carte, à échelle 1 : 10000, obtenue par l'agrandissement mécanique de la première. Sur la carte, l'ensemble du territoire choisi pour la recherche est divisé en carrés dont les côtés correspondent à un kilomètre. Toutes les découvertes sont localisées dans le cadre de cette division.

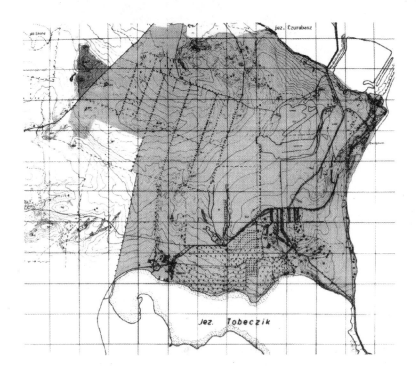

Fig. 3. Carte de la chora de Nymphaion: en gris – superficie de la prospection systématique en 1995-1997

La prospection systématique du terrain (Survey) se fait à pied, en équipes de 5 personnes (équipes composées d'archéologues polonais et ucrainiens). Les travaux sont dirigés, du côté polonais par T. Scholl et, du côté ucrainien, par V. Zin'ko.

Chaque site, ou concentration d'objets, est toute de suite situé sur la carte et obtient sa fiche d'inventaire (fiche du site). Lors de la prospection, on procède à une description du terrain, de son relief et de sa végétation. On recueille tout objet caractéristique qui reçoit sa fiche d'inventaire (fiche d'objet particulier), une photographie, un croquis et une description. La datation des céramiques est confiée à V. Zin'ko. Tous les monuments recueillis restent bien évidemment à Kertch.

Les premiers résultats : il est déjà possible de confirmer l'hypothèse relative au territoire étudié, préalablement délimité. Il s'agit le plus vraisemblablement de la chora de Nymphaion: la plus importante concentration de monuments a été repérée dans le voisinage de la ville; la plupart des sites et du matériel archéologique datent de la période antique.

Les premières traces de la présence humaine sur ce territoire remontent au début du deuxième millénaire av. J.-C. On y a également découvert 4 sites d'habitation datant de l'âge du bronze, une dizaine de villages appartenant à l'époque antique, quelques villages médiévaux, khazares et tartares, ainsi que des nécropoles du XIXe et du XXe siècle.

La prospection systématique et intensive, menée depuis quatre ans, a permis d'inventorier, à part les 42 établissements (dont il a été déjà question), 14 nécropoles antiques et médiévales (VIIIe-IXe s.), des traces de parcellaire à 5 endroits, 6 fragments de voies, 2 carrières, un fragment d'aqueduc, un vallum et de nombreuses concentrations d'objets antiques.

Conformément aux principes formulés lors de la mise sur pied du "Projet Nymphaion", parallèlement aux travaux sur le terrain, on publie les sources et différentes études concernant Nymphaion. Nous pouvons être fiers de quatre publications intitulées "Nymphaion Project" parues en français et en anglais dans la revue "Archeologia" à Varsovie (la cinquième publication "Project" est actuellement sous presse).

Toutefois, il reste encore beaucoup à faire tant dans le domaine des recherches sur le terrain qu'au niveau de la publication de sources et d'études historiques. Au fur et à mesure que nos travaux collectifs avancent, de nombreuses questions apparaissent et demandent d'être résolues.

Parmi ces questions, il faut signaler celle des contacts (contacts locaux et à grande distance) de cette petite et modeste colonie qui restait toujours à l'ombre de Pantikapaion. Il s'agit, premièrement, de contacts réciproques des habitants de Nymphaion avec la population indigène et, plus particulièrement, avec les Scythes. Ces contacts se réalisaient, semble-t-il, dans le voisinage le plus proche de la ville, car à l'intérieur de la chora, et peut-être même en ville. Deuxièmement, il est question des relations entre Nymphaion, Pantikapaion et le Royaume du Bosphore. Lorsqu'on étudie la carte, on constate une proximité évidente de ces deux centres ainsi que la position de Nymphaion situé sur la voie des itinéraires maritimes menant vers la capitale du Royaume du Bosphore. Et enfin, il faudrait étudier attentivement les relations de Nymphaion avec d'autres villes du littoral de la mer Noire ainsi qu'avec d'autres centres méditerranéens. Il s'agirait non seulement de contacts commerciaux mais aussi de relations culturelles et politiques. Dans le cadre de ces dernières, il faut compter le problème souvent débattu, celui notamment des relations entre Nymphaion et Athènes, problème posé à partir du témoignage d'Eschine et de Démosthène (Aesch., in Ctes. 171; Demosth., De corona, 9-11).

112

Choix de bibliographie

A.Wąsowicz, *Nymphaion Project*, in: *Nymphaion Project I*, Archeologia XLV 1994 (1995), p. 69-72.

S.L.Solov'lev, V.N.Zin'ko, *Research on the chora of Nymphaion. Study Problems*, ibidem, p. 73-78.

N.Kunina, T.Scholl, O.Sokolova, A.Wąsowicz, *The Bibliography of Nymphaion*, ibidem, p. 79-89.

O.J.Neverov, *Les bagues et les pierres gravées provenant de Nymphaion*, in: *Nymphaion Project II*, Archeologia XLVI 1995 (1996), p. 71-75.

A.K.Kasparov, *New Data on Faunal Remains from Nymphaion and Neighbouring Settlements*, ibidem, p. 77-80.

W.Olszaniec, *Zródła pisane do dziejów Nymphaion* [Sources écrites pour l'histoire de Nymphaion], ibidem, p. 81-88.

The Bibliography of Nymphaion. Addenda and Corrigenda, ibidem, p. 89-91.

V.N.Zin'ko, *Geroevka-2. A Rural Settlement in the Chora of Nymphaion* (Ancient Period), in: *Nymphaion Project III*, Archeologia XLVII 1996 (1997), p. 85-94.

K.Domżalski, *Terra Sigillata from Nymphaion. Survey 1994*. Appendix: G.Schneider, *Compositional Analysis of Terra Sigillata from Nymphaion*, ibidem, p. 95-112.

T.Scholl, V.Zinko, *Archeologiczna mapa Nymphaion*, Kwartalnik Historii Kultury Materialnej 1997, 1, p. 61-65.

Comptes rendus des conférences "Nymphaion": J.Stępniewski, Kwartalnik Historii Kultury Materialnej, 1994, 2, p. 275-278; R.Karasiewicz-Szczypiorski, ibidem, 1995, 4, p. 545-550; idem, ibidem, 1996, 4, p. 463-466.

Mariusz Mielczarek, Nataliya M. Sekerskaya
Toruń, Kiiv

Polish-Ukrainian archaeological excavations at Nikonion

Nikonion was a small city established by the Greeks on the left bank of the Dniester river (Fig. 1). According to the archaeological data Nikonion was founded at the very end of the VIth century BC[1] - we do not possess any written evidence regarding its metropolis. In this period the lower Dniester region was controlled by the Scythians, but it also acted as a border zone of Scythian and Thracian influences[2]. To the end of the 4th century BC Nikonion played a significant role in the region[3]. The 5th and the first half of the 4th centuries were a period of prosperity for the city[4]. From the end of the 5th and the beginning of the 4th centuries onwards the city lost its dominant position to the neighbouring city of Tyras (located at present-day Belgorod - Dnestrovskii): henceforward Tyras became the leading centre on the lower Dniester[5]. Destroyed at the end of the century, most probably during Zopyrion's campaign, of 331 BC[6], Nikonion

---

[1] N.M. Sekerskaya, Antichnyi Nikonii i ego okruga v VI-IV vv. do n.e., Kiev 1989, passim; eadem, Arkhaicheskaya keramika iz Nikoniya, "Materialy po Arkheologii Severnogo Pricherno - mor'ya", 8, 1976, pp. 84-95; M.S. Sinitsyn, Raskopki Nadlimanskogo i Roksolanskogo gorodishch v 1957-1958 gg., "Zapiski Odesskogo Arkheologicheskogo Obshchestva", 1 (34), 1960, pp. 196-197; S.B. Okhotnikov, Fenomen Nikoniya, [in:] Nikonii i antichnyi mir Severnogo Prichernomor'ya, Odessa 1997, pp. 27-32; cf. M.S. Sinitsyn, Raskopki gorodishcha vozle s. Roksolany Belyaevskogo raiona Odesskoi oblasti v 1957-1961 gg., "Materialy po Arkheologii Severnogo Prichernomor'ya", 5, 1960, pp. 55-56. See also A.V. Gudkova, S.B. Okhotnikov, L.V. Subbotin, I.T. Chernyakov, Arkheologicheskie pamyatniki Odesskoi oblasti (spravochnik), Odessa 1991, p. 94.
[2] S.B. Okhotnikov, Nizhnee Podnestrov'e v VI-V vv. do n.e., Kiev 1990; idem, The Lower Dniester Region in Antiquity, [in:] Nikonion. An Ancient City on the Lower Dniester, Toruń 1997, pp. 13-17.
[3] N.M. Sekerskaya, Antichnyi ...., passim; S.B. Ochotnikov, Tyras i Nikonion. Świat kolonii greckich u ujścia Dniestru, Toruń 1997, pp. 14-15.
[4] N.M. Sekerskaya, Antichnyi ...., pp. 3 ff.
[5] S.B. Okhotnikov, The Lower ...., p. 15; idem, Tyras ...., pp. 18-19. See (other literature in these publications) P.O. Karyshkovskii, I.B. Klejman, The City of Tyras. A Historical and Archaeological Essay, Odessa 1994; T.L. Samoilova, Tira v VI-I vv. do n.e., Kiev 1988; N.A. Son, Tira rimskogo vremeni, Kiev 1993.
[6] N.M. Sekerskaya, Antichnyi ...., p. 48; S.B. Okhotnikov, The Lower ...., p. 16; idem, Tyras ...., p. 26.

experienced an acute crisis. An inscription from Tyras dating to the beginning of the 3rd century BC, mentions that the inhabitants of Nikonion appealed for help from Histria through the mediation of Tyras[7]. From the second half of the 3rd century BC Nikonion practically ceases to exist for two or three centuries. An increase in the density of settlement in the town is noticeable in the second half of the 1st century BC[8].

The historical and geographical situation of Nikonion gives us a significant opportunity to study a small peripherial Greek city located on the very border of the oikoumene. Our general knowledge concerning Nikonion is not good[9]. First of all there is a lack of epigraphical data. The epigraphic evidence recovered from Nikonion is so far represented by a single small fragment of an inscription of uncertain nature (Fig. 2). No traces of monumental public buildings have been identified, and no monumental sanctuaries. We can, however, say more concerning the economic position and trade connections of the polis.

The mound covering the remains of the ancient city of Nikonion[10] is situated on the high, left-hand, bank of the Dniestrovskii Liman lagoon, north-west of the modern village of Roksolany, and about 40 kilometers to the south-west of Odessa. The mound occupies a high river terrace of the Dniester. The lower terrace, with the "lower city" was destroyed by the river in 1904[11]. The mound is bordered by ravines on its northern, southern and eastern sides. These ravines precisely defined the borders of the city. As in any Greek city the borders were delineated by the defensive curtain. The curtain of the 5th century BC was partialy discovered in the north-western part of the mound[12]. In the 16th century

---

[7] See P.O. Karyshkovskii, Novye epigraficheskie nakhodki v Nizhnem Podnestrove, [in:] Problemy issledovaniya antichnogo i srednevekovogo Khersonesa, 1888-1988, Tezisy dokladov, Sevastopol' 1988, p. 57; Yu. G. Vinogradov, Greek Epigraphy of the North Black Sea Coast, the Caucasus and Central Asia (1985-1990), "Ancient Civilisation from Scythia to Siberia", 1.1, 1994, p. 72; idem, Sinoikizm Nikoniya, [in:] Nikonii i antichnyi mir Severnogo Prichernomor'ya, Odessa 1997, pp. 54-55.

[8] The present state of knowledge of Roman Nikonion is still not good - V.I. Kuz'menko, Issledovanie rimskikh sloev Nikoniya, "Materialy po Arkheologii Severnogo Prichernomor'ya", 8, 1976, pp. 218-224; A.G. Zaginailo, N.M. Sekerskaya, Zhilye postroiki v severo-zapadnoi chasti Nikoniya, (in:) Drevnosti Prichernomorskikh stepei, Kiev 1993, p. 57.

[9] Cf. N.M. Sekerskaya, Antichnyi ..., p. 6.

[10] See the discussion concerning the identification of the Roksolany mound with ancient Nikonion - P.O. Karyshkovskii, K voprosu o drevnem nazvanii Roksolanskogo gorodishcha, "Materialy po Arkheologii Severnogo Prichernomor'ya", 5, 1960, pp. 149-162.

[11] V.I. Goshkevich, Zapiski ob arkheologicheskikh issledovaniyakh v Khersonskoi gubernii, "Drevnosti", 22, 1909, 1, p. 176; N.M. Sekerskaya, Antichnyi ..., pp. 17-18.

[12] A.G. Zaginailo, Otkrytye oboronitel'noi steny v Nikonii. Predvaritel'noe soobshchenie, [in:] Novye arkheologicheskie issledovaniya na Odeschine, Kiev 1984, pp. 74-79; A.G. Zaginailo, N.M. Sekerskaya, o.c., p. 52; N.M. Sekerskaya, Oboronitel'nye sooruzheniya Nikoniya, [in:] Drevnee Prichernomor'e. Kratkie soobshcheniya Odesskogo Arkheologicheskogo Obshchestva, Odessa 1993, pp. 55-57; eadem, Ancient Nikonion in the Light of 40 Years of Archaeological Excavation (1957-1997), [in:] Nikonion. An Ancient City on the Lower Dniester, Toruń 1997, p. 24; eadem, Antichnyi ..., pp. 46-48.

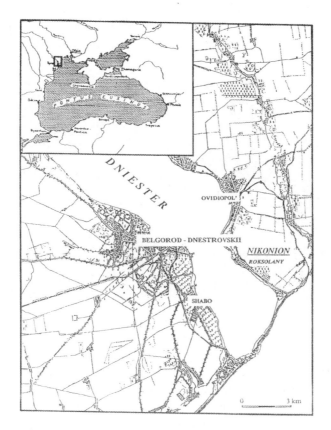

Fig. 1. The Lower Dniester region and the location of Nikomon

the Pole Marcin Broniewski saw stone ruins in this place[13], which, on the basis of Strabo, Broniewski identified as "The Tower of Neoptolemus"[14].

During the first centuries AD settlement spread out from the mound itself to the small plateau lying to its south.

Archaeological research at Nikonion first started in 1957 with an expedition directed by M.S. Sinitsyn[15]. The joint Ukrainian-Polish studies at Nikonion were

[13] M. Mielczarek, Z dziejów zainteresowań Polaków antycznymi zabytkami północnego wybrzeża Morza Czarnego, [in:] Nunc de Svebis dicendum est ..., Warszawa 1995, p. 183; idem, Polish Interest in the Ancient Northern Black Sea Coast. An Outline, [in:] Nikonion. An Ancient City on the Lower Dniester, Toruń 1997, p. 36. See also I.T. Chernyakov, Lokalizatsiya Nikoniya na srednevekovykh kartakh, [in:] Nikonii i antichnyi mir Severnogo Prichernomor'ya, Odessa 1997, pp. 80-86.

[14] Martini Bronovii de Biezdzfelda, bis in Tartariam nomine Stephani Primi Poloniae Regis legati, Tartariae descriptio ante haec in lucem nunquam edita cum tabula geographica eiusden Chersonesus Tauricae, Coloniae Agrippinae 1595. See A.E. Malyukevich, Otkrytie bashni Neoptolema, [in:] Drevnee Prichernomor'e. II chteniya pamyati professora Petra Osipovicha Karyshkovskogo, Odessa 1991, pp. 117-119.

[15] N.M. Sekerskaya, Itogi issledovaniya Nikoniya za 40 let (1957-1997), [in:] Nikonii i antichnyi mir Severnogo Prichernomor'ya, Odessa 1997, pp. 7-13; eadem, Ancient ..., pp. 18-26.

116

begun only three years ago, after a break of several years in the excavations. They have been carried out by the Nicholas Copernicus University in Torun and the Odessa Archaeological Museum, along with the participation of Odessa State University.

Fig. 2. Nikonion. Fragment of marble inscription. The Archaeological Museum in Odessa

The archaeological researches of the Ukrainian-Polish expedition are concentrated upon the southern part of the mound[16]. This quarter of the mound is dominated by remains of the 6th-3rd centuries BC. Whereas the central part of the mound has been excavated by the Odessa State University expedition from the fifties onwards[17], and the south-western part has been excavated by the Odessa Archaeological Museum expedition from the sixties, research upon the area lying to the west has been undertaken only in last few years. The main purpose of the work is to reveal the civic plan of this part of the town. During the last few years the remains of three buildings dug into the ground and of two houses have been discovered.

The cellar of one building located in the southern part of the mound has been partialy destroyed by rubbish pits. The surviving walls are over 3m high (Fig. 3) and have an extraordinery width of 80 cm[18]. The basic building material was clay, as well as mud-brick, and stone.

[16] See N.M. Skerskaya, Antichnyi ..., passim; A.G. Zaginailo, N.M. Sekerskaya, o.c., pp. 51-58.

[17] A.G. Zaginailo, I.T. Chernyakov, L.V. Subbotin, Issledovaniya drevnego Nikoniya, [in:] Arkheologicheskie otkrytiya 1972 goda, Moskva 1973, pp. 280-281; A.G. Zaginailo, Raboty skifo-antichnoi ekspeditsii, ibidem, otkrytiya 1974 goda, Moskva 1975, pp. 278-279; idem, Raboty Nikoniiskoi ekspeditsii, ibidem, otkrytiya 1976 goda, Moskva 1977, p. 293; N.M. Sekerskaya, Antichnyi ..., p. 13.

[18] Cf. A.G. Zaginailo, N.M. Sekerskaya, o.c., p. 53; N.M. Sekerskaya, Antichnyi ..., pp. 51 ff.

Fig. 3. Nikonion. Wall of the cellar (no. 206) of the house excavated in 1997 (upper part during the excavations). Phot. M. Mielczarek

This house, according to a coin found in the inside of the wall, was constructed in the middle of the 5th c. BC[19]. At the end of this century or during the early 4th century the house was destroyed, only to be rebuilt later on in the same century. The second and third quarters of the 4th c. BC constitute the period of greatest building activity at Nikonion[20]. The house was in use in the 4th c. Destroyed once again during the last decades of the century, the house was subsequently covered by a new construction.

The floor of the house was not destroyed, and it consists of material of the 4th century BC. Amphoras from Chios and Thasos, and fragments of black-glazed Attic pottery. The main vessel standing in the excavated part of the cellar was a pithos, placed alongside the northern wall.

Houses constructed during the 5th c. BC often cut through older constructions. The domestic rooms at Nikonion dating from the second half of the 6th century to the first quarter of the fifth century BC were dug into the ground, either completely or partialy[21].

One feature excavated in 1995 was especially interesting: a rectangle in plan of about 16 m. square (Fig. 4), it yielded a beautifully preserved clay hearth. Constructed from amphora sherds and clay[22], it was placed on a special elevation alongside the eastern wall of the room (Fig. 5). Fragments of only a single amphora were used. On the floor coins of Histria[23] and possible issues of Scyles were found.

---

[19] Bronze coins of Histria with the wheel on the obverse and ΙΣΤ on the reverse; see Sylloge Nummorum Graecorum, British Museum 1. The Black Sea, London 1993, nos. 220-222.

[20] N.M. Sekerskaya, Antichnyi ..., pp. 20 ff.

[21] Ibidem, pp. 22 ff.

[22] See other examples: A.G. Zaginailo, N.M. Sekerskaya, o.c.; N.M. Sekerskaya, Antichnyi ..., pp. 24-30.

[23] Bronze coin with the wheel and letters ΙΣΤ - Sylloge ..., nos. 220-222.

During the many years of excavation hundreds of graffiti have been recorded[24]. This category of finds is especially important as we lack any other form of evidence for the religious practices of the citizens of Nikonion. What is suprising is that they testify to the great popularity of the cult of Zeus. Of particular interest is the discovery of graffiti in which the epithet of "king" is added to the name of Zeus[25]. The cult of Zeus Basileus is attested at Olbia but is not encountered in any other city of the north-western Black Sea coast.

Fig. 3b. Nikonion. Wall of the cellar (no. 206) of the house excavated in 1997 (inside). Phot. M. Mielczarek

This is important, as over and above the graffiti only the excavated figurines[26] (Fig. 6) give us any trace as to the religious life of the inhabitants of Nikonion.

[24] I.D. Golovko, Graffiti Roksolanskogo gorodishcha, "Kratkie soobshcheniya o dokladakh i polevykh issledovaniyakh OGU i OGAM za 1960 g.", 1961, pp. 81-84; idem, Epigraficheskie nakhodki, "Materialy po Arkheologii Severnogo Prichernomor'ya", 5, 1966, pp. 77-88; P.M. Sekerskii, Zastol'naya nadpis' iz Nikoniya, [in:] "Materialy po Arkheologii Severnogo Prichernomor'ya", 8, 1986, pp. 215-218.

[25] Cf. I.D. Golovko, Graffiti ..., p. 83; idem, Epigraficheskie ..., p. 78; M.M. Mal'tsev, Posvyatitel'nye graffiti Nikoniya, [in:] Arkheologicheskie i archeograficheskie issledovaniya na territorii Juzhnoi Ukraini, Odessa 1976, p. 182; N.M. Sekerskaya, P.M. Sekerskii, Graffiti s posvyashcheniem Zevsu iz Nikoniya, [in:] Nikonii i antichnyi mir Severnogo Prichernomor'ya, Odessa 1997, pp. 44-47.

[26] For instance: I.B. Kleiman, Terrakoty, "Materialy po Arkheologii Severnogo Prichernomor'ya", 5, 1960, pp. 90-100; idem, Neskol'ko terrakot iz Nikoniya, [in:] Nikonii i antichnyi mir Severnogo Prichernomor'ya, Odessa 1997, pp. 47-50.

Fig. 4. Nikonion. House dug into the ground (no. 196) excavated in 1995.
Phot. M. Mielczarek

Fig. 5. Nikonion. Clay hearth in the house dug into the ground (object no. 197)
excavated in 1995. Phot. M. Mielczarek

120

Among the ceramic material the oldest is Ionian pottery dating to the 6th century BC. In the earliest levels Ionian pottery appears together with a sparse quantity of fragments of Attic pottery; in the next stage Attic pottery predominates[27]. However from the 4th century BC onwards the amount of hand-made pottery rises significantly. The majority of hand-made vessels belong to Scythian and Thracian pottery types[28].

Fig. 6. Nikonion. Clay figurine. 5th century BC.
The Archaeological Museum in Odessa

The composition of the corpus of recovered amphoras is quite typical for the northern Black Sea coast. For the 4th century BC amphoras of Heraclea Pontica, Thasos, and Sinope prodominate. For the end of the 4th and beginning of the 3rd centuries BC (after the destruction of the town) the amphoras of Thasos, Heraclea Pontica, Sinope and Chersonesus prevaile. In smaller numbers amphoras of Chios, Lesbos, Peparethos, Mende and other centres are encountered[29].

---

[27] N.M. Sekerskaya, Antichnyi .... pp. 36 ff.

[28] V.I. Kuz'menko, M.S. Sinitsyn, Lepnaya posuda, "Materialy po Arkheologii Severnogo Prichernomor'ya", 5, 1960, pp. 56-72; I.V. Bruyako, Lepnaya keramika grecheskogo Nikoniya, [in:] Drevnosti Prichernomorskikh stepei, Kiev 1993, pp. 58-71; N.M. Sekerskaya, Antichnyi .... pp. 68 ff.

[29] E.A. Gansova, Kompleksy keramicheskoi tary, "Materialy po Arkheologii Severnogo Prichernomor'ya", 5, 1960, pp. 72-77; B.A. Vasilenko, Drevnegrecheskie keramicheskie kleima, naidennye na vostochnom beregu Dnestrovskogo limana, "Materialy po Arkheologii Severnogo Prichernomor'ya", 7, 1971, s. 137-149; N.M. Sekerskaya, Antichnyi .... pp. 71-92; eadem, Grecheskii import kontsa IV-pervoi poloviny III v. do n.e. iz Nikoniya, [in:] Severo-zapadnoe Prichernomor'e - kontaktnaya zona drevnikh kul'tur, Kiev 1991, pp. 66-71; T.L. Samoilova, Ekonomicheskie svyazi Nikoniya po dannym keramicheskoi epigrafiki v dorimskii period, ibidem, pp. 61-66; A.I. Martynenko, Poslednii etap fasosskogo importa v Nikonii, [in:] Nikonii i antichnyi mir Severnogo Prichernomor'ya, Odessa 1997, pp. 55-60.

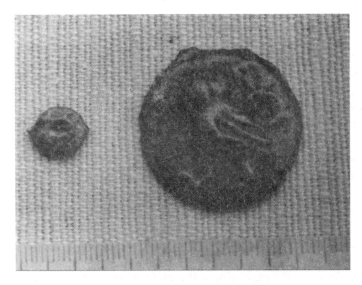

Fig. 7. Nikonion. Bronze cast coins of Scyles.
The Archaeological Museum in Odessa

Among the recovered material are numerous coins[30]. Among them the bronze coinage of Histria prevails[31]. At Nikonion these pieces were also imitated, and consequently these issues should be treated as an indigenous local currency[32]. Specific to Nikonion is the presence of unique cast coins of Scyles (Fig. 7), a Scythian ruler of the first quarter of the 5th century BC[33]. Coins of Olbia, Tyras, Apollonia Pontica and other centres of the northern and western Black Sea area are also represented.

Together with work on the main mound, the necropolis of Nikonion, located to the north-east of the town, has also been excavated[34].

[30] A.G. Zaginailo, Monetnye nakhodki na Roksolanskom gorodishche (1957-1963 gg.), "Materialy po Arkheologii Severnogo Prichernomor'ya", 5, 1960, pp. 100-130; idem, Litye monety iz Nikoniya (K voprosu ob ekonomicheskikh svyazyakh goroda v VI-IV vv. do n.e.), [in:] Severo-zapadnoe Prichernomor'e - kontaktnaya zona drevnikh kul'tur, Kiev 1991, pp. 54-59;

[31] In consequence of this situation M.S. Sinitsyn proposed Histria as the metropolis of Nikonion - M.S. Sinitsyn, Raskopki gorodishcha ...., pp. 55-56.

[32] A.G. Zaginailo, Litye ..., p. 58; N.M. Serkerskaya, Ancient ...., p. 19.

[33] A.G. Zaginailo, Litye ...., pp. 58-59; A.G. Zaginailo, P.O. Karyshkovskii, Monety skifskogo tsarya Skila, [in:] Numizmaticheskie issledovaniya po istorii yugo-vostochnoi Evropy, Kishinev 1990, pp. 3-15; A.G. Zaginailo, Litye monety tsarya Skila iz Nikoniya, [in:] Drevnee Prichernomor'e (chteniya pamyati professora Petra Osipovicha Karyshkovskogo), Odessa 1989, pp. 27-29; idem, Eshche raz o monetakh tsarya Skila, [in:] Drevenee Pruchernoor'e. Kratkie soobshcheniya Odesskogo Arkheologicheskogo Obshchestva, Odessa 1993, pp. 91-95. Cf. P.O. Karyshkovskii, Ol'viiskie assy s izobrazheniem sovy, "Sovetskaya Arkheologiya", 1962, 2, pp. 210-213.

[34] A.G. Zaginailo, I.V. Bruyako, Issledovaniya nekropolya antichnogo Nikoniya, [in:] Problemy antichnoi kul'tury. Tezisy dokladov Krymskoi nauchnoi konferentsii, III, Simferopol' 1988, pp. 241-242; I.V. Bruyako, The necropolis of Nikonion, [in:] Nikonion. An Ancient City on the Lower Dniester, Toruń 1997, pp. 27-29.

Greek burials are known only from the 5th and 4th centuries BC[35]. The archaic cemetery has still not been found.

All burials were in barrows. The kurgans are concentrated in the central part of the necropolis, on both sides of the ancient road, as indicated by air photographs[36]. At present 30 burials of the 4th century BC have been investigated. They took the form of a simple pit or a catacomb. Cremation burials are single.

The most common element in all of the burials are amphoras. Many of them were used to seal off the corridor of the catacomb or to cover the pit. These amphoras come from Heraclea Pontica, Thasos, Chios, and Peparethos.

The burial inventory is not rich. Single finds of black glazed ceramics, hand-made pots, and a number of small knives. Recovered jewellery consists of metal or glass paste beads, bronze pendants and earings: bracelets are rare. Coins are very rare, found only in three graves - two bronze coins of Histria and one of Tyras.

The cemetery of the Roman period has also been excavated over the last few years[37].

In the coming years the main aim of the excavations will continue to be research into the southern part of the town.

---

[35] A.G. Zaginailo, I.T. Chernyakov, L.V. Subbotin, o.c., p. 281; I.V. Bruyako, The Necropolis ..., pp. 27-28.

[36] I.V. Bruyako, N.P. Nazarova, V.G. Petrenko, o.c., p. 39; I.V. Bruyako, The Necropolis ..., p. 27.

[37] I.V. Bruyako, Nekotorye itogi raskopok nekropol'ya Nikoniya rimskogo vremeni, [in:] Drevnee Prichernomor'e. III chteniya pamyati prof. P.O. Karyshkovskogo. Tezisy dokladov. Odessa 1996, pp. 11-12; idem, The Necropolis ..., pp. 29-30.

Anna de Vincenz

Jerusalem

Shuni-Mayumas
A Model of Archaeological Park in Israel
Summary

Archaeology in modern Israel has reached maturity. The "treasure-hunting" and "adventure-trips" of the last century are no more. The involvement of the general public has finally been reached with the setting up of the museums, exhibitions and, most important of all, archaeological studies in high schools and universities.

Research is one of the most important parts of the archaeological discipline. Unfortunately, the general public has been alienated from all this and archaeology has become a science for the select professionals.

However, new ways are now being found to involve the interest of the public. Young people (especially archaeology students) have always been volunteering on excavations, but not everyone's attitude it is to get dirty and to sweat. Hence the overall concept of archaeological parks. An archaeological park combines pleasure with science (in our case, archaeology and history). More and more parks of this kind are being set up in different parts of the world.

In this proposal I should like to show, that the successful planning and building of an archaeological park in Israel is possible.

The proposed park is situated 6 km from Caesarea Maritima in a very fertile region, where even nowadays vines are grown and wine is made. The site has an importance which is known since antiquity, but only lately its importance for modern society has been understood. Archaeological excavations started in 1987 during a general restoration of the site, with its Turkish fortress and the signs of the War of Independence. After the discovery of a Roman theatre, a park was planned at the site, to combine the ancient and modern history.

Today, the theatre has been restored and is used for performances. The excavations proceed with the help of volunteers from all over the world and a small museum is being built at the site which will exhibit the finds from the excavations.

The park, inevitably has become a meeting place for people interested in relaxing but also in visiting an archaeological and historical site. The JNF which is sponsoring the park organises summer camps for Jewish youth from all over the world, and also camps for Israeli soldiers and new immigrants, combining leisure activities with the teaching of history. School children come to Shuni to learn about ancient and modern history, and are directly involved in a variety of activities, for example, grinding corn and baking bread. The archaeological excavations continue under the direction of JNF archaeologist Eli Shenhav who invites Israeli and foreign students to join him in his historical research.

Shuni-Mayumas is a park which combines leisure and scientific activities in a successful exciting fashion.

Gérald Finkielsztejn

Jerusalem

Une fouille de sauvetage d'envergure inhabituelle: la ville byzantine et la nécropole de Kfar Samir (Haifa, Israel)

Résumé

Cette fouille a été effectuée en 22 mois de travail (ètalés sur 27 mois) sur un terrain de 3.2 hectares destinés à la construction de deux accès à un tunnel autoroutier qui doit traverser le mont Carmel du nord au sud de la ville de Haifa. Ce projet a permis de degager le coeur d'une petite ville byzantine et sa nécropole de 46 tombes. Les murs des constructions n'étant généralement conservés que sur 1 ou 2 assises de pierres, immédiatement sous la surface et posés sur la roche-mère qui a fourm le matériau de construction, l'ensemble du plan de la ville a pu être dégagé dans le temps réduit imposé par le constructeur.

Il s'agit d'un établissement qui s'est développé pendant toute la période byzantine et a été peu occupé à la période islamique (IVe-VIIIe s.). La nécropole, dont 46 tombes ont été dégagées, couvre également la période romaine (Ier-VIIe s.) et quelques sépultures du Bronze Moyen y ont été aussi découvertes. Les établissements de la ville comprennent:

- des zones d'habitats ordinaires ou luxueux (avec mosaiques),
- des citernes privées (en "cloche" dans les cours) ou publiques (dont une gigantesque prés d'une source et du débouché d'un wadi et une autre sur l'atrium d'une église),
- 2 églises avec mosaiques (parfois inscrites), baptistères et reliquaires, dont l'une est insérée dans un complexe probablement monastique et de pélerinage,
- 10 pressoirs à vin avec mosaiques, parfois inscrites, représentant 13 cuves, l'un d'eux a été restauré pour nous permettre de faire du vin et comprendre une partie du processus de fabrication, en collaboration avec une firme de vin locale,
- 7 pressoirs à huile (représentant 18 unités de pressage), dont l'un montre les transformations dues à l'évolution des techniques de pressages, le systéme de balancier d'un autre à été restauré (bois et cordages) pour en comprendre le fonctionnement.

L'dentification du site n'est pas totalement assurée. Considéré, au début de la fouille, comme "Castra des Samaritains" (de la toponymie moderne "Khirbet Samir") nous tendons à incliner plutôt vers "Porphyrion", cité épiscopale, établissement nommée, comme "Castra", dans les sources byzantines, tant chrétiennes que juives.

Un intérèt supplémentaire de ce projet rèside dans le débat qui tourne autour de l'antagonisme entre la nécessité de construire le tunnel et celle de conserver ce site exceptionnel par sa taille et par sa signification tant historique que touristique. Il semble qu'un compromis se dessine entre les deux intérêts car un plan nouveau des routes menant au tunnel, permettant de sauver au moins 50% du site, a été proposé et est en cours d'examen et fera l'objet d'un débat public le mois prochain, à l'Université de Haifa (où j'enseigne la période hellénistique).

New studies on ancient art and culture

Józef Wolski

Cracovie

L'archéologie et l'histoire ancienne: L'Iran à la lumière des nouvelles sources archéologiques

Pour mieux comprendre le problème, parcourons rapidement son essentiel. Ce ne sont que les sources grecques et, au moindre degré, latines qui ont fourni les données permettant de reconstruire l'histoire de l'Iran, de ses rapports avec le monde occidental[1]. Certes, grâce à cela, un nombre assez important d'informations concernant la vie politique des dynasties des Achéménides, des Arsacides et des Sassanides a été conservé. Cependant, c'est une image quelquefois assez déformée de l'Iran, de sa culture, de son développement qui surgit et troubla notre aperçue de l'Orient pendant treize siècles de leur domination en Iran. Et c'est l'idée de leur barbarie, une notion négative, commune en Grèce, conséquence des guerres médiques, enracinée dans la littérature et renforcée par l'eurocentrisme excessif,qui fut le produit du XIXe et encore du XXe siècle[2]. C'est précisément l'époque de la dynastie des Parthes-Arsacides (240 av. J.-C. env. - 226/8 ap.J.-C.) qui fut traitée d'une manière défavorable comme dénuée de toutes les valeurs culturelles. Dans cette perspective, on ne tenait que le règne des Achéménides (550-330 av. J.-C.) ainsi que celui des Sassanides (226/8 - 655 ap. J.- C) comme dignes d'être sujet des recherches ce qui a valu pour ces derniers le nom des renovateurs de l'iranisme (néoiranisme). Par contre, l'époque des Arsacides, vide, ne se présentait que comme une lacune dans le développernent de la culture de l'Iran[3]. En conséquence

---

[1] J. Wolski dans: *L'empire des Arsacides*, Acta Iranica vol. 18, Louvain 1993, version polonaise *Imperium Arsacydów*, Poznań 1996, a présenté les conséquences de cette situation pour la reconstruction du processus historique en Iran.

[2] Le temps des Sassanides, grâce aux sources relativement abondantes, a été exposé dans la littérature d'une maniére plus large. Voir, tont récemment : G. Wiesehöfer, Das antike Persien, von 500 v. Chr. bis 650 n. Chr., München – Zürich 1994, où la période arsacide n'occupe que quarante pages, pendant que celle des Sassanides presque quatre-vingt pages.

[3] Malgré l'absence des sources indigènes, sauf quelques inscriptions, on a attribué à l'épisode gréco-macédoniene, une importance exagérée dans l'histoire de l'Iran. Que ce n'était qu'un épisode qui, pour un court laps de temps, a interrompu la continuité de la culture de l'Iran, ce sont les fouilles de

de cet état des choses les recherches sur les Parthes étaient limitées à l'histoire politique dont l'oeuvre de N.C. Debevoise, A Political History of Parthia, Chicago 1938 est le meilleur exemple.

Ii est cependant à noter que ce jugement portant ombrage à une partie importante du monde antique commence à s'écrouler. La preuve en est dans les travaux consacrés à l'histoire de l'Iran qui ont tiré au clair les réalisations des dynasties qui y avient regné. Un jalon dans cette voie c'est la découverte à Persepolis d'archives des textes élamites - Persepolis Fortifications Texts - renfermant la documentation de l'administratrion royale des Achéménides[4]. D'un coup s'évanouit l'idée du primitivisme des Iraniens. Ces documents nous montrent que l'adminiatration de l'empire des Achéménides était très développée ce qui met en doute les opinions des Grecs à cet égard, ainsi que les aspirations des Grecs d'être traités à la cour des Achéménides comme particulièrement priviligiés. En vérité, il y avait d'autres nations dont les représentants, p.ex. les Israélites, étaient tenus pour capables de remplir de hautes fonctions. Bien que ces découvertes aient touché l'époque des Achéménides, elles étaient importantes pour l'Iran dans leur totalité, parce qu'elles démontraient les possibilités des Iraniens tenus jusqu'ici pour peu doués. Comme on le supposait, le « Blitzkrieg » d'Alexandre le Grand devait causer l'effondrement, de tout ce processus, de le réduire au néant. Conformément à ces suppositions, la mise en ruine de la structure politique a dû, peser sur le sort de toutes les manifestations de la vie de l'Iran[5].

Il n'était pas du tout facile de faire tomber cette idée surtout par rapport à l'Iran et pour se servir d'une comparaison c'était d'autant plus difficile que Rome annihilée elle aussi par les barbares politiques, a quand même légué à ses conquérants ses richesses culturelles pour des siècles à suivre. Il est évident qu'il n'était pas ainsi en Iran et qu'ici nouas avons affaire avec un autre processus de l'histoire. Les Grecs et les Macédoniens disposaient d'une culture déjà développée, produit d'un passé millénaire et ils n'avaient pas besoin de s'approprier les biens culturels de l'Iran[6]. De cette façon, il y existaient deux unites séparées ce qui, bien entendu, n'a pas exclu de contacts réciproques. D'autre part la découverte par les Perses de l'écriture cunéiforme, adaptée aux besoins de la langue perse, les reliefs monumentaux, comme celui de Behistoun, les somptueux palais, comme celui de Persepolis, tenu pour le chef - d'oeuvre de l'architecture, nous donnent à penser. Et tout cela devait être d'un coup anéanti sous le choc de l'armée du grand Macédonien pour ne laisser qu'un vide culturel de quelques siècles. Ce n'est qu'à l'époque des Sassanides, renovateurs supposés de l'iranisme, que cette lacune devrait disparaître pour faire place au néoiranisme.

L. Vanden Berghe et de Ed. Haerinck, qui en ont apporté des preuves.

[4] Cf. R.T. Hallock, Persepolis Fortification Tablets, Oriental Institute Publications, vol. CXII, Chicago 1960, 57.

[5] Pour montrer les opinions négatives par rapport aux Arsacides dans la littérature contemporaine, il suffit de citer E.J. Keal, Bibl. Mes. 7, Malibu 1977, 81, qui les dépeint, sur la plate-forme politique, comme «clowns du millénaire».

[6] Il est à noter que cette opinion dominait dans la littérature du XIXe siècle pour ne citer que l'oeuvre de A.v. Gutschmid, Geschichte Irans und seiner Nachbarländer, Tübingen 1888, tenue dans ces temps pour classique.

Conformément à cette opinion, les Arsacides tenus pour barbares, n'étaient pas capables d'entereprendre n'importe quelle activité culturelle[7]. Ces points de vue ainsi que les autres étaient produits, à l'epoque passée, engendrée, comme on l'a dit ci-dessus, par l'eurocentrisme excessif. Pourtant, tont récemment on observe un recul de ces opinions unilateralés, appuées sur les sources grecques et latines. Abstraction faite de sources, il faut envisager l'attitude changée des savants dont l'appréciation de l'Iran et de son rôle occupe une place de plus en plus importante dans les recherches. Grace à cette nouvelle attitude l'époque des Parthes - Arsacides a particulièrement attiré l'attention des chercheurs. La critique, malgre l'incompatibilité des sources litteraires, s'efforce de reconstruire la voie conduisant les Arsacides au sommet de leur puissance en Orient. Il faut tout d'abord citer les résultats des fouilles archéologiques menées dans l'Asie Centrele par les savants soviétiques et russes[8]. C'est grâce à elles qu'on a constaté que les opinions anciennes tenant les tribus qui siégeaient au Nord de l'Iran pour des primitifs nomades, ne répondent pas à la réalité. Ils étaient pour une grande partie des sedentaires. C'est donc sous un jour nouveau qu'il nous faut apprécier leur niveau culturel, leur développement social. Arsace$_1$ chef de la tribu des Parnes-Daha, fondateur de l'Etat parthe, n'était pas, comme nous le font croire les sources grecques, un brigand qui guerroyait en quéte du butin, mais un chef d'armes préparé à faire des conquêtes, et en plus, de fonder un Etat en Iran.

En s'opposant à la communis opinio, je me suis intéressé aux sources ou bien négligées jusqu'ici ou bien interprétées d'une fausse manière. Ce qui m'a aidé dans mes recherches, c'étaient des sources nouvelles puisées dans le sol de l'Iran, suffisament solides pour faire pencher la balance au détriment des opinions antérieures. Pour préparer le terrain à une discussion future, il éttait de tout point de vue important de voir clair ce que l'Iran était au moment de l'invasion d'Arsace et de la fondation de l'empire parthe. C'est grâce aux travaux de H. Kreissig qu'il était possible de constater que la structure socio-économique de l'Iran des Séleucides et des Arsacides ne différait guère de celle de l'époque des Achéménides[9]. En acceptant une telle vision de l'Etat des Arsacides, sans céder à la pression des opinions enracinées dans la science depuis le XVIIIe siècle, je me suis intéressé à l'idée du développement de la culture de l'Iran héritée par les Arsacides de l'époque des Achéménides, donc celui de l'iranisme[10]. Et c'est de cette position

---

[7] Conformément à l'opinion exprimée par H.H. von Osten. Die Welt der Perser, Stuttgart 1956, 118, les Parthes n'étaient pas capables d'entreprendre une oeuvre d'envergure.

[8] On ne peut pas oublier que pour mettre en évidence le rôle de l'Iran dans le processus historique, il ne suffit pas d'exposer ce grand, du reste, ensemble territorial, mais aussi il faut se pencher sur le sort de l'Asie Centrale, liée à ce pays par des liens divérs. Cf. W.J. Vogelsang, The Rise and Organisation of the Achaemenid Empire. The Eastern Evidence. Leiden – New York – Cologne 1992.

[9] Voir pour cette question, l'oeuvre de H. Kreissig, Wirtschaft und Gesellschaft im Seleukidenreich, Schriften zur Geschichte und Kultur der Antike. 16, Berlin 1978.

[10] Mais dans la littérature contemporaine, pour s'opposer à cette hypothèse, on cite le terme de philhellène figurant sur les légendes des monnaies parthes. Pourtomt, aujourd'hui, on est enclin de n'y voir que la preuve de la propagande des Arsacides. Autrement il serait difficile d'expliquer la politique brutale des rois parthes à l'égard des Grecs. Les Arsacides se comportaient comme conquérants orientaux, ce qu'on voit dans le massacre des Grecs à Syrinx pendant l'expedition

que j'ai conçu l'idée d'écrire une synthèse de l'histoire parthe, en publiant at chez E. Peeters, en 1993, mon livre : L'ernpire des Arsacides, accessible aussi en version polonaise sous le titre Imperium Arsacydów, Poznań 1996.

Il est évident que maintenant jen'en présente qu'un raccourci limité aux exemples susceptibles de démontrer le rôle de l'archéologie dans cette approche nouvelle de l'histoire de l'Iran arsacide. Rappelons que sous l'influence d'Arrien, la plupart des historiens, depuis le XVIIIe siècle, a accepté la version des origines parthes basée sur cet écrivain. Conformément au récit d'Arrien, la fondation de l'Etat parthe était l'oeuvre des deux frères, Arsace et Tiridate, sous le règne d'Antiochos II Théos (261-246 av. J.-C.)[11]. Pour ma part, je tiens, et je l'ai déjà fait en 1937, le récit d'Arrien pour non-historique; je me suis appuyé sur Strabon, Pompée Trogue dans l'extrait de Justin. Je tiens Arsace I er et non pas Tiridate pour fondateur de l'Etat parthe sous le règne de Séleukos II Kallinikos (246-226 av. J.-C.). Une violente discussion s'en est ensuivie, à laquelle a pris une part active Domenico Musti, partisan ferme d'Arrien, surtout de sa chronologie. La solution du problème est due aux l'archéologie. Il y a une vingtaine d'années environ on a trouvé un trésor àsavoir des monnaies de l'époque arsacide parmi lesquelles il y avait des monnais frappées par Arsace I er et son fils Arsace II[12]. D'un coup s'écroulèrent toutes les hypothèses avancées depuis quelques siècles à propos de l'historicité ou non-historicité d'Arsace Ier et de Tiridate, ce dernier tenu pour fondateur de l'Etat parthe. Cependant, cette découverte ne se limite pas au problème cité ci-dessus, si important qu'il soit pour l'histoire, pour l'histoire parthe. Ce qui rehausse sa valeur historique c'est la langue des légendes écrites en partie seulement en grec, et en partie en araméen. Alors, les Arsacides, en vraies continuateurs des Achéménides, se sont servis de l'araméen pour documenter leur attitude idéologique. Ces deux faits nous montrent les Arsacides, dès leurs débuts, se laisser conduire par les égards profondément enracinés dans le passé de l'Iran, bien loin de cette barbarie que leur imputaient les sources.

Pourtant les Arsacides ne se sont pas contentés d'être les imitateurs de leurs devanciers. L'introduction de la langue iranienne, pehlevi, dans l'écriture fut un grand pas en avant dans   la formation de la culture iranienne. Autrefois on tenait les Sassanides pour les inventeurs de cette écriture. Mais les faits s'y opposent. Et voità, les fouilles de Nisa ont mis au jour un somptueux ensemble architectonique, palais, temple plain d'objets d'art, ce qui ne permet pas d'accuser les Arsacides du

---

d'Antiochos III en Iran. Cf. Polybe X 27-31. Et les Romains ne se sont pas comportés autrement, l'example en est l'attitude de L. Aemilius Paulus, lui aussi philhelléne.

[11] Le compte-rendu d'une longue discussion concernant les débuts des Arsacides, dans laquelle la valeur de la relation d'Arrien occupe la place principale, est donné par J. Wolski dans : L'empire des Arsacides, p. 37. C'est J. Wolski, qui dans Eos, 1937 et 1938, a abordé la question de l'historicité d'Arrien, et l'a repris dans son article sur Arsace Ier, fondateur de l'Etat parthe, Acta Iranica III, 1974, 159-199, en luttant fermement pour la priorité des relationç de Strabon et de Trogue Pompée dans l' extrait de Justin.

[12] Cf. M.T. Abgarians et D.G. Sellwood, A Hoard of Early Parthian Drachms, Numismatic Chronicle, Seventh Series, vol. 11, 1971, 103-118, qui, dans leurs opinions, se sont ralliés à mes travaux publiés une quarantaine d'années plus tût.

primitivisme. Un a découvert des archives cornposées de pièces d'ostrakons couverts d'écriture en araméen et parmi lesquels ilyen avait un en pehlevi[13]. Alors c'est déjà en l'an 100 av. J.– C. env. que le grand souverain parthe Mithridate II se servit de cette langue dans la partique.

Pourtant, ce n'est pas tout. La découverte sur un rocher en Elymaide, à Hung-i Nauruzi, d'un relief avec une scène d'hommage rendu par un prince au roi des rois Mithridate Ier, en 140-139 av. J.-C. env., nous fournit une preuve nouvelle de l'emploi de pehlevi[14]. L'image du roi est pourvue d'une inscription : Mithridate roi des rois[15]. C'est donc dèjà vers le milieu du IIe siècle av. J. C. que les Iraniens se sont élevés au niveau jusqu'ici non soupçonné. Et c'est de nouveau que l'archéologie nous est venue au secours pour résoudre les problèmes épineux de l'histoire de l'Orient ancien.

Dans ce contexte, il nous semble utile de rappeler que le roi Votogèse (57-77 ap. J.-C.) se décida à remplacer les légendes grecques sur les monnaies parthes par des légendes en pehlevi, en soulignant de cette : manière le triomphe de l'iranisme sur l'hellenisme[16]. On voit que l'Iran s'est montré capable de créer sa propre culture, d'imprégner la culture parthe d'éléments indigènes propres à la faire triompher sur l'hellénisme. Mettre tout cela en évidence sans l'apport de l'achéologie dont les travaux furent en Iran, helàs, interrompus, ne serait pas possible.

Mais, en parlant de l'archéologie, surtout celle de l'Iran, on ne peut pas oublier les archéologues, au moins quelques uns. En première place je voudrais citer Louis Vanden Berghe célèbre archéologue belge, professeur à l'Université de Gand et ancien président de l'Académie Royale de Belgique, membre de l'Académie Polonaise des Lettres et Sciences de Cracovie, décédé malheureusement il y a deux ans. Son activité en Iran comme chef des fouilles et ses publications ont permis non seulement de mettre en évidence le haut niveau artistique de la culture matérielle de l'Iran, (je pense à l'architecture monumentale ou aux reliefs taillés sur les rochers), mais aussi, ce qui est conforme à mes propres recherches, la continuation sous les Arsacides du développement artistique caractéristique de l'époque des Achéménides[17]. C'est grâce à lui que l'idée du vide culturel supposé pour le temps des Arsacides s'écroula definitivement[18]. La direction des études commencées par lui trouve son continuateur dans la personne de son successeur E. Haerinck. En un

---

[13] Cf. D.M. Diakonov et D. Livshitz, Les documents de Nisa jusqu, au Ier siècle de n.e. (en russe), Moskva 1960. Nous leur devons la publication et le commentaire de ces documents.

[14] Cf., pour le commentaire archéologique, L. Vanden Berghe, Le relief de Hung-i Nauruzi, Iranica Antiqua 3, 1963, 154-168.

[15] Voir J. Harmatta, Parthia and Elymais in the 2nd Century B.C., Acta Ant. Acad. Scienc. Hung. 29, 1989, 180-217, à qui nous devons un commentaire linguistique.

[16] Pour ne citer, dans la dernière instance, que J. Wolski, L'empire des Arsacides, 174, qui a inclu cette manifestation de l'iranisme dans le processus global ayant lieu en Iran sous les Arsacides.

[17] Pour me rapporter à la notice biographique du savant publiée dans la livre paru sous sa rédaction : Bibliographie analytique de l'archéologie de l'Iran ancien, Leiden 1971, ainsi qu'une autre oeuvre publiée par J. Duchesne-Guillemin, Bio-Bibliographie de 134 savants. Acta Iranica 20, Leiden 1979.

[18] Cf. E. Haerinck, La céramique en Iran pendant la période parthe (ca 250 av. – C. – à 225 ap. J.-C.), Iranica Antiqua, suppl. 2., Gent 1983.

mot, la collaboration de deux disciplines a contribué d'une façon éclatante à rayer ce mythe, tenu longtemps pour évident, de la barbarie des Parthes-Arsacides, pour céder place à l'opinion que c'est à eux que nous devons le développement de l'Iranisme observé sous les Sassanides. Sans cela, sans ce magnifique essor de Nisa, il serait difficile de reconstruire les grandes lignes de ce centre de la culture orientale.

Zsolt Kiss
Varsovie

Les auriges de Kom el-Dikka

Dans la seconde phase d'existence de l'édifice théâtral de Kom el-Dikka, dégagé par la mission archéologique polonaise à Alexandrie, celui-ci était recouvert d'une coupole soutenue à l'ouverture de l'orchestre par deux puissantes colonnes posées sur deux socles élevés[1]. Le socle Nord a conservé sur deux faces trois représentations gravées accompagnées d'inscriptions. Sur la face Sud du socle nous voyons Doros en course[2], plus bas Kalotychos victorieux sur son char[3] ; sur la face Ouest est représenté en pied Doros[4]. Dans son ouvrage sur l'ensemble des inscriptions et dessins gravés de l'édifice théâtral Zbigniew borkowski en a donné une description minutieuse et la lecture des légendes.

Grâce à une interprétation magistrale d'une autre inscription qui mentionne ces deux auriges Z. Borkowski a pu les dater à 608-610 de n.è.[5]. Pourtant une telle datation des représentations semble trop rigide[6]. En effet la fameuse inscription susmentionnée parle de Doros « le Jeune » (Néos). Ce pourrait être un cocher du même nom (apparenté ?) postérieur à Doros tout court. En ce cas les images de Doros remonteraient nettement à avant 608-610 de n.è.

A l'inverse, il est plausible que la gloire des deux auriges des Verts aie continué après la victoire politique de la faction reflétée par l'inscription. De toute manière tout cet ensemble, puisqu'il est resté intact, illustre la toute dernière phase d'utilisation de l'édifice théâtral. Or, W. Kołątaj a démontré que la destruction des

---

[1] Z. Kiss, *Remarques sur la datation et les fonctions de l'édifice théâtral à Kom el-Dikka*, in : 50 Years of Polish Excavations in Egypt and the Near East, Varsovie 1992, p. 177, fig. 2.

[2] Z. Borkowski, *Alexandrie II. Inscriptions des factions à Alexandrie*, Varsovie 1981, pp. 100-103, n° 8, figs 4 et 49 : inscription, p. 79, n° 7.

[3] Ibid., pp. 102-104, n° 10, figs 4 et 49 : inscription, p. 79, n° 9.

[4] Ibid., pp. 98-100, n° 5, figs 3 et 48 : inscription, p. 79, n° 4.

[5] Ibid., pp. 81-86, n° 39, fig. 24.

[6] C'est aussi l'opinion de C. Haas, *Alexandria in Late Antiquity. Topography and Social Conflict*, Johns Hopkins University 1997, p. 65.

thermes publics voisins doit être liée avec l'invasion perse en 619 de n.è.[7]. C'est une limite également logique pour l'existence du « club » des partisans des Verts[8].

En bref, il nous semble que l'édifice théâtral de Kom el-Dikka put être une salle de réunion des Verts peu avant 608 de n.è. et dut le rester jusqu'em 619 de n.è. Il nous semble impossible de dater les trois représentations avec plus de précision.

Leur iconographie est digne d'intérêt malgré leur exécution fruste. Z. Borkowski considérait que vu «Le niveau technique et artistique de ces représentations, l'affirmation qu'elles éclairent le répertoire de l'art byzantin et de ses diverses sources semble tout à fait abusive, néanmoins pour certains types de représentation du char de course il n'existe aucune analogie en dehors de nos dessins maladroits ». C'est le contraire que nous essaierons ici de démontrer.

Nous n'en reprendrons pas la description détaillée donnée par Z. Borkowski. Commençons par l'image de Doros en haut de la face Sud du socle (fig.1). Nous voyons l'attelage en cours de course : c'est un bige. Le dessin du cocher permet uniquement d'affirmer qu'il brandissait un fouet dans la main droite. Le motif est bien connu sur les représentations de courses de chars sur les mosaïques depuis le IIIe siècle de n.è. Citons en example une mosaïque de Prima Porta montrant l'aurige Liber victorieux dans la course, dressé dans son char et brandissant le fouet dans la main droite[9]. Ce mode de représentation du cocher en compétition, si courante dans la partie occidentale du monde romain (Espagne, Italie, Afrique du Nord), était absente dans la partie orientale. Nous la retrouvons bien plus tard sur le curieux « jeu de billes » (Kügelspiel) du Musée de Berlin, daté au Ve siècle[10]. Ainsi, malgré l'absence de chainons intermédiaires, nous avons la preuve que le schéma occidental fut repris dans le répertoire iconographique de Constantinople. Son utilisation encore au début du VIIe siècle à Alexandrie ne peut donc étonner.

Plus bas sur la paroi Sud du socle est placée l'image de Kalotychos victorieux. La gravure est plus soignée et nous permet de saisir plus de détails. Nous sommes après la course : malgré que le cocher tient le fouet dans la main droite, dans la

---

[7] W. Kołątaj, *La dernière période d'utilisation et la destruction des thermes romains tardifs de Kom el-Dikka*. ET IX, 1976, pp. 217-229 ; id.., *Recherches architectoniques dans les thermes et le théâtre de Kom el-Dikka à Alexandrie*. in : Das römisch-byzantinische Ägypten, Mainz 1983, p. 188 ; id., *Alexandrie VI. Imperial Baths at Kom el-Dikka*, Varsovie 1992, p. 151.

[8] Il est curieux que le socle Sud resta vierge de gravures ou inscriptions de la période étudiée. Par contre y furent trouvées sur les faces Ouest et Nord deux inscriptions funéraires arabes de la fin du VIIe – début du VIIIe siècles, cf. W. Kubiak, *Inscriptions arabes de Kom el Dick*, BSAA 43, 1975, p. 134, pl. I. Cela par ailleurs confirme que peu après l'invasion arabe la partie Nord de l' auditorium et le socle Nord étaient cachés sous la terre et les décombres (ce qui explique les inscriptions des factions ont survécu). Par contre la partie Sud de l' auditoire était visible et fut démantelée ; également le socle Sud émergeait, limitrophe à la nécropole musulmane implantée dans le dallage du portique.

[9] K. Dunbabin, *The Victorious Charioteer on Mosaics and related Monuments*, AJA 66, 1982, pp. 69 et 88, n° 15, fig. 7.

[10] O. Wulff, *Altchristliche Bildwerke*, Berlin 1909, pp.16-17, n° 27; J. Gottwald, *Das byzantinische Kugelspiel*, AA 1931, pp. 152-172; A. Cameron, *Porphyrius the Charioteer*, Oxford 1973, pp.33-36 et 58, figs 16-18; A. Effenberger, in: Das Museum für Spätantike und Byzantinische Kunst Berlin, Mainz 1992, pp. 116-118; A. Alföldi, E. Alföldi, *Die Kontorniat-Medaillons*, II, Berlin 1990, pl. 264, 4-5.

gauche il brandit une couronne. Le cheval de droite a la tête surmontée d'une palme avec couronne, celui de gauche d'une palme plus courte. Mais l'élément marquant est que le cocher victorieux n'exécute pas le tour d'honneur, comme p.ex. sur la peinture d'Ostie, Caseggiato degli Aurighi[11], mais se dirige vers le spectateur (la tribune d'honneur). La représentation de l' attelage de face était déjà connue dans l'art grec[12], mais ici le mode de representation est tout à fait différent : si le char et l'aurige sont nettement de face, les roues du char sont écartées et de profil. De même les deux chevaux sont de profil et s'écartent des deux côtés.

Z. Borkowski voyait ici une influence orientale[13], mais ce mode de représentation du char victorieux est bien connu dans l'art romain, aussi, à juste titre, A. Cameron attribue une origine romaine au motif du char de face[14]. Il rejette la supposition que ce schéma du cocher vainqueur puisse etre une copie de

Fig. 1. Kom el-Dikka (Alexandrie), Edifice théatral, socle Nord, face Sud

---

[11] Dunbabin, op.cit., p. 68, schema WZ, fig. 5.
[12] G. Hafner, *Viergespanne Vorderansicht*, Berlin 1938, pp. 115-120.
[13] Borkowski, op.cit., pp. 105-106.
[14] Cameron, op.cit.., pp. 17-28.

l'empereur lors du triomphe (nous ne nous occuperons pas ici des images d'Hélios en quadrige ni de l'empereur sur les monnaies suivant la même convention). A. Cameron voit plutot l'influence inverse : une influence de l'iconographie de l'hippodrome sur l'iconographie officielle de l'empereur. Nous pouvons à l'étai de cette conception citer la représentation en opus sectile du consul dans la basilique de Junius Bassus à Rome[15]. Remarquons par ailleurs que le consul conduit un bige, brandissant une palme, entre quatre représentations des factions à cheval. La convention de représentation des roues du chariot est identique à celle sur la gravure de Kom el-Dikka. La différence est que les chevaux « divergeants » tournent la tête vers l'intérieur. Cette image est datée à l'an 331 et c'est un chaînon entre la gravure étudiée et de nombreuses images de cochers sur des mosaïques à partir du IIIe siècle comme p.ex. un pavment de Trèves[16], daté vers 250 de n.è., représentant Polydus. Ces images sont plus éloquentes, nous n'en citerons plus tard qu'une mosaïque de Dougga[17] du IVe siècle représentant en quadrige le cocher Eros, brandissant dans la main droite le fouet et une couronne, dans la gauche une palme. Les chevaux du milieu tournent la tête vers l'intérieur, les chevaux de dehors vers l'extérieur. Dans la seconde moitié du IVe siècle le schéma se répète avec une grande fidélité sur une mosaïque de Merida représentant l'aurige Marcianus (sauf que dans la main gauche il tient seulement le fouet)[18]. Nous ne disons rien ici du costume de l'aurige, car nous reviendrons plus loin sur ce sujet. Mentionnons déjà que l'aurige porte juste une tunique et une ceinture sur la mosaïque de Hudston (Angleterre)[19] également du IVe siècle. Enfin, en cette même période, de nouveau le motif est répété sur une autre mosaïque de Trèves[20] avec quatre cochers vainqueurs. Nous voyons donc combien répandu était le motif dans la partie occidentale de l'Empire Romain[21].

On ne le retrouve pas moins couramment dans les arts dits mineurs. Au premier plan se placent les contorniates du Ve siècle[22] sur lesquels la représentation est particulièrement fréquente, quoique simplifiée vu les dimensions du matériau. L'aurige brandit de nouveau la couronne dans la main gauche, tenant une palme dans la droite. Observons encore la représentation des chevaux strictement divergeants, comme sur la gravure de Kom el-Dikka. Très proche est l image sur

---

[15] R. Bianchi-Bandinelli, *Rome. La fin de l'art. antique*, Paris 1970, p. 96, figs 88-89; K.W. Weeber, *Panem et Circenses. Massenunterhaltung als Politik im antiken Rom*, Mainz 1994, fig. 77.

[16] W. Reusch, *Wandmalerein und Mosaikboden eines Peristylhauses im Bereich der Trierer Kaiserthermen*, TrZ 29, 1966, pp. 216-222, pls 32-36; Dunbabin, op.cit., pp. 72, 82 et 89, n° 25, fig. 8; Weeber, op.cit., fig. 84.

[17] Dunbabin, op.cit., pp. 74-75, 82 et 88, n° 8, fig. 17; *La Mosaique en Tunisie*, Tunis 1995, p. 191.

[18] Dunbabin, op.cit., pp. 74, 82 et 88, fig. 15; Weeber, op.cit., fig. 87.

[19] Dunbabin, op.cit., pp. 73 et 88-89, n° 20, fig. 10; J.H. Humphrey, *Roman Circuses. Arenas for Chariot Racing*, University of California 1986, p. 432, fig. 202.

[20] K. Parlasca, *Die römischen Mosaiken in Deutschland*, Berlin 1959, pp. 26-27, pl. 25; Dunbabin, op.cit., pp. 72-73, 82-83 et 89, n° 26, fig. 9.

[21] Humphrey, op.cit., passim (cf. Index, p. 701, s.v. Crown and Palm of Victory).

[22] A. Alföldi, E. Alföldi, *Die Kontorniat-Medaillons*, I, Berlin 1976, pp. 209-211, n°s 166-192; II, pp. 205-208, n° 641; Cameron, fig. 31, 6; Dunbabin, op.cit., p. 76, type WY.

un disque en métal incrusté de Trèves représentant l'aurige porfyrius[23] et sur d'autres plaques apparentées[24] qui restent dans la représentation des chevaux plus proches des mosaiques. D'autre part, le cocher brandit la palme dans la main droite mais de la gauche tient les rênes. Sur une plaque de bronze gravée du Musée de Berlin[25], de la même période, nous retrouvons une version plus soignée exactement du même schéma que sur les contorniates. Il est également répété dans la céramique à relief nord africaine du IVe siècle[26]. Citons enfin les dits verres dorés de la seconde moitié du IVe siècle[27] répétant également le même schéma.

Nous pouvons donc affirmer que l'image étudiée était une des plus courantes dans l'iconographie du cirque (sans parler de ses plus larges implications symboliques de la victoire) aux IVe et Ve siècles dans la partie occidentale de l'Empire Romain. Nous la retrouvons avec grande fidélité dans notre fruste dessin du début du VIIe siècle. Malgré l'absence d'exemples de la partie orientale de l'Empire et malgré la lacune d'au moins un siècle (le VIe), la lignée directe est évidente.

Sur la face Ouest du socle Nord dans l'édifice théatral de Kom el-Dikka nous voyons une seule grande représentation de Doros vainqueur (fig.2). Cette image ne comporte aucun élément explicite lié à l'hippodrome. Seul le centexte des autres gravures et des inscriptions la range incontestablement dans ce domaine. En effet, ici le costume de l'aurige est surprenant ; Z. Borkowski le considérait comme sans analogie. Doros porte une longue et ample tunique serrée à la ceinture et descendant à mi-mollet. Les pieds sont nus ou couverts par une sorte de chausses. Dans la main droite levée il tient la palme de victoire. Ce n'est pas le vêtement caractéristique de l'aurige que nous voyons p.ex. sur la mosaique de Dougga citée plus haut : tunique courte, une haute ceinture lacée formant comme une cuirasse, des hautes bottines lacées, un casque sur la tête. On en connait une bonne illustration dans une statue des Musei Vaticani[28] ou sur la fameuse mosaïque de Baccano au Museo Nazionale Romano, datée vers 200[29]. Nous retrouvons encore ce costume en usage en Egypte au début du VIe siècle comme le montre le fameux papyrus aux auriges d'Antinoé[30].

---

[23] A. Alföldi. E. Alföldi, op.cit., I, p. 190, n° 662, pl. 209; Cameron, op.cit., fig. 31,5; Weber, op.cit., fig. 78.

[24] A. Alföldi. E. Alföldi, op.cit., I, p. 190-191, n°s 663-665, pls 207 et 210.

[25] A. Alföldi. E. Alföldi, op.cit., II, pl. 268,6; A. Effenberger, in: Das Museum für Spätantike und Byzantinische Kunst Berlin, op.cit., p. 99, n° 23.

[26] A. Alföldi. E. Alföldi, op.cit., II, pl. 268,4; R. Brilliant, in: Age of Spirituality. Late Antique and Early Christian Art., Third to Seventh Century, New York 1979, p. 107, n° 98; Dunbabin, op.cit., fig. 22.

[27] A. Alföldi. E. Alföldi, op.cit., II, pl. 268,5; Cameron, op.cit., fig. 31, 1-2.

[28] G. Lippold, Die Sculpturen des vaticanischen Museums, III, 2, Berlin 1956, p. 91, n° 619, pls 45-46; H.v. Heintze, in: Helbig[4], I, Tübingen 1963, pp. 399-400, n° 504; Weeber, op.cit., fig. 86.

[29] S. Aurigemma, Le Terme di Diocleziano e il Museo Nazionale Romano, éd. 5, Roma 1963, p. 139, n° 377. pl. 97; K. Parlasca, in: Helbig[4], III, Tübingen 1969, pp. 421-422, n° 2470; Weeber, op.cit., figs 70, a-b.

[30] S.J. Gąsiorowski, A Fragment of a Greek Illustrated Papyrus, JEA 17, 1931, pp. 1-9; E.G. Turner, The Charioteers from Antinoë, JHS 93, 1973, pp. 192-195; S.R. Zwirn, in: Age of Spirituality, op.cit., pp. 102-103, n° 93.

Fig. 2. Kom el-Dikka (Alexandrie), Edifice théatral, socle Nord, face Ouest

Le schéma même du cocher vainqueur en pied est bien connu. K. Dunbabin le considère comme courant dans l'iconographie de l'hippodrome mais exceptionnel sur les mosaiques. Citons juste une mosaïque de Dougga de la seconde moitié du IVe siècle[31] sur laquelle le cocher en uniforme complet de la course lève le fouet dans la main droite et serre de la gauche une palme contre son flanc. C'est exactement la même situation sur une feuille de dyptique en bronze incrusté, du début du Ve siècle, à Paris, Musée du Louvre[32]. L'agencement est légèrement différent sur un verre doré de Toledo (Ohio)[33] de la seconde moitié du IVe siècle : l'aurige serre la palme contre son flanc gauche mais dans la main droite tient les rênes de son cheval. Ce motif enfin figure sur des tessères en os[34]. Ainsi donc nous avons ici l'étape suivante dans l'iconographie du cirque : d'abord le char en course

[31] Dunbabin, op.cit., pp. 66 et 69, n° 9, fig. 6, schéma T.

[32] E. Coche de la Ferté, *L'antiquité chrétienne au Musée du Louvre*, Paris 1959, n° 33; Alföldi, Alföldi, op.cit., II, pl. 269, 8; S.R. Zwirn, in: Age of Spirituality, op.cit., 103-104, n° 94.

[33] Alföldi, Alföldi, op.cit., II, pl. 269, 1; S.R. Zwirn, in: Age of Spirituality, op.cit., 104, n° 95.

[34] Alföldi, Alföldi, op.cit., II, p. 198, pl. 270, 5-6.

(comme Doros sur la face Sud du piedestal), ensuite venait la présentation de l'attelage du vainqueur (comme l'image de Kalotychos), maintenant ce serait une phase suivante de présentation de l'aurige vainqueur. Mais l'image de Doros en cette situation présente certains traits différents, en particulier le vêtement. Z. Borkowski voyait l'alternative : « ou le cérémonial des jeux exigeait alors que l'aurige paraisse en vêtement solennel, différent de celui porté pendant la course, ou bien c'est l'habit du bigarius »[35]. En définitive Z. Borkowski penchait pour la seconde solution.

Mais revenons aux images de l'aurige vainqueur en pied. Sur quelques contorniates du Ve siècle est ainsi représenté l'aurige Aelianus[36] ainsi que d'autres. Comme sur les exemples précédents le vainqueur brandit le fouet dans la main droite et tient la palme dans la gauche, mais il n'est vêtu que d'une courte tunique. L'image est floue, mais on peut mieux l'interpréter grâce à la représentation de Porfyrios sur le disque de bronze de Trèves cité plus haut et aux effigies de même type sur les disques apparentés[37]. Ici l'aurige tient le fouet et la palme de manière un peu différente. Il est vêtu d'une courte tunique ceinte, sans « cuirasse » ni bonnet. Il ne porte non plus les hautes bottines lacées mais un pentalon serré aux chevilles et formant des plis. C'est le même élément qu'on observe sur un contorniate[38]. Encore une sorte de chausses plissés est porté par des conducteurs de quadriges sur une céramique moulée tardive de Grande Bretagne[39].

Enfin, au début du VIe siècle sur une des bases de Porphyrius à Constantinopole (dite « Ancienne »)[40] ce fameux aurige est représenté en pied serrant la palme contre son flanc gauche, la main droite dressée tenait un élément aujourd'hui brisé : le fouet ou une couronne. Il est vêtu d'une tunique un peu plus longue et d'une sorte de pantalon collant ou de hautes bottines. Or, Prophyrius n'était certainment pas un bigarius, tout comme rien non plus ne permet de reconnaitre des bigarii dans les autres exemples cités. D'autre part, comme le prouve la miniature citée d'Antinoé, certainement en Egypte au Ve siècle le costume « professionnel » des cochers était resté le même que jadis. Aussi, la première solution prévue par Z. Borkowski nous semble plus vraisemblable : que dans une phase ultérieure de la victoire l'aurige apparaissait avec la palme mais en « vêtement civil ». C'est en cette phase que serait ici représenté Doros.

Pourtant son effigie reste exceptionnelle : sa tunique est particulièrement longue, il porte des chausses ou est pieds nus, il brandit uniquement la palme de la victoire dans la main droite (à juste titre Z. Borkowski considère la grande boucle dans l'oreille droite d Doros comme un trait purement individuel). Il est impossible de trancher jusqu'à quel point ces détails refléteraient une réalité nouvelle dans le cérémonial des courses du cirque à Alexandrie au début du VIIe siècle. Si cette image ne reproduit pas fidèlement les schémas des IVe-Ve siècles, elle s'en inspire.

---

[35] Borkowski, op.cit., p. 107.
[36] Alföldi, Alföldi, op.cit., I, p. 212, n° 199, pl. 201, 2-4; II, p. 210.
[37] Cf. Supra notes 23-24; Cameron, op.cit., fig. 31, 4.
[38] Alföldi, Alföldi, op.cit., II, pp. 209-210, n° 650, pl. 206, 1.
[39] Humphrey, op.cit., p. 436, fig. 204.
[40] Cameron, op.cit., pp. 42-48, fig. 13; Dunbabin, op.cit., fig. 20.

En conclusion, nous pouvons affirmer que les schémas de l'iconographie de l'hippodrome, créés en Occident, voient une dernière survivance dans ces modestes dessins à Alexandrie au VIIe siècle. Il ne s'agit sans doute pas d'un emprunt direct, mais d'une transmission par l'intermédiaire de Constantinople, dont l'iconographie du cirque est malheureusement mal connue. Là où Z. Borkowski voyait des influences orientales et des prémices de l'art byzantin nous voyons plutôt un dernier écho, même assez fort, de l'art romain occidental.

Ilona Skupińska-Lovset

Łódź

Portraits of boys with «Youth lock» from Syria.

In this paper a group of portraits of boys, carrying a characteristic hairstyle, all with a Syrian provenience, will be discussed. This hairstyle, characterized by a longer strand of hair on the right side of the head, variously arranged, has been defined as the «youth lock» or «youth plait» and traditionally connected with the cult of the Egyptian Isis. A plait on the right side of the head is known from Pharaonic Egypt, where it was a sign of high birth. It is known, that in Antiquity hairlocks could be grown to various deities and semideities, in Syria for instance to Dea Syria. In some cases, in particular when concerning reliefs of Palmyra, the hairstyle, and its variants with longer hair on the back of the head, not only on the right side, have been defined as «slave locks»[1]. In the Roman period, because of the spread of the cult of Isis and her son Harpocrates, whose iconography shows him wearing a lock of hair on the right side of the head, the hairstyle has been called the «Horus lock».

A monograph touching the subject of the cult of Isis was written in 1957 by V. von Gonzenbach, who relates chronological limits for such representations to the Ist - IV th. centuries A.D., and connects the type with the « Adoption to the state of

---

[1] This interpretation, leaning on H. Ingholt and older literature is accepted by G. Ploug. However, neither written nor iconographical evidence favor the interpretation of children with partially long hair as slaves. This author is inclined to treat the above representations as « servants of the Godhead», not slaves. Ploug considers the following as slaves: G. Ploug., Catalogue of the Palmyrene Sculptures Ny Carlsberg Glyptotek. Copenhagen 1995. cat. Nos. 84 I.N. 1069 (a girl richly dressed, hair in rows of curls in the front with looped plait on the right side of the head, hair on both shoulders), 85 I.N. 1153 (a young man in embroidered long sleeved tunic, hair in rows of curls in the front, long strands falling on both shoulders and a woman without turban, Antonine-type hairstyle, her right hand on his right shoulder). The hairstyle of both can be compared with that of Roman camillus. Cat. No. 126, I.N. 1024 shows a well known relief of a grown up male with schedula and a teenage boy with the hair in curls in front and a lock on the right side. A priest modius with laurel wreath and an oval stone in the centre is placed between them on the pillar. The boy carries a cylindrical scrinium in his right hand, a polyptichon in the left.

divinity», accordingly the adoption of boys to the rank of «sons of Isis» through a ceremony of initiation.[2] This assumption, although to begin with not sufficiently documented was followed in archaeological literature. Two additional documents as to the above aspect of the Isis cult have been supplied by L. Castiglione[3], new research as to the Isis cult has been published[4], and a number of new evidence from Egypt [5], Athens [6], southern Dacia[7], Rome [8], Asia Minor[9], Syria [10] or items without any closer provenience[11] have been supplied. Also portraits of girls with a plait have been registered in small number.

Growing archaeological evidence shows that the «youth lock» was located on any place on the head, such as above the right ear, on the back of the head, on the crown of the head, above the temples, which compared with the great geographical spread may indicate possible connections with various deities, or alternatively with various functions in the cult.

From Syria, with the exception of a portrait from Palmyra[12] showing an effigy of Bitti, the daughter of Yarhai, only representations of boys with «youth locks» are known. They are carved in the round or form a part of a relief composition. With the exception of the head of a boy found in Samaria, today in Oslo, whose contextual function is impossible to establish, they all belong to a funerary context. It should be mentioned, that Syrian portraits show both locks and plaits. Plaiting is not uniform,

---

[2] V. von Gonzenbach, Untersuchungen zu den Knabenweihen im Isiskult der römischen Kaiserzeit. Antiquitas I.4, Bonn 1957.

[3] L. Castglione, Gnomon 31, 1959, 539-541.

[4] R. E. Witt, Isis in the Graeco-Roman World. London 1971; F. Dunand, Le culte d'Isis dans le bassin oriental de la Mediterranée, vol. III., Leiden 1973.

[5] K. Parlasca, Mumienportraits 52 n. 255, 70 n. 68, 71, 93, 116, 132, 181, 263 n. 1, 291. Idem. Repertorio d'arte dell'Egitto Greco-Romano. Serie B. Rittrati di mummie. Roma. I (1969) nos. 35, 36, 58, 83, 86, 172, II (1969) nos. 254, 257, 411, 473 - 475, III (1980) no. 674; G. Grimm, Mumienmasken p. 105 Pl. 58.3.

[6] Conze IV (1911/12) nos. 1973, 1987, 1999, 2001, 2010, 2054; A. Mühsam, Berytus 10 (1952/53) p. 113.

[7] G. Bordenache, Dacia 2(1958) p. 277 figs. 6,7, I. Berciu - C.C. Petrolescu, Les Cultes Orientaux dans la Dacie Méridionale (1976) p. 30 no. 12 pl. 7.

[8] G. Fallani, Raccolta archeologica del Prof. Dott. Angello Signorelli, Rome 1951 no. 14 p. 13 Pl. I.3.

[9] Turkey, Izmir, formerly garden of the Basmahane Museum inv. No. 3581, S.Sande, Greek and Roman Portraits in Norwegian Collections, Roma 1991 p. 65 n. 2.

[10] K. Parlasca, A New Grave Relief from Syria, in Brooklyn Mus. Annual, 11 (1969/70 pp. 173 f. N. 8, Idem. Syrische Grabreliefs hellenistischer und römischer Zeit. 3. Tr.W.Pr 1981, Mainz 1982 p. 12 pl. 6.

[11] W. Hornborstel et al., Kunst der Antike. Schätze aus norddeutshem Privatbesitz, Mainz 1977 no. 33 pp. 55 ff.

[12] Ploug 1995 op.cit. no. 84 I.N. 1053, Løytved. Size: 0.56 x 0.435cm. Hard, grayish limestone. Dated ca. A.D. 230 - 250.

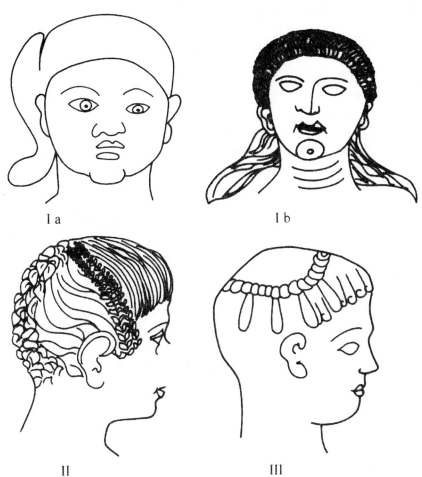

I a   I b

II   III

Fig. 1, I a. - Type I a. , text no.2. From Harbata, today in Paulist convent at Harisa, Lebanon. Author's drawing, I b. - Type I b., text no. 4. From Palmyra, today in Ny Carlsberg Glyptothek, Copenhagen no. 1153. Author's drawing, II - Type II, text no. 5. From Samaria-Sebaste, in The National Gallery, Oslo. Author's drawing, III - Type III, text mo. 10. From Epiphamea, today in The National Museum, Copenhagen, no. 8 A 14. Author's drawing.

and will be described in the following. Plaiting appears not common outside Syria, but instances of a looped or semicircular plait have been recorded[13].

---

[13] A head in a private collection in Switzerland, E. Simon, Eikones. Festschrift H. Jucker. (Antike Kunst, Beiheft 12), Bern 1980 pp. 173ff Pl. 69; reliefs in Istanbul, E. Pfuhl, H. Möbius, Die ostgriechischen Grabreliefs II, Mainz 1979 no. 2182 p. 522 Pl. 312; and Rome, A. Giuliano (ed.) Museo Nazionale Romano. Le sculture I. 8, Rome 1885, VII, 3, pp. 331f.; D.E.E. Kleiner, Roman Imperial Funerary Altars with Portraits, Rome 1987 cat.no. 126 pp. 272 ff Pl. LXVIII.4 (with bibliography).

Types of hairstyle with «Youth lock» in Syria (Fig.1).

In Syria three types of «youth lock» may be recorded:

I. Long strands of loose hair:

I a. (Fig.1. I a) A lock hanging down from behind the right ear. This variant stands closest to the Roman period representations of Horus-Harpocrates and his circle in Egypt. On a relief from Palmyra described below, probably a young assistant to a priest has been shown, which may indicate an active role of boys in the cult.

Two in size almost identical statuettes: ca. 0.46 m., at present not available for study, are known from photographs and descriptions. They were part of a larger lot found in the Lebanese village of Harbata, situated north-west from Baalbek, in May 1931 by a local farmer. Antiquarian authorities managed to register 10 items, reliefs and three-dimensional representations, but several had already reached private hands in Beirut and Damascus[14].

Both statuettes were made in local limestone in the popularist style. They represent a fattish child, clad in a girdled, knee-length tunic, right hand lifted in a gesture of adoration, the left holding possibly a porphyry bird, a childhood attribute. They carry a circular amulet (or a bulla)[15] appended in front on a circular string. They are barefooted. The very chubby face is similar in appearance to that of children ex voto in the Eshmun temple in Sidon[16]. Their hair appears shaven, except for a rich, long lock falling to the right shoulder. Such a hairstyle is found on many Egyptian terracottas of Harpocrates or his attendants dated to the Roman period[17].

1. **Harbata**. First statuette, said to be 0.46 m. high is headless, and has the right leg restored. It is said to be kept in Beirut[18].

2. **Harbata** (Fig. 1. I a). The second one is complete. It is said to be of the same size as the first item, but possibly 10 cm. should be added for the head. It is referred to as kept in the collection of the Paulist convent at Harisa[19].

---

[14] M. Chehab, S. Ronzevalle, Antiquités de Harbata, in MUSJ XXI (1937-38) pp. 74-85 Pls. XIX - XXV. Ronzevalle propose to date the entire group to the second part of the third century A.D. (p. 77).

[15] Such amulet? together with four rod-like pendants on a necklace is known from a statuette of a naked, fat boy from Roman Egypt cf. I. Skupinska-Løvset, The Ustinow collection. Terracottas. Oslo-Bergen-Tromsø 1978, Cat nos. UT 143 (Pl. XXIX).

[16] N. Jidejian, Sidon, 1971 figs. 185-86, 188-1991. Among these has been found a statuette of Ba´alcjillem, son of king Ba`ana, dated 425 B.C.

[17] Skupinska-Løvset 1978 op.cit. Cat nos. UT 117, 118 (Pl. XXI), UT 122, 123 (Pl. XXIII), UT 131, 132 (Pl. XXVI). However, the dissatisfied expression of the face, and its would-appear elderly look resembles the Egyptian «Patäken», as sit. loc. UT 137 fig. XXVII.

[18] Chehab, Ronzevalle op.cit. p. 75 Pl. XX. 3.

[19] Ibid. p. 78 Pl. XXIII.11.

3. **Palmyra**. NCG 1024[20] shows in relief a group of a boy and an adult male (his head is lacking). The grown-up palliatus stands on the right with a schedula in his left hand, a fat teenage boy, placed on the left carries a cylindrical scrinium in his right hand, and a polyptichon in his left. The boy's hair is fashioned in rows of short curls combed onto the forehead and a lock of hair on the right side of the head, behind the ear, which falls to his shoulder. A priestly modius encircled with laurel wreath and decorated with an oval stone in the center, is placed between them, on a pillar. Disregarding Ploug's insistence on calling the Palmyrene children with long locks or partially long hair as slaves, an identification as a ministrant who is assisting the priest and probably also serving during a religious ceremony will here be promoted.

I b. Long strand of hair behind, apparently of some thickness as the hair is shown on both shoulders. An analogy in a marble portraitbust, executed in a cosmopolitan style, but without any closer provenience can be given[21].

4. **Palmyra** NCG 1153[22] (Fig. 1. 1 b), a loculus cover showing a young man in embroidered long sleeved tunic, hair in rows of curls in the front, long strands falling on both shoulders[23] and a woman wearing an Antonine-type hairstyle, her right hand on his right shoulder.
Here also a representation of a girl named Bitti, cf. no. 20.

II. The hair is plaited in front of the right ear and led diagonally up, toward the back, or towards the front, ending close to the crown of the head.
This variant is to the present recorded only in Palestine. However items with the hair plaited in the front of the right ear and hanging down in a loop[24] are known from elsewhere. Of popularist style is a stele in neighboring Phrygia, showing in a naiskos a bust of a young man, clad in a chiton and a cloak, with on each side of the stele such attributes as: 2 astragals, ivy leaves over balls (or medallions?), a garland[25].

---

[20] Ploug 1995 op.cit. Cat. No. 126 pp. 255-257.

[21] E.A. 4394. H: 0.495 m., dated to the Hadrianic period, private collection Beynuhnen.

[22] H. Ingholt, Studier over palmyrensk skulptur, Copenhagen 1928 p. 143 PS 452, ibid. Berytus 2 (1935) 80 pl. 37.2; M. A. R. Colledge, The Art of Palmyra, London 1976 pp. 71 & 263 fig. 94; K. Parlasca, Ein Frauenkopf aus Palmyra, in, Ancient Portraits in the J.P. Getty Museum, vol. 1, Malibu 1987 p.11 fig. 4, n. 11; Ploug 1995 op.cit. cat. No. 85 I.N. 1153

[23] Here also a girl, described below as no. 18, should be considered because of the long hair falling on both shoulders.

[24] Here a quality marble head, with no provenience, and a relief on a stele from Phrygia should be mentioned. Cf. , E. Simon op.cit. pp. 173ff Pl. 69 (marble head), and Pfuhl/Möbius op.cit. no. 2182 p. 522 Pl. 312 (Phrygian stela).

[25] Istanbul Arch. Mus. Inv. 4085, size: 1.32 x 0.73 x 0.2 m. , The name of his parents, were Stratoneikos and Markia. The attributes are uncommon. Cf. Pfuhl/Möbius op.cit. no. 2182 p. 522 Pl. 312.

5. **Samaria - Sebaste** (Fig. 1. II & Fig. 2 a-d). Hair led backwards. A detailed description of this item can be given, thanks to the good preservation of the head, today in Oslo. «The Oslo head» was found in the village of Sebastyeh (Roman Samaria - Sebaste) in Palestine[26]. Subsequently it was bought by Plato von Ustinow and sold to a Norwegian consortium, to become from 1955 deposited at the National Gallery in Oslo[27].

The item is executed in crystalline, sparkling white marble. Its dimensions are as follows: H: 0.202 m., from chin to crown: 0.177 m W: 0.159 m., D: 0.158 m. Diam. at forehead: 0.49 m., mid-lips - hairline: 0.085 m., outer eyecorners: 0.084 m., inner eyecorners: 0.031 m., Plait: length. 0.114 m., lower width: 0.023 m (of this the plait close to the face: 0.011 m.), upper width: 0.019 m., Thickness of the plait: down: 0.011 m., up: 0.01 m.

It is broken off diagonally from the neck towards crown of the head, an artificial way, which may indicate intent. The neckdimensions of the breakage in plane are 0.11 x 0.08 m., the surface of breakage is finished by chiseling. The shape of the head at the upper part of the neck may indicate a neck support, usual in the area.

Demolishing of the face is apparent in its lacking a nose and a chin. Chipped off are the upper lip, fragments of the lower lip, eyelids and ears. A sunken area, 0.021 m. X 0.017 cm. in size, is to be observed above the fastening of the end of plait. Brownish deposits are seen on the large part of the hair. This exhibits under miscroscopic examination the structure of a paint. Deposit under the breakage on the neck has crystallized structure and bigger particles.

The head shows a careful modelling on the front and the sides, less careful but still satisfactory on the back, as the arrangement of the hairlocks is generally clear. Least careful is the execution of the meeting place between the bangs and the hair behind. The light turning of the head towards the boy's left is marked by a descending curve of the bangs towards the left ear, which appears placed slightly lower (10.5 cm.), than the right one (10.8 cm.) from an ideal horizontal. His looking towards the left is marked by an extending of the tearduct on the left eye, diminishing on the right one. Tearducts, mouth corners and noseholes are drilled by slowmoving drill. The surface of the face is subtly modelled, in the eyes the upper eyelids are slightly protruding, eyebrows are marked by delicate diagonal incisions. The ears, especially the left one is less carefully worked out.

[26] RB 1904 p. 84 plate no. 1. According to the same source, Ustinow believed that the head represented Augustus as a child. On the history of the Ustinow collection cf. I.Skupinska-Løvset, Ustinov collection. The Palestinian Pottery, Oslo-Bergen-Tromsø 1976 pp. 17-23. The head with the auction number R 36, was valued to 3 500 NOK. It is now in the possession of the Ethnographical Museum, Oslo.

[27] Sande op.cit. No. 52 Pl. LI pp. 64-66 (with further bibliography). However, Sande's description of the plait is wrong, she does not mention traces of paint on the head, she gives a wrong provenience of the item (Cesarea Maritima). Negatives: National Gallery nos. 984 a-d and 743 a-d.

Fig. 2a, Head of a boy found at Samaria-Sebaste. Oslo, National Gallery.
Courtesy of The National Gallery in Oslo.

However, the head appears to be locally produced, because of local peculiarities in style [28], such as clear outlining of the hairline on the forehead and of the plait and ears, and pronoucing of the corners of the lips, not directly connected with a Corinthian workshop, as indicated by Sande[29].

The face of the boy is oval, full but not fatty. His forehead, partially covered by bangs, must have been high. The hairstyle consists of bangs starting from a place close to the crown of the head and combed onto the forehead. The strands part above the inner corner of the right eye. On the left side the hair is cut to the ear, on the right, it is long and plaited in two plaits, which are fastened diagonally, side by side. They end just below the crown of the head, and are not tucked under, as Sande

[28] I. Skupinska-Løvset, Portraiture in Roman Syria. A Study in Social and Regional Differentiation within the Art of Portraiture» to appear shortly.
[29] Sande op.cit. p. 65.

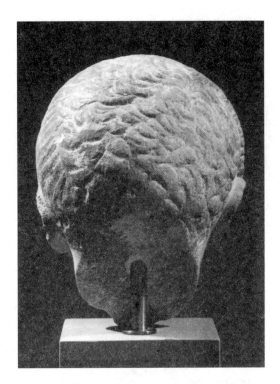

Fig. 2b, Head of a boy found at Samaria-Sebaste. Oslo, National Gallery.
Courtesy of The National Gallery in Oslo.

says[30], as the ends of plaits are clearly indicated, as well as thinness of the plaits at that point. Behind, the hair is cut in short curls, irregularly arranged, generally in vertical rows.

6. **Seleukeia on the Euphrates**. A representation of an apparently 6 - 8 year old boy in the Adana Museum, no. 1214[31] is a quality work. The boy stands in a rounded niche, framed by two pilasters crowned by Corinthian capitals, with conventionalized palmettes above. At the base a funerary inscription is cut, giving the name of the boy as Broutios Koskonios.The stele is dated to the second part of the second century[32].

---

[30] Sit.loc.

[31] Adana Mus. no. 1214. Size: 0.82 m. x 0.45 m. , T: 0.29 m.; M.F. Mousche, in BCH 33 (1959) 543f. Fig.1. Pfuhl/Möbius op.cit. vol.1 no. 791 p. 209 pl. 116; J. Wagner, Seleukeia am Euphrat/Zeugma, Wiesbaden 1976 pp. 220-221, dated to the 2 nd part of the second century A.D.. Plait not observed by the all above authors. To the plait: I.Skupińska-Løvset, Funerary Portraiture of Seleukeia-on-the-Euphrates, in Acta Archaeologica 56-1985, Copenhapen 1987 p. 116 fig. 21.

[32] Wegner op.cit. p. 221.

The boy is shown in a slight contraposto, head slightly turned towards his right shoulder. therefore the possibility of interpretation of the hairstyle is limited. His hair is short cut and curly, three rows of curls, alternatively turned are shown. The youth plait is thicker and looser braided than in the case of the Caesarea head. It goes in a slightly curved line from the front of the ear up across the right temple. On his right shoulder a lock of hair? may be discerned.

The boy wears a mid-leg length outer tunic (as an inner tunic is indicated on the left shoulder), but no cloak. The tunic has long sleeves, is draped but not girdled. On his neck he wears a ring - shaped necklace with a pendant in the middle, interpreted as a bulla. He has a finger ring on his left hand. In his bent hands at the height of the hips he holds his childhood's attributes, in the right hand a porphyry? bird (neck and head are lacking) in the left a bunch of grapes (or other fruit?)[33]. He is wearing sandals with a decorated strap between the first and second toes and with a strap around the ankles.

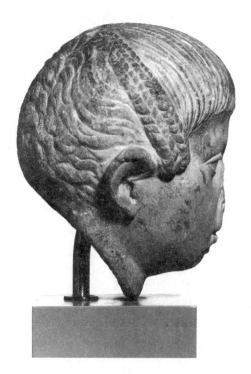

Fig. 2c, Head of a boy found at Samaria-Sebaste. Oslo, National Gallery. Courtesy of The National Gallery in Oslo.

---

[33] Similar attributes have been interpreted differently e.g. A. Sadurska - A. Bounni., Les sculptures funèraires de Palmyre. RdA Supplementi 13. Rome 1994 cat. No. 92..»Une grape de dattes, faucon.». cat. No. 94.. «colombe, olivier.». cat. No. 95.. «oiseau, grape.»

His face is chubby, nose short and broad, large eyes, small lips, similarly to the Epiphanean boy.

7. **Northern Syria**. A family representation on an elongated, inscribed stele in a private collection[34]. This relief shows characteristics of Northern Syria, and is probably of an early Antonine date.

In a rectangular frame a woman, a boy and a man are represented to the height of the waist. The woman wears a turban, from which wavy strands of hair, parted in the middle are led to behind the ears, the man wears his hair in long strands combed onto the forehead. The boy has crop cut hair in the front, a plait led from the height of the right ear towards the front, and additionally a vertically placed plait behind. A similar hair arrangement, although not plaited, may be observed on a marble item in Romania[35].

8. **Palmyra**. A funerary portrait of Nurbel, son of Barnebo, dated to A.D. 160 - 180[36]. The boy is standing frontally, legs splayed, holding a bird (identified as a falcon) in his left, and a bunch of fruit identified as dates in his right hand. He carries a large ring in his right ear. His hair is combed in large curls onto his face, a plait is led from behind the right ear towards the front. Some analogy to his cousin Habibata may be pointed out[37]. She has the hair similarly dressed in the front, but no plait may be recognized. She carries a similar bird (identified as a dove!), and in the right hand a bunch of fruit (identified as olives!). On a spirally twisted chain she carries a round medallion, similar to that of the boys with «youth locks». She carries a mid-leg length tunic draped similarly to that on the Egyptian terra-cotta representations of Harpocrates and of women connected with cult, namely adhering to the belly and forming folds between the legs[38].

9. **Palmyra**. Palmyra Museum A.N. 1079. Ploug informs that « this plait is not arranged in a semicircle, but runs straight across the centre of the crown to the rear.» [39]

---

[34] Parlasca 1982 op.cit. pl. 6.1 p. 12.

[35] V. Popova-Moroz, Roman Portraiture from III. C. in Tracia and Moesia, in Ritrato ufficiale e ritrato privato. Atti della II Conferenze Internazionale sul Ritrato Romano. Roma 26 - 30 Settembre 1984. Quaderni de «La Ricerca Scientifica» 116. Roma 1988, p. 429 Fig. 15 «head of an Isis boy from Appiaria (Riachovo) Rousse, Historical Museum. Crop cut hair in the front, on the right, a thin lock led forwards, a thick one hangs behind. The head is dated to the third century A.D..

[36] Sardurska, Bounni op.cit. cat. No. 92 Fig. 18. Palmyra, Museum Inv. 1984/7076. Found in the hypogeum no. 6 called Sassans hypogeum, in loculus 1. Dimensions: 0.5 m. X 0.32 m.. The plait has been not identified to the present.

[37] Ibidem cat. No. 94 Pl. 12. Palmyra Museum inv. 1986/7078. Dimensions 0.4 m. X 0.22 m..

[38] Skupinska-Løvset 1978 op.cit. UT 122 Pl. XXIII (Harpocrates), UT 134, 135 Pl. XXVI (women with tambourines).

[39] Palmyra A.N. 1079 = H. Ingholt., Inscriptions and sculptures from Palmyra, II. Berytus. Archeological Studies, The American University of Beirut, V, Copenhagen 1938 p. 138 note 6, Ploug 1995 op.cit. p. 206.

II b. Complex braid placed low, close to the ear.

10. **Skythopolis**. Bronze head found nearby Beth Shean described as „ a Jewish boy with side-locks and braids"[40] is a quality work. The head shows a boy with a full face, regular features, relativly short, broad nose and full lips forming a Cupid's bow. The hair except of the flat, broad braid, is short and its modelling exhibits inclination towards `a penna treatment. This, together with a melancholic outlook of the face would probably date the head to the Severan period.

III. The most characteristic of the third group is that plaited hair, or part of it, is arranged in a loop (or multiple loops). It may be supplemented by another plait directed vertically, or loose hair on the back of the head. As most of examples are reliefs, the arrangement of supplementary hair is not certain. Most generally the group may be defined as comprising a loop (loops) of hair only, and loop of hair and other hair.

11. **Epiphamea** (Fig. 1.' III & Fig. 3) The most important, because of its threedimensionality and good state of preservation is a portrait statue, less than natural size, found in a hypogeum in Hama (Epiphamea)[41]. This statue has been found accompanied by a statue of a female, size less than natural, which because of the hairstyle and the belt could be interpreted as active in the cult of Isis[42]. The boy is standing frontally, legs apart, feet directed slightly towards the centre, arms bent, hidden under the cloak, hands sticking up, one above the other.He is wearing a mid-leg length tunic[43] and a cloak of the same length, on the feet boots reaching the ankles. His face is chubby, squarish, with short, rather broad nose, small lips, fairly large, almond-shaped eyes. His hairdo consists of a row of large curls above the forehead, carefully modelled, the hair on the back more generally indicated. The youth tress adheres to the head and consists of a plait forming a semicircle with four rod shaped ornaments hanging from it. The tress is colored bright red, between the 2nd and 3rd plait traces of gilding may be seen. Gilding of the «youth lock» is observed on the mummy portraits[44].

---

[40] Only preliminarly published by C. C. Vermeule, in Berytus 26 (1978) 99 - 101 fig. 7.

[41] G. Ploug., Fouilles et recherches de la Fondation Carlsberg 1931 - 1938. II.3 The Graeco-Roman objects of clay, the coins and the necropolis, Nationalmuseets skrifter. Større Beretninger X, København 1986 pp. 82-85 figs. 25d, 29 b-c.

[42] Skupinska-Løvset 1983 op.cit. pp. 333-4.

[43] Ploug 1986 op.cit. p. 81 is telling us that the tunic is short-sleeved, but how should she know? Her description is far from accurate. She is also stating that both the shoes and the cloak are ankle - length, which is not the case. His face is not round in shape and his eyes are almond-shaped, not almost round.

[44] Parlasca 1980 op.cit. no. N 674, colorplate F (J.P.Getty's Museum, Malibu inv. 78 AI 262, size: 0.13 X 0.207 m.. Bought in 1979).

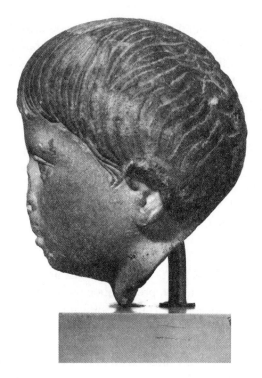

Fig. 2d, Head of a boy found at Samaria-Sebaste. Oslo, National Gallery.
Courtesy of The National Gallery in Oslo.

12. **Palmyra**. An effigy of a teenage boy in the Archaeological Museum in Istanbul[45], dated to ca. 190 A.D.[46], shows still another version of the hairstyle. He has hair in long curled strands combed onto the forehead and a plaited portion of hair along the top of the head. It forms two plaits passing in a loop on the right side of the head. One plait goes from the middle of the head to the right, another from the right towards the middle. He is wearing a tunic and a cloak with an end falling straight down on the left side of the body.

13. **Palmyra**. Head of a boy found in the grave no. 36[47]. Curled hair in rows, a single plait descending from the middle of the head in a circular line, ending above the right ear. Antonine date.

---

[45] Istanbul inv. 3795; Ingholt op.cit. p.138 Pl. XLIX. 4.

[46] Ploug 1995 op.cit. p. 206.

[47] A. Smidt-Colinet, Das Tempelgrav Nr. 36 in Palmyra, in Damascener Forschungen 4., Mainz 1992 no. B 20 a fig. 54, pl. 46. a - b.

14 **Palmyra**. A stele dated to ca. A.D. 190, reproduced by Tanabe[48].

15. **Palmyra**. PS 429, a woman with a little boy standing behind her, having a hairstyle with a looped plait, dated to ca. A.D. 190 - 210[49].

16. **Palmyra**. PS 513 = CIS 4459 as above, the boy is seated on her hand[50].

17. **Palmyra**. Bust of ... ba, son of Ate`aqab[51], found in 1937 in the tomb of Abd`astor. A teenage boy in both tunic and an embroidered cloak and carrying a little circular medallion on his neck. He holds a little bird in his left hand, the right one rests in the folds of the cloak. His hair is in rows of curls combed on the forehead and supplemented with braided lock, which passes from the crown of his head to the middle of the forehead, and thence in a double loop to a point over the right ear[52].

18. **Palmyra**. Heavy, thick plait covering almost the whole crown on the front, published by Parlasca[53].

19. **Palmyra**. Circular plait, stele dated to ca. A.D. 230 - 250, published by Parlasca[54].

20. **Palmyra**. NCG. 1053[55] a girl (teenage?) richly dressed, in embroidered both tunic and coat, pearl necklace and a necklace of twisted wire with an oval medallion, twisted bracelet and ear-rings. Dated by Ploug to A.D. 239 - 250. She has her hair cut similar to boys in rows of curls in the front with looped plait on the right side of the head. Supplementarily she is carrying long hair falling to both shoulders[56]. Ploug interprets her as a Lesbian[57].

---

[48] K. Tanabe ed., Sculptures of Palmyra. Memoires of the Ancient Orient Museum I. Tokyo 1986 fig. 264, Ploug 1995 op. cit. p. 206.

[49] Ploug op.cit. p. 206.

[50] Sit.loc.

[51] Palmyra Museum inv. A 898/898, Ingholt 1938, op.cit. Pl. XLIX.3, p. 138; Parlasca 1983 op.cit. note; Ploug 1995 op.cit. p. 206, dates the item to 210 - 230 A.D.

[52] According to Ingholt's description. Ingholt op.cit. p. 138. By studying the picture an other direction could also be possible.

[53] K. Parlasca., Ein antoninischer Frauenkopf aus Palmyra in Malibu. Ancient Portraaits in the Paul Getty Museum 1. Occasional Papers on Antiquity 4 pp. 107 - 114. Malibu 1987 pl.45 a., Ploug 1995 op.cit. p. 206, dated A.D. 210 - 230.

[54] Parlasca 1987 op.cit. pl. 46 a; Ploug 1995 p. 206.

[55] Ploug 1995 op.cit. cat. No. 84 pp. 205 - 207, with bibliography.

[56] Long hair on the back of the head falling freely to the shoulders is typical of Roman camillus. Ploug, however, insist on its being a slave hairstyle, as in case of I.N.1153, Ploug 1995 pp. 208 - 210, no. 85 (a man and a woman, dorsale behind her, accompanied by an illegible inscription. The woman interpreted as a mourner, as she puts a comforting hand on his shoulder).

[57] Op.cit. p. 206. The view is not documented.

Uncertain:

21. **Palmyra**. Paris Louvre A 18174[58], the portion with the plait now broken, has according to literature had a single looped plait. Parlasca identifies the boy as a schoolboy as on his dyptich, the letters may be read.

22. **Seleukeia on the Euphrates**. Belkis[59]. This hairstyle can not be fully identified as the boy is shown on a stela in relief. It appears as the hair form a loop around the crown of the head. Dated to the second part of the second century A.D.

Fig.3. Statue of a boy found in Hama, ancient Epiphamea. Copenhagen, National Museum. Courtesy of The National Museum.

---

[58] Colledge op.cit. fig. 82.
[59] Size: 0.77 x 0. 32 x 0.14 m. Wegner op.cit. no. 84 p. 221-2, Skupinska-Lovset 1987 op.cit p. 117 fig. 22. Standing chubby boy with a staff of two rods in his left hand. Wearing a mid-legs tunic and a cloack (chlamys?) fastened by a fibula. An inscription gives the name: Kirillos Apolinarou.

Concluding remarks.

Age of the children, their garments and attributes.

Young age at the time of death is settled in the case of a boy wearing «lock of youth» portrayed in Terenuthis in Egypt [60], as he died only one year old. On the basis of present material the age of Syrian boys remains unknown, but may be guessed from small child to teenage. F. Poulsen considers the age of the boy in Oslo as four years[61], however, the age is not easy to establish judging from physical appearence only. On an altar of Florus, found in Rome, dated to A.D. 280 - 320[62] a chubby boy, his hair cut short and combed onto the forehead, a looped plait hanging down in front of his right ear is shown. He looks 10 years old but the accompanying inscription states that he died at the age of exactly two years, 10 months and 24 days.

Most of the Syrian boys are dressed in plain tunic and cloak. When represented in full figure, the tunic and the cloak reach mid-legs. Most often the tunic is ungirdled. The cloak may be draped as a pallium, or in one case fastened as a chlamys. On their feet they wore boots or sandals or are shown barefoot. Two Palmyrene boys wear embroidered tunics and cloaks. Of adornments they may carry collars, a circular pendant interpreted as a bulla, ear-ring and finger ring. Of attributes they may carry a bird (a porphyry bird?) and a bunch of fruit (grapes, dadles), a dyptichon, a polyptichon and a scrinium.

The girl, dressed in tunic and cloak, both embroidered, carries necklaces, oval medallion, bracelet and ear-rings.

In service of the Godhead.

Only representations with shaven head and a lock of hair behind the right ear (group I a) has direct iconographical connections with Egyptian representations of Harpocrates and his attendants. In Palmyra, a boy with curled hair in front and a lock of hair at the right ear, carrying writing and reading utensils, is shown close to a pillar with a priestly head-gear on, which may characterize him as an assistant in a religious context.

Clear religious surroundings are lacking for children of groups II and III.

---

[60] K. Parlasca MDIK 26 (1970) p. 193 no. 6 Pl. 65.

[61] F. Poulsen. La collection Ustinow. La sculpture. Videnskapsselskapets Skrifter II. Historisk-Filosofisk Klasse. 1920. No. 3.

[62] Museo Nazionale delle Terme, ph. DAIR 65.12., D.E.E. Kleiner, Roman sculpture. Yale University Press 1992 p. 460 fig. 421. Kleiner suggests that his parents, Bassaeus and Servea because of their single names were of servile origin, but Florus was not marked as slave, but as in service to the Isiac cult.

Because of the find context[63], and the presence of the «youth-lock» the statue found in the hypogeum at Epiphanea ought to be interpreted as representing a boy connected with the cult of Isis[64]. This opinion has been contradicted by G.Ploug, who, leaning on research by R.E.Witt[65] would like to consider the boy as «Son of Isis» only because of his untimely death. Such interpretation, however, finds no justification in the archaeological material. Although we find plentiful representations of children in a funerary context of Syria only few are shown with the «Youth plait». Although one should consider death at a young age as untimely, scarsity of portraits with a «Youth plait» adds to them an extraordinary significance, which may indicate rank or function.

Ploug also considers children with long hair on the back of the head as slaves[66], but inconsistency in interpretation lies among others in the fact, that some youngsters are shown with a pendant identified as a bulla, traditionally interpreted as an attribute of a freeborn.

It is not possible to select a group of children in service of Dea Syria, or any other Syrian gods, an attribute in the shape of a bunch of rods, however, may be connected with northern Syria. On a stele of Seleukeia (here no. 22) a boy, with an uncertain arrangement of long hair on the back of the neck is shown with a bunch of two rods. Similar rods are carried by a seated female in a diadem from Hierapolis[67] interpreted as a goddess, and by a boy on a rectangular pillar from the same area, today in the gardens of the Municipial Museum of Aleppo[68].

Date of the representations.

As indicated by Parlasca, one of the earliest mummy portrait of a youth with a «youth lock», is exhibited in the National Museum in Warsaw[69]. Syrian portraits of

---

[63] The figure of a female found in the same tomb, but placed more centrally, carries, however, not decisive attributes such as the knotted cloak or Isis symbols. But her religious functions are marked by girdle and hairstyle.

[64] Skupinska-Løvset 1983 op.cit. pp. 333-4.

[65] Witt, op.cit. p. 221 note 49, states that the untimely death may be alone the reason for consideration of the boy as «Son of Isis» Cf. G. Ploug 1986 op.cit. p. 85.

[66] It appears unlikely, that any of two postulates of G. Ploug as to the children with «youth plait» namely as demarking solely children who died too early, and secondly the slaves, could be supported by Syrian material.

[67] Syrian National Museum, Damascus inv. No. 3738, Sélim Abdul-Hak & Andrée Abdul-Hak., Catalogue illustré des Antiquités Gréco-romaines au Musée de Damas., Damascus 1951 p. 60 no. 12 Pl. XXVIII.1., H: 152 cm.(base included).

[68] Museum garden no. 5099. On a pillar, in separate reliefs, a grown male and a boy, both are represented with double rods in their left hands, right hands with palm directed towards the viewer, a gesture of prayer.

[69] Inv. MN 127191 size: 0.336 m. x 0.139 m., Parlasca 1969 Volume B I op.cit. no. 35 Pl. 10.1.

all groups show items of similar early date. Early are statuettes of Harbata (here nos. 1,2), to around A.D. 100 date the Samaria-Sebaste head (here no. 5), only slightly later is the Ephiphanean statue (here no. 11).

All variants of «youth plait» seem popular in the second century A.D. Hadrianic - early Antonine is probably a variant with hair in rows of curls combed onto the forehead, and a thick long loose hair behind (group I b).

Of third century date are several reliefs from Palmyra, showing looped plait of complicated composition.

Iwona Modrzewska-Pianetti
Varsovia

Gli scavi polacchi nell' isola di Torcello
visti dopo trent' anni

Qual' e' la ragione di tornare a commentare i risultati degli scavi polacchi svoltisi nella laguna veneziana gia' trentacinque anni fa? (fig.1) Indipendentemente dalla ragione di ricordare i successi delle ricerche polacche nel Mediterraneo, ci sono anche i motivi forniti dalle ricerche odierne.Indubbiamente le ricerche della missione PAN diretta da Lech Leciejewicz hanno permesso di confrontare la realta' archeologica e le leggende sulla storia di Venezia create dai cronisti medievali. Chissa' se non e' ancora piu' importante che hanno provocato l' interesse per l'archeologia del terreno nel territorio veneto ed anche lo sviluppo degli studi complessivi sia sull' alto medioevo che sulla romanita' della costa veneziana.

C'e' anche la mia ragione privata data dalla partecipazione alle ricerche veneziane dagli anni ottanta fino ad ora (fig.2). Come si sono trovati gli archeologi polacchi nell' isola di Torcello nel 1961?. Ce lo rivela in parte G.P. Bognetti (1961) che fu' direttore dell' Istituto di Storia della Societa' dello Stato Veneziano, della Fondazione Cini di Venezia, mentre i particolari avevo il piacere sentire direttamente da Lech Leciejewicz che dirigeva lo scavo.

La iniziativa nacque durante i congressi dei medievalisti svoltisi a Salerno e Varsavia ove G.P. Bognetti conobbe A. Gieysztor e W. Hensel e sopratutto i risultati dei lavori dei medievalisti polacchi.

Cosi' nacque l' idea di assegnare all' allora Istituto di Storia della Cultura Materiale dell' Accademia Polacca delle Scienze (PAN) l' esecuzione dello scavo svoltosi in due campagne consecutive.

Parallelamente, la Soprintendenza archeologica del Veneto, che autorizzava lo scavo, eseguiva, con la dirigente G.Fogolari (1961) un altro scavo nella parte meridionale del isola, presso la chiesa di San Giovanni Evangelista.

I risultati completi dello scavo polacco sono stati pubblicati piu' avanti nel 1977 (Leciejewicz,Tabaczyńska,Tabaczyński 1977) che e' stato fino a poco fa' l'unico, e sicuramente il primo, scavo stratigrafico nelle zone lagunari dell' Alto

Adriatico (fig.3). Esso e' stato effettuto nell' isola di Torcello, la quale e' situata una decina di chilometri a Nord-Est di Venezia.

La scelta e' stata fatta con riguardo alla importanza dell' insediamento insulare veneziano della gente spostatasi dalla parte della costa di Altino, come voleva la tradizione, gia' durante gli invasioni degli Unni di Attila nella meta' del V secolo (Ortalli 1981; Modrzewska,Pianetti 1996).

Infatti, presso la cattedrale e' stata trovata la lapide commemorativa della fondazione della basilica del 639, che pero' secondo alcuni potrebbe provenire da Cittanova e spostata poi dalle autorita' ecclesiastiche a Torcello. Cio' che, data la mancanza di materiali lapidei nella laguna, veniva praticato in tutto il corso della storia.

Il periodo bizantino e altomedievale per tutta la costa e' stato tempo di grandi trasformazioni per i popoli della Cisalpina Orientale per gli insediamenti goti e longobardi cosi come a causa dei grandi eventi climatici che, piu' che normalmente, in questa regione, hanno cambiato l' immagine della costa da Grado ed Aquileia a Torcello e verso gli sbocchi dei fiumi Brenta e Po (Brambati 1985).

Ambedue i fattori venivano piu' tardi descritti dai cronisti medievali come Paolo Diacono, Giovanni Diacono e dai cronisti altinati, che descrivevano diversi fenomeni dopo secoli secondo le necessita' dei sovrani.

Indubbiamente, dopo le ricerche archeologiche lungo tutta la costa altoadriatica e la laguna, si e' attestata la cosi detta "alluvione" descritta da Paolo Diacono, cronista longobardo del VIII sec., che doveva essere dovuta all' aumento dei livelli dei fiumi e del mare. Cio' dovrebbe essere successo nello Alto Adriatico nel VI-VII secolo.

I piu' recenti scavi a Concordia Sagittaria e Jesolo hanno dimostrato rialzamenti dei pavimenti delle prime chiese dei secoli IV e V D.C.(Croce Da Villa 1984, 45; Sandrini 1987, 99; Tombolani 1985, 73-90). Cio' che gia' prima risultava dagli scavi polacchi a Torcello.

Infatti, la stratigrafia torcellana, fatta separatamente per i due scavi: una presso la chiesetta di San Marco, luogo di leggendario deposito della salma di San Marco prima della sua traslazione a Venezia nel IX secolo, (scavo 1, Leciejewicz 1981), un' altra (scavo II) rilevata nello scavo davanti la cattedrale di Santa Maria Assunta e la chiesa di Santa Fosca, ambedue ubicate presso una piazza non abitata dal Medioevo.

Come hanno dimostrato le ricerche di archivio, nel XVI secolo esistevano ancora nella isola varie chiese e monasteri scomparse oggi dalla superficie (Vecchi 1981). E' un fenomeno che non e' isolato nella laguna, ove la subsidenza ha provocato vari spostamenti dei monasteri situati nelle isole dal medioevo. Come esempio si puo' dare l' abbandono dei monasteri esistenti dal medioevo nella isola di San Lorenzo di Ammiana situata a Sud-Est di Torcello e tante altre ora quasi coperte dalle acque salmastre della laguna (Dorigo 1996; Marabini, Veggiani 1992). Il abbassamento del suolo e' il fenomeno fisico piu' importante che influisce sulla storia degli insediamenti nella laguna veneziana, formata dai sedimenti di fiumi che con una densa rete coprono le terre venete. Fenomeno provocato dal

Fig. 1. Veduta da satellite della laguna Veneta,
edizioni Geogramma S.P.A. Olbia 1996

costipamento dei sedimenti e da eventi neotettonici (Pianetti, Zanferrari 1980;
Pianetti 1968).

Questo fenomeno cambiava l' ambiente lagunare nel passato, come lo cambia
finora, esso viene studiato da vari specialisti di Istituti del Consiglio Nazionale
delle Ricerche di Venezia, studi iniziati da G.Morandini 1960.

Torniamo alla prima missione polacca che doveva confrontare tutti questi
problemi nel terreno, cioe' in una delle duecento isole veneziane (Leciejewicz,
Tabaczyńska, Tabaczyński 1961).La parte che stupisce dopo tanti anni, e' la
documentazione preparata dai membri della missione, specialmente i favolosi
disegni colorati dei profili e delle sezioni fatti con la grande capacita' di
E.Tabaczynska.

Abbiamo potuto consultarli presso la Fondazione Cini; una parte della
documentazione si trova presso la PAN di Varsavia.

I quaderni dello scavo, gli inventari di materiali scelti, la documentazione
mostrataci da L.Leciejewicz, hanno sono stati elaborati nella pubblicazione edita
dall' Istituto Nazionale di Archeologia e Storia dell' Arte di Roma (Leciejewicz,
Tabaczyńska, Tabaczyński 1977).

Nelle varie parti dello scavo: davanti la cattedrale, chiamato "in piazza" (scavo II); presso la chiesetta di S.Marco (scavo I), la missione polacca ha scavato fino a quattro metri di profondita' dal piano campagna(fig.4).

I dieci strati stabiliti avevano lo spessore medio di 4O-7O cm. La missione ha raccolto i campioni del terreno sottoposto poi allo studio chimico-pedologico da A. Comel (1975) dell' allora Stazione chimico-agraria sperimentale di Udine dell' allora Ministero dell' Agricoltura.

Lo studio, un po' dimenticato, ci e' servito per gli studi attuali (Modrzewska, in stampa 1).

Sarebbe in questo luogo troppo lungo disegnare il quadro cronologico-stratigrafico datoci dallo scavo 1961-1962, pero' accenniamo, che ora abbiamo intrapreso i lavori di verifica.

Bisogna pero' dire alcune parole sullo scopo, sulla scelta del posto e sui risultati dello scavo.

Per lo scavo principale(scavo II) e' stata scelta la piazza davanti la cattedrale dove fu collocata la sede vescovile di Altino-Torcello dal VII-IX secolo.

Il battistero antistante e' datato al VII secolo e proprio qui qualche mese fa' e' stato fatto lo scavo-sondaggio da parte di M. De Min della Soprintendenza ai beni

Fig. 2. Ideogramma di nave e territorio veneto,
studio Gerardi di Dolo(Padova)

culturali di Venezia.Esso dovrebbe servire per confronto con i sondaggi fatti qualche anno fa' davanti alla basilica di San Marco a Venezia (Ammermann, De Min 1994), ma piu' con quello rigorosamente effettuato e studiato da E. Bonatti (1968) alle Motte di Volpego (laguna Sud).

A Torcello, accanto alla cattedrale, vicino alla chiesa di Santa Fosca (scavo II) e presso la chiesetta di San Marco (scavo I) sono state scoperte delle tombe.

Era la zona centrale del isola, se anche non sembra la piazza del mercato, ma con funzione religiosa, e' qui che la missione polacca ha scoperto numerose sepolture antistanti alle chiese dalla parte Ovest.

Fig. 3. Particolare dalla carta del regno lombardo veneto dell' I.R. Istituto Topografico Militare 1843 (reprint Istituto Veneto di Scienze Lettere e Arti)

La piazza del mercato si ipotizza fosse verso la chiesa di S.Giovanni Evangelista, zona pero' non sufficientemente scavata dagli archeologi italiani.

Nella zona di scavo la missione ha riconosciuto le varie fasi insediative.

I carotaggi sulla piazza sono stati effettuati dall' allora Istituto di Studi Adriatici del CNR di Venezia da A.Marcello e suoi collaboratori che hanno effettuato analisi botaniche, antropologiche e chimico-pedologiche.

I risultati degli studi sono stati pubblicati fra il 1961 e il 1970 nel Bollettino dell' Istituto per la Storia della Societa' e dello Stato Veneziano della Fondazione Cini di Venezia e nelle Memorie di biogeografia adriatica dell' allora Istituto di studi adriatici del CNR di Venezia nello stesso intervallo di tempo (Marcello et al. 1968). Lo studio faunistico e' stato continuato da A.Riedel (Riedel 1981).

Nello scavo nella piazza, la missione dopo le due campagne, ha delimitato dieci strati scendendo dallo strato comprendente il suolo all' argilla di tipo lagunare

Fig. 4. Stratigrafia torcellana secondo Leciejewicz et al. 1961

trovata a circa quattro metri di profondita' reale (le quote della documentazione sono invece riferite allo zero convenzionale posto circa due metri e cinquanta sopra la superficie della lastra commemorativa nel pavimento nella chiesa di S.Fosca).

Nella parte meridionale dello scavo verso la locanda Cipriani (famosa per le visite dello scrittore Hemingway) ove il terreno si abbassa e la isola e' tagliata da canali, le rive erano state rafforzate da pali di legno, come si fece da allora in tutta Venezia.

I pali sono stati importanti per le datazioni radiocarbonio, effettuate dall' allora Centro per lo studio dei sedimenti recenti del CNR di Roma (Alessio et al. 1967) Dati recentemente calibrati da A.Pazdur che assieme con altri studi vengono ora di essere pubblicati dall' Universita' di Venezia.

In base alla stratigrafia, le varie fasi insediative nella piazza a Torcello sono state delimitate fra il XVI e il I sec.D.C.

Uno dei ritrovamenti piu' importanti e' stato fatto nello strato quinto , ove c'e', a circa due metri sotto la superficie dell' isola, la officina vetraria datata al VII-IX secolo (Leciejewicz, Tabaczyńska, Tabaczyński 1977, 57-73) (fig.5).

A parte i forni, sono state rinvenute le scorie vitree e frammenti dei prodotti fino a poco fa custoditi nel piccolo museo torcellano protette dal custode, che da bambino aiutava la missione polacca negli scavi.

Ora i vetri, scrupolosamente inventariati da E.Tabaczyńska, sono stati spostati, come il resto dei materiali dello scavo polacco nei magazzini della Soprintendenza Archeologica dei Beni Culturali di Venezia nell' isola di Murano, protette dalle alte maree, ma non accessibili agli studiosi. Senza dubbio questa officina vetraria testimonia che nel VII-IX sec. ivi fioriva una grande attivita' produttiva. Poi, questo luogo e' stato trasformato nel grande cimitero medievale, che e' stato scavato nella zona circostante da L.Leciejewicz nel 1983 nella breve campagna di scavo organizzata dal Dipartimento di Studi Storico Archeologici dell' Universita' di Venezia diretto dal G.Traversari.

Questa nuova attivita' e' cominciata dal simposio italo -polacco a Venezia dedicato alle origini di Venezia (Le origini di Venezia 1981).

Nel quadro di questa nuova collaborazione sono state effettuate anche le prospezioni geofisiche nella parte vicina alla cattedrale e nella parte meridionale dell' isola ove le ricerche archivistiche indicavano l' ubicazione della chiesa di San Tommaso e forse un tempietto romano, ora invisibili in superficie (Modrzewska, Herbich in stampa; Modrzewska, in stampa 1). In questa campagna ha partecipato dott. Mirosław Mizera del IHKM PAN scomparso tragicamente nel gennaio 1999. Fu caro collega e buon compagno dei lavori del nostro gruppo durante molti anni.

Un altro gruppo diretto da W.Hensel faceva ricerche geofisiche e archeologiche davanti la chiesa di San Donato nell' isola di Murano. I risultati delle ricerche sono ancora in elaborazione.

A nostro avviso, molto soggettivo, tutto cio' che e' stato scoperto dalla missione polacca nel 1961-1962 sotto le fornaci per vetro, cioe' prima del VII secolo, e' piu' importante.

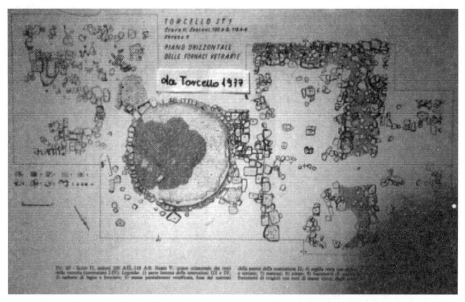

Fig. 5. Lo strato V con i forni vetrari secondo Leciejewicz et al.1977

Sono i risultati concernenti l' epoca bizantina (strato VII, scavo II) e , piu' in profondita,' nella piazza si sono avuti i dati concernenti l' Antichita' romana (strato VIII e IX, sempre scavo II) (fig.6).

Queste due epoche sono state sopratutto obiettivo della nuova ricerca intrapresa nel 1993 per un triennio e che ora proseguira' per altri tre anni di un progetto comune di ricerca dell' Istituto di Archeologia ed Etnologia PAN Varsavia (un tempo IHKM PAN primo realizzatore dello scavo) e dell'Istituto per lo Studio della Dinamica delle Grandi Masse del Consiglio Nazionale delle Ricerche di Venezia.

Nel quadro di questa collaborazione finora si sono svolti vari studi archeologici, fra essi quelli sulle ceramiche torcellane (Modrzewska in stampa; Modrzewska

168

1996), geologici, storici, analitici (hanno partecipato F. Pianetti, L. Leciejewicz, G. Calderoni, Z. Hensel, T. Baranowski, M. Pawlikowski, I. Modrzewska, A. Buko).

I risultati di questi primi anni degli studi sono pubblicati come Rapporti Tecnici del CNR di Venezia con n° 226, 1998.

Tutti gli studi avevano come scopo la verifica e precisazione delle datazioni torcellane sulla base di vari materiali avuti a disposizione, fra essi le ceramiche in funzione delle datazioni stratigrafiche.

Cosi' e'risultato che durante la alluvione, descritta da Paolo Diacono, gia' nominato, la isola non e' stata abbandonata ma solo e' stato rialzato il livello del terreno della piazza. La ceramica ivi ritrovata dimostra la continuita' della vita, almeno dal IV -VII sec., per l'epoca tarda discussa qui.

In breve commentiamo l' importanza dei ritrovamenti degli strati piu' profondi nella piazza di Torcello 1961-1962.

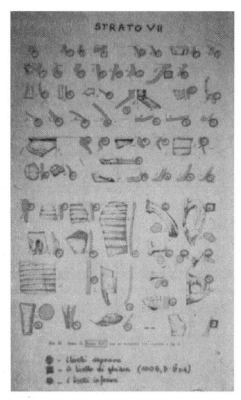

Fig. 6. L' insieme della ceramica dello strato VII secondo
Leciejewicz et al.1977

Esse giacevano alla profondita' di circa quattro metri sotto il livello attuale dell' isola e sono sopratutto i materiali ceramici datati all' epoca giulio claudia.

Questo fatto ha aperto la forte disscussione sulla romanita' della laguna. Fin oggi e' l' argomento che divide i ricercatori fra quelli che, come W.Dorigo, ritengono che

Fig. 7. Veduta della laguna presso Torcello, Francesco Tiron (1745-1797)
Museo Correr di Venezia. Reprint Il Gazzettino di Venezia, 1994

la laguna nell' Antichita' fosse tutta terra e potesse essere abitata nel I sec.D.C.
(Dorigo 1994). E quelli studiosi, specialmente della scuola padovana, che
ritengono che la laguna fosse terreno piu' o meno come ora, cio' che avrebbe dato
la possibilita' di comunicazioni endolagunari tramite le "fosse" (Rosada 1990).

Le nuove ricerche a Cittanova Eracliana, ove risiedevano le autorita' della
comunita' marittima delle citta' venete nel VII sec., D.C., hanno dimostrato che la
citta', ora circa a venti chilometri dalla riva, nei tempi romani fosse un' isola
(Salvatori 1989).

Fra discordanze, discussioni, leggende e le difficolta' date dal terreno lagunare
gli studi iniziati dai polacchi, ha continuato E.Canal Ispettore Onorario della
Laguna. Egli da quarant' anni ha fatto prospezioni, specialmente nella laguna Nord-
Est, scoprendo piu' di duecento stazioni con i vari ritrovamenti mobili e in situ
(Canal 1995; Canal 1998).

I suoi scavi fatti qualche anno fa' a San Lorenzo di Ammiana, a pochi chilometri
da Torcello, confermano la possibilita' della vita nelle varie isole veneziane dall'
epoca romana almeno. Ivi e' stato trovato un pavimento datato, dai ritrovamenti
ceramici, post quem alla fine del I sec. D.C.

L' idea della vita che continuava malgrado i cambiamenti climatici nel VI-VII
sec. (Fersuoch, Canal et al., 1989), la scoperta di E.Canal, come una volta la prima
scoperta delle traccie della romanita' fatta a Torcello, ha i suoi ammiratori ed
avversari.

Ci son quelli che ritengono ,che gli strati romani sono formati dal rafforzo delle isole con i materiali romani e terra portati qui da Altino che doveva essere abbandonato con i primi insediamenti barbarici (fig.7). Nonostante cio', la uniformita' dei materiali ceramici, indica la formazione in loco dello strato romano. E.Canal, grande amico dei polacchi, ha deciso di pubblicare tutte le sue scoperte, che potevamo consultare dal vivo e nel manoscritto. Abbiamo avuto occasione di pubblicare assieme (Modrzewska, Canal 1993) alcuni dei suoi ritrovamenti.

Ora pero' e' troppo presto per rivelare le sue sensaziozionali scoperte, che risalgono ai tempi quando la missione polacca ha cominciato a scoprire la laguna.

Gli studi sono in corso e dopo gli anni ,quelli fatti dalla missione polacca diretta da Lech Leciejewicz sono la base piu' valida per gli studi lagunari veneziani.

BIBLIOGRAFIA ED ABBREVIAZIONI

Alessio et al. 1967
M. Alessio, F. Biella, F. Bacchechi, C. Cortesi, University of Rome Carbon-14 dates V, Radiocarbon IX, 1967, 349-351.

Ammerman, De Min 1996
A.J. Ammerman, M. De Min et al., More on the origins of Venice, American Antiquity 69 (264), 1996, 501-510.

BISSSV
Bolletino dell' Istituto per la Storia della Societa' e dello Stato Veneziano, Fondazione Cini ,Venezia

Bognetti 1961
G.P. Bognetti, Una campagna di scavi a Torcello, in Scavi a Torcello (1961). Relazioni provvisorie, BISSSV 3, 1961, 1-25.

Bonatti 1968
E. Bonatti, Late-Pleistocene and postglacial stratigraphy of a sediment core from the lagoon of Venice (Italy), Memorie di Biogeografia Adriatica VII, suppl. 1968, 9-26.

Brambati 1981
A. Brambati, Modificazioni costiere nell' arco lagunare dell Adriatico settentrionale, Antichita' Altoadriatiche XXVII, 1985, 13-47.

Canal 1995
E. Canal, Le Venezie sommerse:quarant' anni di archeologia lagunare in La laguna di Venezia, Venezia 1995, 193-226.

Canal 1998
E. Canal. Testimonianze archeologiche nella laguna di Venezia. L'etā antica, Mestre 1998.

Croce Da Villa 1984
P. Croce da Villa, Scoperte recenti a Concordia. Studi su Portogruaro e Concordia, Antichita Altoadriatiche XXV, 1984, 41-45.

Dorigo 1994
W.Dorigo, Venezie sepolte nella terra del Piave, duecentomila anni fra il dolce e il salso, Roma 1994.

Dorigo 1995
W.Dorigo, La via acquea endolitoranea fra Chioggia ed Equilio, in La laguna di Venezia, Verona 1995, 193-226.

Fersuouch, Canal et al. 1989
L.Fersuoch, E.Canal et al., Indagini archeologiche a San Lorenzo di Ammiana (Venezia), Archeologia Veneta XVII, 1989, 72-90.

Fogolari 1961
G. Fogolari, Relazione dello scavo archeologico a San Giovanni Evangelista di Torcello, BISSSV 3, 1961, 46-49.

Le origini di Venezia 1981
Le origini di Venezia.Problemi, esperienze, proposte, Symposium italo-polacco Venezia 28 febbraio -2 marzo 198O, Marsilio Editori, Venezia 1981.

Leciejewicz 1981
L. Leciejewicz, Alcuni problemi dell' origine di Venezia alla luce degli scavi di Torcello, in Le origini di Venezia 1981, 55-63.

Leciejewicz, Tabaczyńska, Tabaczyński 1977
L. Leciejewicz, E. Tabaczyńska, S. Tabaczyński, Torcello. Scavi Scavi 1961-1962, Istituto Nazionale d' Archeologia e Storia dell' Arte, monografie III,Roma 1977.

Marabini, Veggiani 1992
F. Marabini, A. Veggiani, Le fluttuazioni climatiche degli ultimi milleni e la loro influenza sul litorale e la laguna di Venezia, Bolletino dell' A.I.C. 84-85, 1992, 79-84.

Marcello et al. 1968
A. Marcello, A.M. Fabbri, P.Tarchi, P.Paladini, Interpretazione dei reperti archeologici vegetali nell' isola di Torcello durante gli scavi del 1961 e del 1962, Memorie di Biogeografia Adriatica VII, 1968, suppl., 27-30.

Modrzewska, Canal 1993
I. Modrzewska, E. Canal, Anfore della laguna veneta. Scelta di ritrovamenti, Technical Report C.N.R. 168, Venezia 1993.

Modrzewska 1996
I. Modrzewska, Anfore romane e bizantine nella laguna di Venezia. Problemi da risolvere, Terra incognita. Rivista di Antropologia, Archeologia e Storia 1, 1996, 25-40.

Modrzewska, Pianetti 1996
I. Modrzewska, F. Pianetti, Una lettura della storia della laguna di Venezia, in Słowianszczyzna w Europie, vol.1, Wrocław 1996, 191-196.

Modrzewska in stampa
I. Modrzewska, Note sulle ceramiche dello strato VII dello scavo di Torcello. Nuove ricerche archeologiche, Suppl Rivista di Archeologia, a cura di L. Leciejewicz, in stampa.

Modrzewska in stampa 1
I. Modrzewska, Sulla storia della laguna di Venezia, Udine, in stampa 1.

Modrzewska, Herbich in stampa
I. Modrzewska,T. Herbich, Prospezioni geofisiche nell' isola di Torcello. Nuove ricerche archeologiche, in stampa.

Morandini 1960
G. Morandini, Elementi geografici ed aspetti morfologici della laguna, in Atti del Convegno per la conservazione e difesa della laguna e della citta' di Venezia, giugno 1960, Venezia 1960, 65-82.

Ortalli 1981
G. Ortalli, Il problema storico delle origini di Venezia, in Le origini di Venezia 1981, 85-89.

Pianetti 1968
F. Pianetti, I fiumi della terraferma veneziana nel quaternario, in Convegno sull' idrografia delle terraferma veneziana, Venezia 1968, 37-51.

Pianetti, Zanferrari 1980
F. Pianetti, A. Zanferrari, Dati preliminari sulla neottetonica degli fogli 51, Venezia e 52 di s.Dona' di Piave ed evoluzione plioceno-quaternaria della pianura e dell' area prealpina del versante veneto orientale, in Contributi alla realizzazione della carta neotettonica d' Italia, parte I, CNR ed., Roma 1980.

Riedel 1981
A. Riedel, la fauna dell' antica Torcello (scavi 1961-62), in Le origini di Venezia 1981, 115-116.

Salvatori 1989
S. Salvatori, Ricerche archeologiche a Cittanova (Eraclia) 1987, Quaderni del Archeologia del Veneto V, 1989, 92-96.

Sandrini 1987
G.M. Sandrini, Concordia Sagittaria.Ripresa dello scavo all' interno della basilica paleocristiana, Quaderni dell Archeologia del Veneto III, 1987, 99.

Vecchi 1981
M. Vecchi, Metodo archivistico e archeologia:ipotesi di ricerca a Torcello, in Le origini di Venezia 1981, 65-69.

Barbara Lichocka

Varsovie

Les monnaies locales et les monnaies impériales à Chypre au IIIe siècle. Le témoignage de Nea Paphos

Les monnaies émises au nom du *Koinon Kyprion* sous Caracalla et Géta attribuées à Paphos sont les dernières connues du monnayage local à Chypre. La fermeture de cet atelier n'était pas un fait isolé. Au IIIe siècle, après la période des Sévères, de nombreux ateliers provinciaux cessent leur activité[1]. C'est la période de changements dans le domaine de la politique monétaire et de l'administration des finances de l'Empire. Il est évident que l'arrêt de production de la monnaie à Chypre a impliqué une modification importante dans la structure du volume monétaire en circulation sur l'île. Au début du IIIe siècle les monnaies du *Koinon Kyprion* pouvaient jouer un rôle considérable dans les transactions locales sur l'île, mais l'analyse du matériel des fouilles archéologiques permet de déduire que ce la monnaie exportée remplissait un rôle essentiel.

Parmi les monnaies du IIIe siècle trouvées dans les fouilles archéologiques à Chypre les deniers sont rares. Pourtant les antoniniens et théoretiquement frappées en argent les pièces avec la marque XXI à l'exergue (les "*antoniniani* XXI" ou les *aureliniani*) sont bien attestées. La présence des monnaies en bronze est confirmée par de nombreux exemplaires.

Au cours des recherches de la Mission polonaise ont été trouvés aussi bien les *antoniniani* que les bronzes. Le monnayage en bronze est représenté par les monnaies frappées à Rome et dans les autres ateliers impériaux, mais aussi par des monnaies produites dans les ateliers provinciaux. Les bronzes impériaux prédominent. En confrontant ces trouvailles avec celles des autres sites à Paphos, de Curium, de Salamine ou de Soloi, de différentes nécropoles, nous pouvons constater l'afflux constant et l'importance de la monnaie impériale à Chypre au IIIe siècle[2].

---

[1] Cf. T. B. Jones, A Numismatic Riddle: The So-called Greek Imperials, Proceedings of the American Philosophical Society 107,4, 1963, p. 331-333; J.-P. Callu, La politique monétaire des empereurs romains de 238 à 311, Paris 1969, p. 17-25.

[2] Cf. aussi Callu, op. cit., p. 51.

Sur l'emplacement du palais romain, connu sous le non de Villa de Thésée à Paphos[3], quelques sesterces témoignent de l'approvisionnement en bronzes impériaux frappés à Rome sous la dynastie des Sévères. La figure de Libertas debout est représentée au revers d'une pièce de Caracalla datée de 213 (n° 167)[4]. La figure de Sol orne les revers de deux monnaies de Sévère Alexandre datées de 232 (n°177[5] et n° 503[6]).

Les monnaies les plus intéressantes pour cette période sont celles d'Elagabal portant au revers le sigle ΔE (désignant peut-être δημαρχικῆς ἰξουσίας) et une étoile au-dessous à l'intérieur d'une couronne, attribuées par W. Wroth à l'atelier d'Antioche en Syrie[7]. La légende accompagnant le portrait d'empereur au droit est en latin. L'état de préservation de ces bronzes est mauvais, la légende effacée. Parmi les monnaies trouvées sur le chantier polonais, nous pouvons citer uniquement deux pièces avec la légende partiellement préservée, IMP C M AVR ANT[ONINVS AVG] (n° 203) et [IMP C M AVR] ANT[ONINVS AVG] (n° 286, fig. 1). Les détails du portrait impérial sont également difficiles à distinguer. Il est probable que le type fut continué par Sévère Alexandre. A part des huit exemplaires trouvés par la Mission polonaise[8], nous pouvons citer plusieurs exemples inventoriés jusqu'à nos jours à Paphos même - dans l'Odéon[9], à Curium[10], dans les tombeaux à Ama-thonte[11], à Kyra[12], à Vasa[13]. La pièce notée par la Mission suédoise à Soloi, a été analysée par C. Bosch qui a suggeré de l'attribuer à l'atelier chypriote sous Sévère

---

[3] Sur l'ensemble de constructions découvertes par la Mission polonaise, dirigée par W. A. Daszewski, à qui j'adresse mes remerciements, cf. Daszewski, dans: Daszewski et al., p. 294-307; dernièrement, id., Nea Pafos 1965-1995, dans: Cypr w badaniach polskich. Materiały z sesji naukowej zorganizowanej przez Centrum Archeologii Sródziemnomorskiej UW im. prof. K. Michałowskiego, Warszawa, 24-25 luty 1995 (éd. W. A. Daszewski, H. Meyza), Warszawa 1998, p. 8-11, fig. 1; S. Medeksza, Willa Tezeusza w Nea Paphos. Rezydencja antyczna, Wrocław 1992 (avec le résumé en anglais), p. 22-74, fig. 2-22; id., Willa Tezeusza w Nea Paphos na Cyprze: powstanie i fazy rozwoju, dans: Cypr w badaniach polskich..., p. 25-35, fig. 2-7.

[4] Cf. BMCRE V, p. 476, n° 246; RIC IV,1, p. 294, n° 498 b.

[5] B. Lichocka, Les monnaies 1976-1983, dans: Daszewski et al., p. 308, note 36, référence erronée; cf. BMCRE VI, p. 200, n° 865-866, pl. 29; RIC IV,2, p. 112, n° 531.

[6] Cf. BMCRE VI, p. 200, n° 865; RIC IV,2, p. 112, n° 531.

[7] BMC Galatia, p. 205, n° 447-450; cf. SNG Cop. Syria, n° 248-249.

[8] Il est probable que ce type représente encore quelques monnaies, mais elles sont très abîmées, ce qui ne permet pas une identification certaine.

[9] Paphos II, p. 185, n° 23-24 et n° 25 (?), Elagabal et n° 27-28 (?), Sévère Alexandre, pl. XXXVI.

[10] D. H. Cox, Coins from the Excavations at Curium 1932-1953, New York 1959, p. 19, n° 144, 16 exemplaires, Elagabal; n° 145, 19 exemplaires, Sévère Alexandre, pl. VI; n° 146, 21 exemplaires, Elagabal ou Sévère Alexandre.

[11] I. Nicolaou, The Coins, dans: Etudes Chypriotes XIII. La nécropole d'Amathonte. Tombes 110-385, Nicosie 1991, p. 181, n° 26-30, pl. IX et p. 184, n° 56, pl. X, 56, Elagabal ou Sévère Alexandre.

[12] A. Pieridou, A Hellenistic-Roman Tomb at Kyra, RDAC 1963, p. 120, Sévère Alexandre.

[13] P. Grierson, Appendix II. The Coins. General Observations, RDAC 1940-1948, p. 64, n° 14-16, Elagabal.

Alexandre[14]. La présence de la légende latine, caractéristique pour Laodicée, a incité E. T. Newell et A. R. Bellinger à supposer qu'on pourrait attribuer ce type à Laodicée justement[15]. Si on accepte cette opinion, il faudrait admettre que ce serait le seul type exporté de Laodicée. D. Waagé était plutôt d'avis que les monnaies au type ΔE au revers ont été produites à Antioche, la ville qui traditionellement n'a pas frappé son *ethnikon*, pendant que Laodicée l'omettait uniquement sous Caracalla et Macrinus, pour un type ROMAE FEL[16]. L'attribution de monnaies étudiées à Antioche n'a pas été acceptée par D. H. Cox, qui penchait pour Laodicée et aussi la production à Chypre[17]. Une hypothèse admettant la possibilité de la frappe dans deux centres différents était proposée déjà par A.R. Bellinger[18].

Le matériel dont nous disposons est encore trop limité pour tirer des conclusions définitives. Il faut pourtant souligner que ce type est très bien attesté à Chypre. Le nombre d'exemplaires attribués à Elagabal, est considérable, environs 30 pièces, pendant qu'Antioche nous a fourni cinq monnaies et Doura Europos une.

Le règne d'Elagabal est aussi représenté par les monnaies en bronze inscrites des lettres SC à l'intérieur d'une couronne de laurier au revers, également d'habitude attribuées à l'atelier d'Antioche, qui a profité du droit de frapper monnaie pour l'utiliser aussi en dehors de la ville. Contrairement aux monnaies avec les lettres ΔE au revers, portant au droit la légende latine, les monnaies avec le sigle SC se caractèrisent par la légende grecque au droit. Ce type a été frappé à Antioche depuis longtemps et il comprend quelques variantes. Les monnaies d'Elagabal portant au revers les lettres SC, ΔE au-dessus et un aigle au-dessous sont bien confirmées sur l'ensemble de différents sites à Chypre[19]. Dans la Villa de Thésée on en a trouvé un exemplaire, malheureusement partiellement endommagé (n° 252)[20].

Au IIIᵉ siècle, l'atelier d'Antioche fonctionne sous la dépendance de l'atelier de Rome. Les lettres SC (*Senatus Consultum*), indiquent qu'il s'agit d'une émission

---

[14] Opinion citée par A. Westholm. The Temples of Soli. Stockholm 1936. p. 135; p. 147; cf. Grierson, op. cit., p. 61.

[15] A. R. Bellinger. The Excavations at Dura - Europos VI. The Coins, London 1949, p. 156, commentaire au n° 1827.

[16] D. B. Waagé. Antioch on-the-Orontes IV.2. Greek, Roman, Byzantine and Crusaders' Coins, Princeton - London - The Hague 1952, p. 57, commentaire au n° 600.

[17] Cox, op. cit., p. 109, commentaire au n° 144; cf. supra, note 10.

[18] Cf. supra, note 15.

[19] Cox, op. cit., p. 23-24, n° 177-179; p. 111-112; Paphos II, p. 78, n° 586, pl. XXI; p. 185, n° 26, pl. XXXI; B. Helly, dans: G. Argoud et al., Le temple de Zeus à Salamine, RDAC 1975, p. 137, Sal. 7552; O. Callot, B. Helly, Monnaies et Sceaux, dans: G. Argoud, O. Callot, B. Helly, Salamine de Chypre XI. Une résidence byzantine "l'Huilerie", Paris 1980, p. 40 et 42, Sal. 6531-6532, 6879; J. Des Gagniers. V. Tran Tam Tinh, Soloi I. Soloi, Dix Campagnes des fouilles (1964-1974), Saint-Foy 1985, p. 88, n° 14, fig. 149. Selon Callu, op.cit., pp. 50-51, à Chypre on trouve les bronzes "copiés ... sur les petites dénominations antiochènes, le sigle SC ΔE étant amputé de sa partie latine".

[20] Cf. BMC Galatia, p. 203, n° 426-432; pour un aigle, dont la partie est très effacée ou mal exécutée, cf. SNG Cop. Syria, n° 242; Waagé, op. cit., p. 56, n° 593.

sénatoriale, exigeant l'autorisation directe du sénat ou son approbation[21]. Sur les monnaies inscrites des lettres ΔE avec une étoile au-dessous, ces lettres sont absentes. Cela suggère que par rapport aux monnaies avec les lettres SC, ces monnaies avaient une importance mineure. Leurs émissions n'étaient pas contrôlées par le sénat, même d'une manière symbolique. La faible valeur de la dénomination au type correspondant à un semis romain suggère sa portée très limitée, locale. Une émission locale ou bien une émission à Antioche destinée à l'étranger ne peuvent être exclues.

Une des monnaies au type ΔE frappée sous Elagabal (no 286, fig. 1) fut trouvée avec une autre pièce d'Elagabal (?) du même type (n° 285) et une monnaie non datée de Probus, frappée à Antioche (n° 284, fig. 5), représentant au droit le buste drapé de Probus, la tête ornée d'une couronne radiée et au revers Jupiter donnant à l'empereur une Victoire placée sur un globe avec la légende CLEMENTIA TEMP(oris)[22]. Pourtant nous ne pouvons accepter sans réserve la supposition de la circulation de ces pièces émises entre 218 et 222 jusqu'au temps de Probus, régnant de 276 à 282. Même si le volume monétaire n'était jamais très abondant à Chypre et que la longue circulation des monnaies est bien attestée aux Ier et IIe siècles, le contexte dans lequel ont été trouvées ces trois pièces, permet uniquement de signaler le problème de la circulation des monnaies d'Elagabal quelques décennies après leur émission, puisque les trois monnaies furent trouvées dans une pièce de la partie Est de la Villa de Thésée[23], dans une couche difficile à préciser: un niveau d'habitation de terre battue ou une couche de remblais touchant directement à ce niveau.

L'infiltration à Chypre de monnaies d'autres centres provinciaux est confirmée par les pièces isolées, par exemple un bronze représentant le buste de Caracalla au droit et la tête de Tyché au revers frappé à Carrhae en Mésopotamie (nr. 315)[24], atelier florissant sous le règne de Caracalla. Un exemplaire représentant le même type a été trouvé à Curium[25].

---

[21] Callu, op. cit., p. 13, 26, 174; id., Approches numismatiques de l'histoire du 3e. Siècle (238-311). dans: Aufstieg und Niedergang II,2, Berlin - New York 1975 (éd. H. Temporini), p. 601; cf. K. Butcher, Roman Provincial Coins: An Introduction to the Greek Imperials, London 1988, p. 98.

[22] Cf. RIC V,2, p. 120, n° 922; cf. infra, p. 181.

[23] Salle 68, cf. le plan de la Villa de Thésée, Daszewski, op. cit. p. 295, fig. 1.

[24] Cf. BMC Arabia, p. 85, n° 30, pl. XII, 30; SNG Cop. Palestine-Characene, Copenhagen 1961, n° 182.

[25] Cox, op. cit., p. 26, n° 203.

Figures

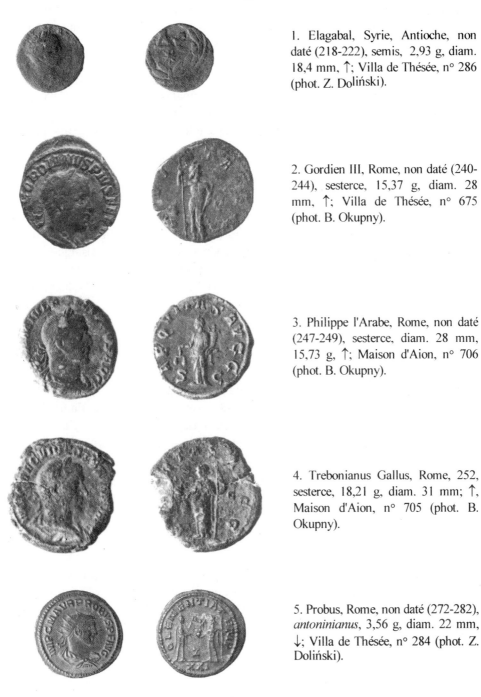

1. Elagabal, Syrie, Antioche, non daté (218-222), semis, 2,93 g, diam. 18,4 mm, ↑; Villa de Thésée, n° 286 (phot. Z. Doliński).

2. Gordien III, Rome, non daté (240-244), sesterce, 15,37 g, diam. 28 mm, ↑; Villa de Thésée, n° 675 (phot. B. Okupny).

3. Philippe l'Arabe, Rome, non daté (247-249), sesterce, diam. 28 mm, 15,73 g, ↑; Maison d'Aion, n° 706 (phot. B. Okupny).

4. Trebonianus Gallus, Rome, 252, sesterce, 18,21 g, diam. 31 mm; ↑, Maison d'Aion, n° 705 (phot. B. Okupny).

5. Probus, Rome, non daté (272-282), *antoninianus*, 3,56 g, diam. 22 mm, ↓; Villa de Thésée, n° 284 (phot. Z. Doliński).

Le nombre d'empereurs régnant au IIIe siècle est imposant: depuis Septime Sévère, régnant de 193 à 211, jusqu'à Dioclétien et Maximien Hercule - Augustes et Constance et Galère - Césars, qui battrent monnaie entre 294-305, nous avons 31 empereurs régnant et 24 co-empereurs et usurpateurs. Il est évident que l'administration de chaucun de ces 55 empereurs au total ne disposait pas de moyens pour retirer assez vite les monnaies du prédécesseur et de couvrir la demande avec des monnaies du souverain actuel. De plus la situation géographique de Chypre, éloigné du centre administratif de l'Empire, rend difficile la possibilité d'y trouver les monnaies de tous les empereurs, par exemple celles des empereurs gaulois. Carausius ou Allectus.

La période après le règne des Sévères est caractérisée par un afflux constant de monnaies impériales[26]. Du règne de Gordien III, quatre sesterces frappés à Rome, nous sont connus à ce jour, dont deux (n° 166, 675) représentent le même type au revers, à savoir, Jupiter debout nu avec un sceptre et un foudre, accompagné d'une légende [IO]VI STRAT[ORI][27]. Une des ces monnaies (n° 675, fig. 3) a été trouvée à l'intérieur du canal dégagé dans un sondage ouvert sous la mosaïque dans le portique Est de la Villa de Thésée[28]. Dans le même endroit on a également trouvé deux monnaies de IIe ou de IIIe siècle (n° 676, 678) et la monnaie de Gallien, la plus récente dans cet ensemble (n° 677)[29].

Sur deux autres sesterces de Gordien III, nous retrouvons l'image de Sol nu, la tête radiée, tenant un globe, AETERNITAS S C (n° 317)[30] et la figure de l'empereur en costume militaire debout, tourné vers la droite, tenant un sceptre et le globe, P M TR P V COS I[I] P P (n° 658)[31].

Les monnaies de Philippe l'Arabe, trouvées à Nea Paphos sont également les bronzes émis à Rome. Citons deux sesterces très bien conservés datés de 247-249: au type d'Aequitas debout tenant une balance et la corne d'abondance, AEQVITAS AV<V>GG S C (n° 506)[32] et un autre, au type d'Annona tenant des épis au-dessus d'un modius et la corne d'abondance, ANNONA AVGG S C (n° 443)[33]. Les autres pièces bien préservées représentent au revers la personnification de Laetitia avec l'inscription au pourtour LAET(itia) FVNDAT(a)

---

[26] Cf. Callu, op. cit., p. 51.

[27] Cf. RIC IV,3, p. 484. n° 298 a.

[28] Salle 50, dans l'axe de l'entrée d'*atrium* (salle 71); pour le plan de la Villa de Thésée, cf. p. ex.. Daszewski, op. cit. p. 295, fig. 1. Dans cet endroit on a encore trouvé les fragments de lampes datées de IIIe/IVe siècle et quelques tessons romaines *African Red Slip Ware*. Ce sondage est mentionné par W. A. Daszewski, Nea Paphos 1989, Polish Archaeology in the Mediterranean 1988-1989, 1990, p. 35.

[29] Cf. infra, note 42.

[30] Cf. RIC IV,3, p. 48, n° 297.

[31] Cf. RIC IV,3, p. 49, n°308 (a).

[32] Cf. RIC IV,3, p. 89, n° 166 a, au revers la légende comporte une lettre V doublée par erreur.

[33] Cf. RIC IV,3, p. 90, n° 168*, pl. 9,5.

AVGVST(i) (n° 311)[34] et Victoria avec l'inscription VICTORIA AV[G] (n° 635)[35].

Une des monnaies de Philippe l'Arabe (n° 706, fig. 3), représentant le type déjà mentionné, celui d'Aequitas[36], fait partie d'un petit ensemble comportant cinq pièces trouvées sur le terrain d'une villa connue sous le nom de la Maison d'Aion. Ces monnaies ont été retrouvées dans une couche de remblais comportant la céramique des IIe et IIIe siècles dans la partie Ouest de la Maison[37]. Dans ce groupe trois exemplaires peuvent être bien identifiés: un sesterce de Philippe l'Arabe déjà présenté, attribué à 247-249, un sesterce de Trebonianus Gallus au type de Libertas, daté de 253 (n° 705, fig. 4)[38] et encore un sesterce, de Septime Sévère, représentant au revers Roma assise, daté de 195 (n° 707)[39]. Deux monnaies sont corrodées. Il s'agit d'un bronze du IIe ou IIIe siècle, portant au revers une représentation d'une figure féminine debout (n° 708) et d'une monnaie d'un petit module (diamètre de 14 mm) du IVe siècle, illisible (n° 709).

La circulation des monnaies de certains empereurs est confirmée par une seule pièce. Mentionnons par exemple un sesterce de Maximin I portant au revers la personnification de Providentia (n° 466)[40], un sesterce de Trajan Decius, représentant la personnification de la Dacie au revers (nr. 312)[41], un antoninien de Gallien au type de VIRTVS AVGVSTI (n° 677)[42], un autre antoninien, de Quintillus au type de PAX AVGVST[I], daté de 270 (n° 324)[43] ou une pièce d'Aurélien représentant l'empereur et Victoria debout, [R]ESTITVOR ORBIS (n° 628)[44]. La monnaie portant au droit le portrait de Claude II le Gothique en couronne radiée, représente PAX AVG(usti) au revers. La lettre T à l'exergue suggère la série de l'atelier à Milan (n° 52)[45]. Le dessin linéaire de la draperie de la représentation de Pax est très caractéristique.

Nous avons plus des pièces de Probus, portant au droit l'effigie de l'empereur ornée d'une couronne radiée et au revers l'empereur qui se tient debout devant un autre personnage avec la légende CLEMENTIA TEMP au pourtour et la marque

---

[34] Cf. RIC IV,3, p. 90, n° 175 a.

[35] Cf. RIC IV,3, p. 92, n° 191.

[36] Cf. supra, note 32.

[37] Pour la stratigraphie, cf. E. Papuci-Władyka, Nea Paphos. Studia nad ceramiką hellenistyczną z polskich wykopalisk (1965-1991), Kraków 1995 (avec le résumé en anglais), couche correspondante à p. 87, fig. 5, n° 3, au-dessus des niveaux d'occupation figurés p. 79, fig. 4, n° 11-12.

[38] Cf. RIC IV,3, p. 172, n° 114 a.

[39] Cf. BMCRE V, p. 138, n° 558, pl. 24, 2; RIC IV,1, p. 186, n° 691.

[40] Cf. BMCRE VI, p. 223, n° 17, pl. 33; RIC IV,2, p. 145, n° 61*.

[41] Cf. RIC IV,3, p. 135, n° 112 (a-b).

[42] Cf. RIC V,1, p. 159, n° 330; cf. supra, p. 182.

[43] Cf. RIC V,1, p. 241, n° 26.

[44] Cf. RIC V,1, p. 306, n° 369.

[45] Cf. RIC V,1, p. 223, n° 157.

XXI à l'exergue (n° 284 et 374)[46]. Un autre exemple de ce monnayage est fourni par une monnaie representant au revers l'empereur tenant le globe et le sceptre, debout, devant une femme qui lui tend la couronne, RESTITVIT ORBIS (n° 372)[47].

Les monnaies mentionnées proviennent de différents ateliers impériaux, y compris Rome (n° 312, 324, 466, 677), Antioche (n° 284, 372, 374) et Cyzique (n° 628).

Citons enfin les monnaies de Maximien Hercule émises avant la réforme monétaire de Dioclétien, une pièce représentant au revers Jupiter et Hercule tenant une Victoire, IOV ET HERCV CONSER AVGG de l'atelier à Tripoli (n° 74)[48] et une pièce au type de Jupiter tenant un sceptre et un foudre avec la légende IOVI CONSERVATORI de Siscia (n° 84)[49]. On a aussi trouvé les monnaies représentant les fractions radiées de *follis* au type de CONCORDIA MILITVM, figurant Jupiter donnant une Victoire à l'empereur, frappées plus tard, entre 295-299 à Cyzique (n° 298)[50] et à Alexandrie, entre 296-297 (n° 373)[51]. Avec la monnaie émise au nom de Constantius César à Alexandrie ou à Antioche en 297-307 (n° 92) ce sont des exemples du monnayage de la Tétrarchie qui débute en 284.

Le IIIe siècle est le siècle des guerres et des luttes politiques. Chypre, éloignée de la grande politique et des opérations militaires, devait pourtant ressentir les conséquences de l'invasion des Goths qui atteignaient les côtes de l'Asie Mineure, entre 260 et 270. La coupure des autres centres de l'Empire et l'invasion probable de l'île[52], ne pouvaient rester sans influence sur la vie économique. Le témoignage évident de cette période semble se réfléter dans les imitations barbares, frappées hors de Chypre et apportées par les troupes dans l'île. On a identifié une pièce irrégulière de Victorinus, figurant au revers un personnage marchant vers la gauche (n° 77)[53].

Il est évident que la vie économique à Paphos au IIIe siècle n'était pas très intense. Peut-être même l'économie de l'île n'était pas entièrement monétarisée. Les crises économiques du IIIe siècle, les réorganisations des ateliers et les réformes du système monétaire, l'inflation[54] - la hausse des prix, la chutte du monnayage en

---

[46] Cf. supra, note 22; Lichocka, op. cit., p. 308, pl. LXIX, 2.

[47] Cf. RIC V,2, p. 120, n° 925.

[48] Cf. RIC V,2, p. 294, n° 624.

[49] Cf. RIC V,2, p. 284, n° 557.

[50] Cf. RIC VI, p. 581, n° 15 b.

[51] Cf. RIC VI, p. 667, n° 46 b.

[52] Cf. Jones, op. cit., p. 340.

[53] Cf. RIC V,2, p. 397-398.

[54] Cf. M. Christol, Effort de guerre et ateliers monétaires de la périphérie au IIIe s. ap. J.-C. L'atelier de Cologne sous Valérien et Gallien, dans: Armées et fiscalité dans le monde antique, Colloque national du C.N.R.S., Paris 14-16 octobre 1976, Paris 1977, p. 242; contre "une vision catastrophi-que de ce phénomène", J.-M. Carrié, Les finances militaires et le fait monétaire dans l'Empire tardif, dans: Les "Dévaluations" à Rome. Epoque Républicaine et impériale (Rome, 13-15 novembre 1975), Paris - Rome 1978, p. 236-237; cf. aussi M. Corbier, Dévaluations et évolutions des prix (Ier - IIIe siècles), RNum Ve sér., XXVII, 1985, p. 107.

argent, la dépréciation du denier et sa disparition définitive, l'introduction des nouvelles espèces, touchèrent Chypre. Malgré sa situation géographique, comme plaque tournante entre l'Ouest et l'Est, malgré ses précieuses mines de cuivre, Chypre ne joue pas de rôle important dans les événements du IIIe siècle. Les légions n'y stationnent pas, ce qui causerait des charges financières mais aussi l'afflux important d'argent. Cela pouvait entraîner une stagnation de l'économie, sans provoquer pourtant un krach financier dans la province. Les plus grandes difficultés du IIIe siècle semblent plutôt tourmenter l'Italie et la partie occidentale de l'Empire alors que Chypre restait dans la sphère d'influence de la partie orientale de l'Empire[55].

Dépourvue de sa propre monnaie, Chypre "cherche de l'aide auprès" du monnayage d'Antioche, qui a un "statut" spécial. Avec la décentralisation du monnayage impérial, Antioche deviendra un des ateliers centraux qui continue à approvisionner le marché à Chypre. Plus tard, laissant de côté les affaires financières et des ambitions politiques de divers empereurs, Chypre se soumet à une unification graduelle et à la "romanisation" du monnayage qui se réalisera dans le siècle suivant dans tout l'Empire romain*.

Abréviations

BMC - Catalogue of the Greek Coins in the British Museum
BMC Arabia - G. F. Hill, BMC. Arabia, Mesopotamia and Persia, London 1922.
BMC Galatia - W. Wroth, BMC Galatia - Cappadocia and Syria, London 1899.
BMCRE - Catalogue of the Coins of the Roman Empire in the British Museum
BMCRE V - H. Mattingly, E. A. Sydenham, BMCRE V, London 1950.
BMCRE VI - R. A. G. Carson, BMRRE VI, London 1962.
Daszewski et al. - W.A. Daszewski et al., Fouilles polonaises à Kato Paphos. Chantier de Maloutena, RDAC 1984, p. 294-314.
Paphos II - I. Nicolaou. Paphos II, The Coins from the House of Dionysos, Nicosia 1990.
RIC - Roman Imperial Coinage
RIC IV,1 - H. Mattingly, E. A. Sydenham, RIC IV,1, London (1ère éd. 1936) 1972.
RIC IV,2-3 - H. Mattingly, E. A. Sydenham, C.H. Sutherland, RIC IV,2-3, London (1ère éd. 1938-1949) 1972.

---

[55] Sur la situation à l'Est de l'Empire au IIIe siècle, R. A. G. Carson, The Inflation of the Third Century and its Monetary Influence in the Near Est, dans: The Patterns of Monetary Development in Phoenicia and Palestine in Antiquity. International Numismatic Convention, Jerusalem 27-31 December 1963, Proceedings (éd. A. Kindler), Tel-Aviv - Jerusalem 1967, p. 239- 244.

*Je tiens à remercier et M. H. Meyza pour les informations concernant la céramique trouvée avec les monnaies étudiées et aussi Mme A. Destrooper-Georgiades et M. Z. Kiss pour leur aimable correction de la rédaction française de mon texte.

RIC V,1-2 - P. H. Webb, RIC V,1-2, London (1ere éd. 1927-1933) 1968.
RIC VI - C. H. V. Sutherland, R. A. G. Carson, RIC VI, London 1973.
SNG Cop. - Sylloge Nummorum Graecorum. The Royal Collection of Coins and Medals Danish National Museum.
BMC Cop. Syria - SNG Cop. Syria: Cities, Copenhagen 1959.

Małgorzata Martens-Czarnecka
Warsaw

Faras and Dongola - Milestones in Discoveries
of the Nubian Painting

In the years 1960 - 1964 in the Sudan and Egypt, UNESCO undertook the international action aimed at saving the monuments of Nubia from getting flooded as a result of construction of the Assuan dam.

Excavation works planned on a large scale resulted in learning, so far very little known Nubian culture and art which flourished in the area stretching south off the present Egyptian borders up to the sixth Nile cataract, from the third millennium BC until late Middle Ages i.e. 14th - 15th century.

As it is known, the Polish Archaeological Mission led by Prof. Kazimierz Michałowski took active part in that action. The most important result of work of Polish archaeologists was the discovery of the cathedral in Faras.[1] The cathedral built typically for Nubia, on cruciform plan with a wealth of ornament in architectural details, had the interior decorated with wall paintings. All that directed attention of Polish researchers to the Nubian art of a Christian period, the Faras cathedral being one of its best examples.

The Faras cathedral was used as a place of worship over 700 years, from the 8th century until the 14th - 15th century.

Several times the cathedral was subjected to reconstruction, its walls were restored, the painting decoration of the interior changed. Some of the older paintings were covered with a new layer of plaster, some were repainted and in course of time

---

[1] The results of the Polish excavations have so far been published in the works of K.Michałowski: *Faras, fouilles polonaises 1961*, Warszawa 1962; *Faras, fouilles polonaises 1961-62*, Warszawa 1965; *Polish Excavations at Faras 1961*, KUSH X (1962), pp.220-244; *Polish Excavations at Faras, Second Season 1961-1962*, KUSH XI (1963), pp.233-256; *Polish Excavations at Faras, Third Season 1962-63*, KUSH XII (1964), pp.195-207; *Polish Excavations at Faras, Fourth Season 1963-64*, KUSH XIII (1995), pp.177-189; *Faras, die Kathedrale auis dem Wüstensand*, Zürich 1967, (hereinafter: *Die Kathedrale*).

new paintings were added on yet unpainted parts of the walls. Scenes from the Old and New Testament, representations of Christ, The Holy Virgin, apostles, saints and Nubian church and court dignitaries make a rich iconographic repertoire. Distinctness of different styles together with an epigraphic material[2], first of all the list of bishops giving dates of their ingresss and death, enabled classification and basic dating of Faras murals, which contributed to understanding of the development of painting in the cathedral throughout centuries.[3] In no other building discovered in Nubia, the chronological spectrum of the wall painting was as wide as in the Faras cathedral. The iconographic types and particular representations and compositions from the cathedral in many cases served as analogies and basis for dating and interpretation of paintings discovered in other Nubian buildings. Conclusions concerning Faras painting can thus be applied to that branch of art on the entire Nubian territory.

In view of the above remarks and on the ground of broad research, the Nubian painting can be divided into three main periods:

- Early period - from the end of the 8th or perhaps even the 7th century up to the second half of the 10th century
- Classic period - from the end of the 10th century up to mid 11th century
- Late period - from the second half of the 11th century up to the 14th - 15th century.

Up to the 8th century an architectural sculpture had made the main decoration of building interiors in Nubia. As it seems, the radical change in favour of figural wall painting took place in the 8th century.

---

[2] S.Jakobielski, *La liste des éveques de Pachoras*, EtTrav 1 (1966), pp.151-170; id., *Faras III, A History of the Bishopric of Pachoras*, Warszawa 1972; id., Inscriptions, in: K.Michałowski, *Faras. Wall Paintings in the Collection of National Museum in Warsaw*, Warszawa 1974, (hereinafter: *Wall Paintings*), pp.279-312; id., *Portraits of the Bishops of Faras*, Nubian Studies, Proceedings of the Symposium for Nubian Studies, Sylwin College, Cambridge 1978, ed., J.M.Plumley, Warminster 1982, (hereinafter: *Nubian Studies*), pp.127-141.

[3] K.Michałowski, *Die Wichtigsten. Entwicklungsetappen der Wandmalerei in Faras, Christentum am Nil*, Recklinghausen 1964, pp. 79-94; id., *Faras, centre artistique de la Nubie chrétienne*, Leiden 1966; id., *Die Kathedrale*; id., *Wall Paintings*; K.Weitzmann, *Some Remarks on the Sources of the Fresco Painting of the Cathedral of Faras*, KuGN, Recklinghausen 1970, pp.325-346; M.Martens, *Observations sur la composition du visage dans les peintures de Faras (VIIIe- IXe siècles)*, EtTrav VI (1972), (hereinafter: *Observations I*), pp.207-250; M.Rassart,*Visages de Faras, caracteristiques et évolution stylistique*, Et.Trav VI (1972), pp.251-275; Martens, *Observations sur la composition de visage dans les peintures de Faras (IXe - XIIIe siècles)*, EtTrav VII (1973), (hereinafter: *Observations II*), pp.163-226; Martens-Czarnecka, *Faras VII. Les éléments décoratifs sur les peitures de la catédrale de Faras*, (hereinafter: *Faras VII*), Warszawa 1982; W.Godlewski, *Some Remarks on the Faras Cathedral and its Paintings*, Journal of Coptic Studies 2 (1992), pp.99-116; id., *The Early Period of Nubian Art; Middle of 6th - Beginning of 9th Centuries*, Etudes Nubiennes, conférence de Genève, actes du VII congres international d'études nubiennes, 3-8 sept.1990, vol.I, éd. Ch.Bonnet, Genève 1992, pp.287-291, 295-301.

Fig. 1. Faras. Saint Anne (phot. A. Dziewanowski)

An analysis of the earliest preserved paintings from Nub (8th - 9th century) reveals specific uniformity and maturity of style,[4] linearism and simplicity of form in application of both colours and line. Figures are represented in accordance with established rules depending on particular iconographic type (Holy Virgin, Christ, saints, angels). Empty gaze of wide open eyes (Fig.1), similar set of robes and strictly defined, limited repertoire of forms of attributes and decorative motifs are apparent (Fig.2). It all testifies activity of qualified painters and their followers. The painters, probably monks, most likely came to Nubian territory from Coptic Egypt or Syro-Palestine, which is indicated by strong connections between early Nubian painting and the art from those territories. Those painters undoubtedly started that branch of art in Nubia, for from 9th century the Nubian painting gradually develops, local features become more and more apparent[5] and in course of time very specific Nubian school of painting can be recognised. In terms of preferred iconographic types as well as secondary stylistic features, the Nubian painting, particularly of the

[4] Cf.Michałowski, *Die Kathedrale*, pp.72-73, Figs.23-33,35; Martens, *Observationa I*, pp.211-236. Michałowski, *Wall Painting*, pp.30,78-122; P.van Moorsel, J.Jacquet, H.Schneider, *The Central Church of Abdallah Nirqi*, Leiden 1975, (hereinafter: *Abdallah Nirqi*),pp.55-56, 76-85, Figs.70,7; Martens-Czarnecka, *Faras VII*, pp.13-29.

[5] Martens-Czarnecka, *Faras VII*, pp.30-49; ead.,*The Birth of the Multicolour Style*, Nubian Letters 12 (1989), pp.6-14.

classic period (10th - 11th century), acquired a homogeneous appearance developed under direct influence of contemporary Christian world - Egypt, Syro-Palestine, Bizantium and even Ethiopia. Tendency to stylization (Fig.3), lively contrasting colours and *horror vacui* apparent in decoration of robes and other objects were undoubtedly taken from an atmosphere of Africa.

Fig. 2. Faras. Saint bishop Ignatios (phot.W. Jerke)

Fig. 3. Faras. Bishop Marianos protected by Holy Virgin
(after Michałowski, Die Kathedrale)

In the classic period particular representations and also scenes containing narrative cycles, although repeating known iconographic types, are painted in the way specific only for Nubia.[6] The local character of the Nubian painting manifests itself in a certain manner in which faces are represented (*en face* or 3/4 profile) as well as in the decoration and arrangement of folds on robes (fig.4). There is a defined repertoire of decorative motifs and patterns which are applied depending on the type of represented figure as well as on the kind of decoration. Colouring of particular details of pictures is always the same. Foreign and local elements blended into original character of the pictures, which at the first glance can be recognised as Nubian (Fig.5).

[6] Michałowski, *Die Kathedrale*, pp.82-93, Figs.48-89; Martens, *Observations II*, pp.176-207; Michałowski, *Wall Paintings*, pp.30, 171-242; *Tamit (1964), Missione Archeologica in Egitto dell'Università di Roma*, éd. S.Donadoni, Roma 1967, pp.35, 54-60; S.Donadoni, *Les fouilles à l'église de Sonqi Tino*, KuGN, pp.209-216, Figs.190-192; van Moorsel, *Abdallah Nirqi*, pp.111-115, Figs.69,81, 101;

Fig. 4. Faras. Three Youths in the Fiery Furnace (phot.A. Dziewanowski)

Fig. 5. Faras. Nativity (phot. A.Dziewanowski)

Fig. 6. Faras. Bishop Georgios protected by Holy Virgin and Christ (unpreserved)
(phot.W. Jerke)

Fig. 7. Faras. Madonna Eleusa (phot.W. Jerke)

From the second half of the 11th century onwards Byzantine influence on the Nubian painting is getting predominant. Although favoured Nubian iconographic subjects, like scenes of protection (Fig.6), compositions of Holy Trinity, representations of donors and men of merit, and church and court dignitaries are still preferred, the style of paintings looses to, considerable extent, its purely Nubian character (Fig.7) and becomes more universal and closer to painting art cultivated at that time on the territories under an influence of Byzantine culture.[7] It should be stressed that mural painting as a form of decoration of interiors is, during that period in Nubia, getting more and more popular. Apart from paintings of high quality, very simple, even primitive compositions also appear. It seems that this kind of art is in great demand. Painters start signing their compositions.

Fig. 8. Dongola. Nativity (phot.W. Chmiel)

Started in 1964, Polish excavations in Old Dongola, lead originally by Prof. Michałowski and afterwards by Dr S. Jakobielski of the Polish Academy of Sciences on behalf of The Polish Centre of the Mediterranean Archaeology of the University

[7] F.Ll. Griffith, *Oxford Excavations in Nubia*, in: LAAA XIII (1926), pp.25-93; id., *Oxford Excavations in Nubia*, in:LAAA XV/3-4 (1928), pp.63-68; *Tamit*, pp.35, 54-60; W.Y.Adams, *The University of Kentucky Excavation at Kulubnarti*, in: KuGN, pp.141-154, Pl.121; Michałowski, *Die Kathedrale*, pp.93-96, Figs. 86, 90-96; Martens, *Observations II*, pp.214-223; van Moorsel, *Abdallah Nirqi*, Figs.65, 66, 77; Martens-Czarnecka, *Faras VII*, pp.89-116; ead., *Late Christian Painting in Nubia*, Etudes Nubiennes, pp.307-316; ead., *New Look at the Wall Painting of the Rivergate Church in Faras*, in: Bibliotheca Nubica III, Pars II, éd., P.O.Scholz, Albstadt 1992, pp.363-383.

193

of Warsaw, also immensely contributed to the knowledge on Nubian painting. The set of paintings decorating the interior of so called House A displays all the features specific for the early period of the Nubian painting.[8] We have here a local continuation of that homogeneous style, so well known from the Faras cathedral.[9] However it is only since 1991 that we can consider Dongola as a place of discoveries of equivalent to those from Faras cathedral for the excavations being carried out on the Kom H[10] systematically reveal rooms of a monastery with walls preserved up to the height of 3 - 4 m, richly decorated with mural paintings.

Fig. 9. Dongola. Three Youths in the Fiery Furnace (phot. M. Pietrzak)

[8] S.Jakobielski, *Polish Excavations at Old Dongola in 1976 and 1978*, Nubian Studies, pp.116-126; W. Godlewski, *Some Comments on the Wall Painting of Christ from Old Dongola*, Nubian Studies, pp.96-99.
[9] Martens- Czarnecka, *Caractéristiques du stule "violet" dans les peitures à Dongola*, EtTrav XIV (1990), pp.223-237.
[10] S.Jakobielski, *Old Dongola 1993*, PAM V, Reports 1993, pp.115-126; id., *Old Dongola 1993/94*, PAM VI, Reports 1994, pp.84-92; id., *Old Dongola, Monastery 1995*, PAM VII, Reports 1995, pp.105-113; id., *Old Dongola: Excavations 1996, Kom H, Site NW*, PAM VIII, Reports 1996, pp.159-168;id., *Monastery of the the Holy Trinity at Old Dongola - A short Archaeological Report*, in: The Spirituality of Ancient Monasticism, Acts of the International Colloqium Held in Cracaw - Tyniec, 16-19th nov.1994, Cracaw 1995, pp.35-45; B.Żurawski, *The Service Area in North Eastern Corner of the Monastery on Kom H in Old Dongola, A Preliminary Report*, Nubica III/1, éd.P.O.Scholz, Warszawa 1994, pp.319-360; id., *Old Dongola 1984-1993. The Mortuary Complex. A Priliminary Report*, EtTrav XVII (1995), pp.327-364; id., *Kom H. Southwestern Unit*, PAM VIII, Reports 1996, pp.169-178.

Fig. 10. Dongola. Christ healing the blind man (phot.W. Chmiel)

So far we discovered some 70 representations and compositions preserved on the walls and innumerable amount of pieces of plaster with fragments of paintings found in the debris. Some of those pieces supplement paintings on the walls, some like puzzles, can be put together into complete representations or their fragments, all supply important information concerning those murals. Architectural analysis of the part of the monastery discovered so far, and all the features characteristic for that painting indicate that the murals should be dated to the period from the second half of the 11th century up to 14th century i.e. to the late period of the Nubian painting.

Generous iconography enriched the repertoire of so far known Nubian iconographic types. Paintings from Dongola enhanced our knowledge on the late Nubian painting, known before mainly from northern Nubian territories. Examples from that period were scarce and in bad state of preservation. Also in Dongola only few fragments of painted plaster from walls of a few churches were preserved.[11] It should also be stressed that for the first time, the paintings discovered on the kom H compose a set probably representative and typical for decorations of walls of Nubian monastery, because the monastery in Dongola is the only example of the

---

[11] For example cf. S. Jakobielski, *Polish Excavations at Old Dongola 1969*, in: KuGN, pp. 171-180; W. Godlewski, *The Mosque Building in Old Dongola*, in: New Discoveries, Leiden 1984, p. 26; K. Innemé, *A Wall Painting in the Former Throne-Hall of Dongola*, EtTrav XVI (1992), pp.21-28.

building of that kind, so far discovered in Nubia, with its painting decoration found in relatively good condition.

The repertoire of scenes and representations in the monastery is of great variety.[12] Beside scenes from the Old and New Testament the figures of angels and archangels can be seen as well as those of Christ, the Holy Virgin, Holy Trinity, apostles and last but not least scenes of protection of kings and bishops. A cycle of narrative representations connected, as it seems, with the life of monks or perhaps only their prior bishop Georgios.

To the most interesting representations from the monastery in Dongola belong the scene of Nativity (Fig.8) repeating the Byzantine iconographic canon with selection of figures according to apocryphical sources, and the Youths in the Fiery Furnace. There are three compositions of that latter scene: one monumental (Fig.9) with composition arrangement the same as in Faras, the second one small but seemingly being the true copy of the former and the third one entirely original, from which two

Fig. 11. Dongola. Madonna Galaktothrophusa (phot.B. Żurawski)

[12] M.Marten-Czarnecka, *New Mural Paintings from Old Dongola*, in: Actes de la VIIIe conférence international des études nubiennes, Lille 11-17 sept.1994, CRIPEL 17/2, pp.211-226; ead., *Wall Paintings from the Monastery on kom H at Old Dongola*, in: Acts of the Six'th International Congress of Coptic Studies, Münster 1996, (in press); ead., *Malowidła z Klasztoru na Komie H w Starej Dongoli*, Sympozja Kazimierskie poświęcone kulturze świata późnego antyku i wczesnego chrześcijaństwa, Lublin 1998, pp. 73-102; ead., *Mural Paintings from Old Dongola*, Gdańsk Archeological Museum, African Report, vol. I, 1998, pp. 95-113; ead., *An Attempt to Define the*

figures of firemen and fragment of the furnace have been preserved. Out of the evangelic scenes, the scene of Christ healing the blind man at the Siloam spring in Jerusalem (Fig.10) is also worth mentioning. Also very interesting is the series of representations of Madonna Galaktothrophusa, one of those of an unique iconography ; the Holy Virgin is spinning and at the same time feeding the Child (Fig.11).

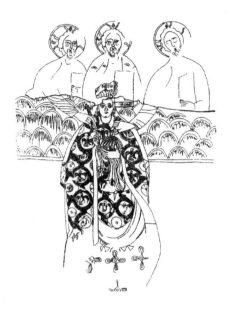

Fig. 12. Dongola. A Nubian king orotected by the Holy Trinity
(reconstruction of the painting by the author)

Scenes of protection became very popular in the late period. Perhaps, however, in case of Dongola great number of such representations resulted also from the specific character of the monastery building. A king under protection of the Holy Trinity[13] protruding from clouds (Fig.12) belongs in my opinion to the best Nubian paintings of that kind. The king held by the shoulders by the two side Persons of the Trinity is crowned with a heavenly crown put on his head by the central Person - Christ according to the preserved fragment of the legend. One of the side Persons hands a cruciform sceptre to the king. The king holds his earthly crown in his hand. Nubians' favoured subject has been here skilfully connected with an imperial iconography of investing the ruler with authority from the hands of a divine protector.[14]

Function of selected Rooms at the Monastery in Old Dongola, Gdańsk Archeological Museum. African Report, vol. I, 1998, pp. 81-93.

[13] M.Martens-Czarnecka, *A Nubian King - Painting from the Monastery from Old Dongola*, Nubica III, ed. P.O.Scholz, (in press).

[14] A.Grabar, *L'Empereur dans l'art byzantin*, London 1971, pp.114-122; Ch.Walter, *Art and Ritual of the Byzantine Church*, London 1982, pp.117-120.

Fig. 13. Dongola. A Holy rider (phot. W. Chmiel)

Analogy to that painting can be found in the representation of an eparch from the Faras cathedral,[15] not so well preserved as the painting from Dongola, nevertheless showing clearly hands of protectors on the eparch's shoulders. In his left hand the eparch also holds a crown and in the right one, the attribute of his authority - the bow. The decoration of robes is similar. The painting like that from Dongola, is very colourful and creates an impression of a coloured drawing.

It seems worthwhile to draw your attention to other paintings, representing the apostles and the holy rider on the horse back. The horse, its muzzle gaping, the eye wild, turns its head back, strongly reined in by the rider with a stern face (Fig.13). All that gives the representation particularly dynamic expression. The harness painted in great detail matches the real thing, namely an iron bridle with a double bit that was discovered during the latest campaign in Dongola.

I have shown you only some of the most interesting paintings from Dongola. There are many more worth presenting for many reasons. Unfortunately it is impossible to show all of them within the limited time of this presentation.

It so happened that since the UNESCO action, practically only Poles have been lucky to discover new monuments of the Nubian painting. The monastery in

---

[15] cf. Michałowski, *Wall Paintings*, pp.263, 265.

Dongola can become the new source of information permitting to extend the knowledge on that subject. In the Faras cathedral seemingly all trends in Nubian painting were represented. Dongola yielded so far examples from early and late periods of Nubian painting. The classic period remains to be discovered. We hope that when we reach older ruins of the monastery, deep inside the kom, we will find the walls decorated with paintings also from that period.

Elke Blumentahl

Leipzig

Statuentypen und Gottkönigtum
Bemerkungen zur Pyramidenzeit
Zusammenfassung

In seiner 1964 erschienenen Schrift „Die Heraufkunft des transzendenten Gottes in Ägypten" zeichnet Siegfried Morenz eine religionsgeschichtliche Entwicklungslinie nach, die einen schrittweisen Abbau der Göttlichkeit des Königs zugunsten der wachsenden Dominanz einzelner prominenter Götter bezeichnet. In und hinter diesen konkreten Göttern vermutet er die Existenz einer umfassenderen göttlichen Größe, die den König und die von ihm vertretene ägyptische Welt transzendiert.

Im Alten Reich markiert Morenz mehrere Etappen dieses geschichtlichen Verlaufs. Nachdem der König seit der 1. Dynastie nach Ausweis seines Horusnamens mit dem Himmels- und Weltgott Horus identisch gewesen war, tritt eine Minderung seiner Position zuerst im Wandel der Pyramidenanlagen von der 3. zur 4. Dynastie und mit dem neuen Königstitel „Sohn des Re" in Erscheinung, der zuerst bei Radjedef belegt ist und Abhängigkeit und Unterordnung des Königs gegenüber dem Sonnengott ausdrückt. Eine weitere signifikante Station des Prozesses macht Morenz am Ende der 5. bzw. zu Beginn der 6. Dynastie aus. Zu ihren Symptomen gehören zwei Statuetten Phiops' I. im Brooklyn Museum. Die eine (Acc. no. 39.121) zeigt den knienden König, wie er einer Gottheit zwei Weingefäße opfert, also als Priester und in einer Haltung besonderer Devotion. Die zweite Statuette (Acc. no. 39.120) gibt den thronenden König wieder und hinter seinem Kopf, im rechten Winkel zu ihm, den Falken des Gottes Horus. Im Vergleich mit der Sitzstatue des Königs Chephren (Kairo CG 14), auf deren Rückenpfeiler zwar ebenfalls der Horusfalke sitzt, aber in gleicher Blickrichtung mit ihm und ihn mit seinen Flügeln umfangend, nimmt Morenz eine gewachsene Trennung und Distanzierung zwischen beiden Partnern wahr.

Es soll nicht in Frage gestellt werden, daß sich im Laufe des Alten Reiches Göttertum und Königtum auseinanderentwickeln und daß der König dabei an Eigenständigkeit verliert. Aber die beiden Statuetten stehen nicht dafür, daß eine

Zäsur dieses Geschehens am Ende der 5. bzw. zu Beginn der 6. Dynastie stattgefunden hat. Das Fragment einer Statue des Chephren (Hildesheim Inv. 69) beweist, daß es den später häufigen Statuentyp der zweiten Statuette Phipos' I. ist bereits für Chephren bezeugt. Eine kopflos erhaltene Statue (Kairo CG 9) läßt Reste eines Falken erkennen, der in der gleichen Ausrichtung auf dem Rückenpfeiler steht und hier wie dort den Horusnamen des Königs einleitet. Der von den Flügeln des Falken umfangene König der Statue Kairo CG 14 gehört zu einem anderen Statuentyp.

Es gilt als sicher, daß der Horusfalke dieser Statue die Flügel zum Schutz um den König legt und somit gleichfalls göttliche Überlegenheit bekundet. Man könnte aber diesen Statuentyp als rundplastische Umsetzung von Reliefszenen mit königlichem Akteur verstehen, denen der Falke mit abgespreizten Flügeln beiwohnt und die ihn nicht nur als Schützer, sondern in einem allgemeineren Sinne als Begleiter des Königs darstellen. Trifft diese Vermutung zu, so hat die Trennung zwichen Horus-Gott und Horus-König schon unter Djoser Gestalt gewonnen. Dann würde der von Morenz skizzierte Vorgang nicht erst in der 4. Dynastie beginnen, sondern deren Neuerungen in Architektur, Königstitulatur und Ikonographie würden - sofern sie nicht auf Überlieferungszufall beruhen - ein weiteres Stadium in einem älteren Prozeß signalisieren.

Francine Blondé
Lyon

Thasos et ses céramiques au IVe s. avant J.-C.
Résumé

Notre intervention traitera quelques aspects de l'étude des céramiques d'usage quotidien du IVe s. avant J.-C. provenant de Thasos, île dans le Nord de la mer Egée. On s'est intéressé aux céramiques à vernis noir, aux céramiques communes et aux céramiques culinaires, produites localement et importées à Thasos même, et on a élargi l'étude en examinant plusieurs sites dans la pérée de Thasos et ses abords. L'apport du laboratoire a été essentiel dans cette recherche, non seulement pour l'identification des pâtes, mais aussi pour une meilleure compréhension dans le domaine des échanges, des techniques, et de la structuration de l'artisanat.

Günther Schörner

Jena

Die Pan-Grotte von Vari. Ein ländliches Heiligtum in Attika

Zusammenfassung

Die Pan-Grotte von Vari ist eine der wichtigsten Kulthöhlen des antiken Attika[1]. In Zusammenarbeit mit dem Deutschen Archäologischen Institut, Abteilung Athen (Prof. Dr. K. Fittschen, Dr. H. R. Goette), und mit der Erlaubnis der zuständigen griechischen Ephorien und der American School of Classical Studies war es möglich, diese im südlichen Attika gelegene Stätte genauer zu untersuchen: So konnte die Höhle neu vermessen und photographisch dokumentiert werden, außerdem wurden erstmals sämtliche künstliche Abarbeitungen (Bettungen für Reliefs und Statuetten, Zapfenlöcher etc.) dokumentiert. In Verbindung mit der Behandlung des vorliegenden Fundmaterials vorwiegend aus der amerikanischen Grabung zu Beginn unseres Jahrhunderts konnten die Nutzungsphasen der Grotte chronologisch eingeordnet werden: Nach einer Frühphase der Nymphenverehrung - belegt durch eine Inschrift des beginnenden 5. Jhs. v. Chr. - wurde die Höhle durch den aus Thera stammenden Archedemos ausgestaltet und für den Kult der Nymphen und des Pan, aber auch anderer Götter wie Kybele, hergerichtet. Seine Arbeiten in der Grotte - das Einmeißeln von Inschriften und Bettungen, die Fertigung von Skulpturen aus dem anstehenden Fels, das Anlegen eines Kultweges - führten zu einer Blüte in der Nutzung während des Endes des 5. und des gesamten 4. Jhs. Nach einer mit dem 2. Jh. v. Chr. einsetzenden Lücke im Fundmaterial ist erst wieder in der Spätantike der regelmäßige Besuch archäologisch nachweisbar, vermutlich in Verbindung mit einer christlichen Nutzung.

---

[1] Die ausführliche Publikation der Ergebnisse wird als Monographie erscheinen: G. Schörner - H. R. Goette, *Die Pan-Grotte von Vari*. Schriften zur Historischen Landeskunde Griechenlands 1 (1998) (in Drucklegung). Ich danke den Kollegen der Jagiellonen-Universität Krakau, insbesondere Herrn Prof. J. Śliwa, für die Einladung zum Kongreß und die Publikation meines Vortragsresümees in dieser Form.

Pan-Grotte von Vari, Gesamtansicht der Osthöhle nach Norden
(Photo Dr. H. R. Goette)

Aufgrund der Befunde läßt sich auch die Topographie des Kultes klassischer Zeit weitgehend klären: Deutlich ist die Trennung zwischen einem noch nicht kultisch rein zu haltenden Eingangsbereich, der auch für die Deponierung von Votiven genutzt wird, und der eigentlichen Kulthöhle für Opfer und anschließendem Fest. Durch die Anstrengungen des Archedemos wurde in dieser der Kultablauf durch Anlage eines Weges neu geregelt, der nun deutlich initiatorische Züge besaß, und bestens die natürlichen Gegebenheiten der Höhle mit ihrer Zweiteilung in eine kleine, dunkle West- und eine große, helle Ostkammer nutzte.

Bożena Rostkowska
Warsaw

Lower Nubia and the Institutio Michaelis
Summary

Among parchment fragments discovered in Lower Nubia there have been found two leaves of the *Institutio Michaelis* - one in the Greek with an illustration, other in the Old Nubian, the text which for years was known only in the Coptic versions.

Both fragments are preserved on single leaves and from the same portion of the text although they have been found in distant places - the Old Nubian fragment at Qasr Ibrim, the Greek one at Serra East. Both provide confirmation for popularity of Archangel Michael in that society. Discussed separately they pose problems, as:

- the history of the Greek original,
- scriptoria,
- a link that bound the culture of the Nubian Christianity to that of the remainder of the Byzantine world in the Nile Valley and others.

Bogdan Żurawski
Warsaw

The Divine Kingdom of Dongola
Some Reconsiderations
Summary

The sovereign of Dongola was the pinnacle of medieval Nubian political structure and society. He was also one's own master in religious matters of the Nubian church. His extraordinary status, deeply rooted in the institution of African divine kingship was affluently inspired by the position of Byzantine emperor. An attentive study of the organisation of the Kingdom of Dongola reveals a medley of Byzantine terminology and African pattern.

Also the Nubian regalia reveal striking resemblance to the Byzantine and African royal emblems. They are also styled on ancient Kushite models transmitted into Christian times by the Ballana kings.

The sacral status of the Dongolese monarch was reflected in his unique privileges enjoyed within the Nubian Church. Similarly to the Byzantine emperor, the Dongolese sovereign was a providential ruler chosen by God and conceived as God's representative on Earth.

The "Byzantine archetype" omnipresent in Nubian kingship might have caused the Nubian kings to take the same "philanthropic" procedure to receive salvation and to win the high reputation among their subjects. The *xenon* building recently exposed in Old Dongola seems to be an institutional manifestation of Nubian royal philanthropy.

It is highly plausible that after the introduction of Christianity to Nubia the Old Testament imagery provided some models for the iconography of Nubian kingship. The Old Testament kings were ideal prototypes for the Byzantine emperors and apparently were the iconographical models for Nubian royal portraiture.

The same way some elements of Old Testament symbolism penetrated Nubian art and decoration; the *pentagram* on the Nubian eparch's headgear is the best illustration of this phenomenon.